THE SEVEN
DEADLY SINS

Raül Garrigasait is a translator and writer. His first novel, *Els estranys*, won numerous prizes and was published by Fum d'Estampa Press in its English translation as *The Others*.

Jordi Graupera is a journalist and university professor, working on self-determination and international relations.

Oriol Ponsatí-Murlà is an editor, translator, writer and musician. He has published widely in both Catalan and Spanish.

Marina Porras is a literary critic, cultural journalist and associate professor at the Universitat Pompeu Fabra in Barcelona.

Adrià Pujol is an anthropologist, writer and translator. Writing essays, biographies, fiction and non-fiction, his work has won numerous prizes.

Anna Punsoda is a journalist and writer. Her first novel, *Els llits dels altres* won the 2018 Roc Boronat prize and will be published in English translation by Fum d'Estampa Press this year.

Oriol Quintana is a professor of ethics and Christian thought at the Universitat Ramon Llull. He has published a number of books on philosophy.

Mara Faye Lethem is an award-winning translator of contemporary Catalan and Spanish prose, and the author of *A Person's A Person, No Matter How Small*.

This translation has been published in Great Britain
by Fum d'Estampa Press Limited 2022

001

© 2019 Oriol Ponsatí-Murlà for *L'avaricia*
© 2019 Marina Porras Martí for *L'enveja*
© 2019 Adrià Pujol Cruells for *La gola*
© 2019 Oriol Quintana Rubio for *La mandra*
© 2020 Raül Garrigasait for *La ira*
© 2020 Jordi Graupera Garcia-Milà for *La supèrbia*
© 2020 Anna Punsoda Ricart for *La luxúria*
© Fragmenta Editorial for the series "*Pecats capitals*"
Translation rights arranged by Asterisc Agents. All rights reserved

English language translation © Mara Faye Lethem, 2022

Set in Minion Pro

Printed and bound by TJ Books Ltd, Padstow, Cornwall
A CIP catalogue record for this book is available from the British Library

ISBN: 978-1-913744-04-5

www.fumdestampa.com

This work was translated with the help of a grant from the Institut Ramon Llull.

Catalan Language and Culture

THE SEVEN DEADLY SINS

RAÜL GARRIGASAIT
JORDI GRAUPERA
ORIOL PONSATÍ-MURLÀ
MARINA PORRAS
ADRIÀ PUJOL
ANNA PUNSODA
ORIOL QUINTANA

Translated by

MARA FAYE LETHEM

CONTENTS

SLOTH

ORIOL QUINTANA

I – SLOTH IN THE WEST

To what extent is sloth an essential human characteristic? If sloth and the other vices are undesirable – as we tend to believe – then humans must have a true nature that those vices obscure and adulterate. If vices are bad – and they are, by definition – then that means humans are in need of redemption or, at the very least, improvement. This makes humans some sort of failed saints: called to perfection, they stumble again and again over the same rocks.

This vision was born of Christian anthropology, according to which humans have fallen from their initial state of permanent sanctity. There was no sloth then, no lust, no gluttony, none of that. Prior to original sin, humans lived in a divine setting, in paradise, by God's side and under His protective wing. As soon as they aspired to something other than living by God's side, they allowed in evil, imperfection, suffering, and all the current defects of human existence. According to this view of human-kind, all of life's defects were undesirable, and had to be rejected because they deprived us of something better: paradise, sanctity. It was that sanctity, that communion with God, that was the true human vocation. As such, lust, gluttony, sloth, wrath and all the other deadly sins had to be overcome or, at the very least, tempered by the grace of the divine force that counteracted them.

The Church provided the material needed to go through this life in the most dignified way possible, until the pre-lapsarian situation was restored. In the 19th century, Father Claret, for example, wrote a book whose title perfectly summed up this idea: *The Sure and Straight Path to Heaven*. Human life in this earthly world was only a transitory state. According to Christianity, human life was merely a preparation for achieving your true vocation and nature after death. You couldn't expect anything significant during your time on earth as (Christian) life was just the groundwork for death.

It was traditional Christianity that first took to attacking sloth. You couldn't sleep in and have the house all in disarray in case the big boss – death – turned up unexpectedly and you were forced to leave the world with unfinished business.

Christianity is pessimistic about the human capacity for improvement. Humanism, on the other hand, is optimistic. Humanism is utopian and has many schools, but basically says that, with or without original sin (because there is also Christian humanism that has, in fact, almost completely replaced its older variant), humans are capable of building a better world and improving themselves. In humanism's foundational text, *Oration on the Dignity of Man*, by Giovanni Pico della Mirandola, humans are attributed almost divine qualities and encouraged to strive to be like the angels, rather than the beasts. Countless later European texts copied that model, placing the responsibility for human improvement in human hands; in the earliest texts of the Renaissance, they counted on having God's help (like in the premodern texts of Saint Ignatius' *Spiritual Exercises*), but as humanism gradually became dominant, trust in human possibilities grew: the enlightened faith in reason and progress was perhaps the best example. The humanist era therefore also represented a rejection, a condemnation of sloth. The defence of progress, armed with reason, science (as became fashionable in the 19th century), or through mere economic development (the laws of which were so well studied by Adam Smith in *The Wealth of Nations*), was against the vice of sloth. There were so many things to be done! Even Protestantism, which emerged with a very negative vision of human possibilities and a rejection of the humanism of the Renaissance, would eventually succumb to a productivist philosophy that was, by its very nature, opposed to sloth, as Max Weber explained so long ago in his classic book on the origins of capitalism. Deep down, it is from this Central European root that sprouts the notion that work makes us free and, by extension, sloth enslaves us.

Thus, despite humanism gradually substituting Christianity in every aspect of culture, sloth remained verboten. The 20th century saw the birth of new schools of humanism. Fascism, Nazism, socialism, they were all calls to action, calls to build a new society. Marx is famous for his diatribes against the vampiric unproductive classes, and no one – except for his master Hegel – ever made such a strident defence of the need for and dignity of work. According to this view, sloth made the actualisation and expression of true human nature impossible. It was in the USSR where perhaps the most rabid refutation of sloth emerged. We are referring, of course, to Stakhanovism: of their own volition, some of Stalin's workers decided to increase production above the regime's quota. And they were not executed for it, but praised and held up as an example. Ironically, historians blamed later inefficiency and the lack of stimuli – in other words, sloth – for ultimately leading to the fall of that regime. It is ironic because something similar to Stakhanovism flooded the parts of Europe that had remained faithful to liberal humanism and capitalism. Efficiency, the search for productivity, and the need to compete demanded that sloth be vilified. And the idea that sloth had to be vilified was exported with surprising success to those Asian countries who also imported capitalism after World War II. Japan and South Korea are famous for their levels of productivity – as well as their high rates of suicide, work related stress disorder, and mortality rates for overwork.

No longer does anyone retreat from a world crazed by productivity. Nobody ever now retires to a monastery. That's how deeply the proscription against sloth has penetrated our society, despite Christianity – sloth's first predator – being substituted by humanism. By the way, no one ever went to a monastery to laze around: the Benedictine motto *ora et labora* prohibited that. But the primary task at the monastery was contemplation; even work was tinged with the unproductivity of reflection. The ancient Greeks, those aristocratic men, also considered leisure and the contemplative life as the highest goal. Work and productive activity was for slaves, the lowest of men. This first idea the Greeks held – that it is better to retire to the monastery, working little and doing the least productive of jobs, which is to pray – is rejected today for its sterility, even in a physical sense, that was better understood within a paradigm of waiting for the end of times, a paradigm that we have inevitably left behind. The second one, the idea that it is better that women and slaves do the work, seems, correctly, to be an eminently rejectable patriarchal and classist model.

The Western World has, in theory, definitively rejected that initial idea that humans had to be redeemed from their sins and vices, including sloth: humanism does not have a negative view of mankind. But it has surprisingly continued, in practice, to act as if mankind needs redemption, as if we must overcome and get past our defective condition. At times this mission to redeem mankind has appeared in a more kindly disguise, affirming that we must develop all of our potential. Yet either way, it has been constant in its persecution of sloth.

II – COMPENSATORY VINDICATIONS OF CONTEMPLATION... AND SLOTH

It is now possible to gather quite a number of texts that speak in favour of contemplation. Noteworthy among the most recent is

Byung-Chul Han's *The Burnout Society*. Han aligns himself with a small tradition of authors who argue for deacceleration and the contemplative life. Other cultural products have denounced the disappearance of free time, the disappearance of the ruminative impulse, and vindicated the need to recover unproductivity. Alongside the thousands of self-help books that tell us how to be more productive and effective, there are thousands of other titles that encourage us to take everything more in our stride: they teach us to meditate, to breathe, to acquire new awareness. They are clearly compensatory cultural phenomena: shredded pieces of a suit torn by the pressure of dominant culture.

If we look further back, into the 20th century – the century that idolized productivity, technology, and wars, and that worshipped power – it is possible to find authors who defend not so much the contemplative life, but it's younger sibling, sloth. These are more radical books. They don't seem capable of nourishing your soul. Yet they do. Those among us who still remember them and read them occasionally do so for their literary quality more than as ethical guides. After all, the lives they narrate are not exemplary ones. Who could model their life after the stories of Charles Bukowski (1920-1994) or the early works of Henry Miller (1891-1980)? They were men who made sloth their way of life. Undoubtedly, they were drawn to write as a rejection of a hyper-productive world, a world that aspired to efficiency, wealth, triumph, and ever-increasing power. In their way, they were prophetic figures that were somehow comparable to the original Franciscan movement. Both Bukowski and Miller were, in practice, great defenders of poverty, as was Saint Francis. However, they did not defend the chastity and meekness promoted by the saint from Assisi. We don't really know what to do with these figures, just as the church didn't really know what to do with Saint Francis and persecuted the Franciscan brotherhood until it was tamed and absorbed by the institution, but with the essence sucked out of it. Humanism doesn't know what to do with professional sloth: it sees no use in it. Or perhaps it does. In the end capitalism ends up incorporating the slackers, co-opting them, converting them into successful writers, for example. Like all prophets, these figures are excessive. We can admire them, but we cannot imitate them. We can understand their defence of laziness (or poverty) as a reaction against a world that is too pressurized and that proscribes sloth as a fundamental way of life. Deep down, even today we usually consider those who decide to marginalize themselves as crazy kooks. We see someone who has chosen to place sloth and unproductivity at the centre of their life as either sympathetic, or parasitic. But generally, we consider them unredeemable, useless. The typical protagonist of Miller or Bukowski's novels is just not inspired to make something of his life. The professional idler sometimes makes us laugh (such as in *The Big Lebowski*) but generally we're distrustful of them.

III – BUT WHAT IF WE WERE JUST FINE AS WE WERE?

Pico della Mirandola situated man at the midpoint of the great hierarchy of beings. Human dignity consisted of the freedom – only available to humans – to choose whether they wanted to ascend or descend within the hierarchy. They could aspire to resemble angels, or beasts. Humanism is a new religion, different from Christianity (in humanism it is man, not God, which is most sacred), but it's new wine in old wineskins: it reproduces the patterns and mistakes of Christianity. From the possibility of ascending or descending, humanism derived the idea that humans had the *obligation* to ascend. That humans needed to ascend. Ascension is good, degradation is bad. All technological development, all the progress of the West, responds to this idea: we need power, we need to ascend.

It didn't occur to any humanist that perhaps it was better for humans to remain in the middle position that Pico della Mirandola believed was their natural place, and everything was developed based on this idea of constant betterment, as if humans were obliged to perfect themselves. Just as they had previously been in Christianity, laziness and other vices were an obstacle to this betterment, an obstacle to human redemption.

No humanist ever seriously considered the possibility that humankind, in its middle ground, had no need for redemption or betterment. No humanist ever believed that we were just fine as we were and that the best thing for us was to remain right at that intermediate point on the chain of beings. Deep down, not even the first humanists understood or loved humankind. They all believed we weren't good enough.

No one put forth the idea that, just maybe, humankind needed sloth, wrath, envy and all the passions, in order to be human. No one suggested that the human task was not ascension, but learning to live with those passions. Passions that were not undesirable, but precisely what made them who they were: good – though not perfect – beings, but good enough beings in their own way. No one suggested that humans are defined by their chaotic passions, and that that's okay. No humanist ever believed that humankind was good enough as it was.

After all, it's impossible to live fully without sloth, wrath, lust, gluttony and all the other chaotic passions. It's impossible to live a fully human life.

One could say that the traditional Christians wanted to replace man – with all his typical imperfections – with something else. According to their anthropology, man had a supernatural calling so they never worried much about discovering human fulfilment. They postponed it for another life or a better world.

However, at least seen through contemporary eyes, that substitution didn't really make the grade. The explanations about life in paradise or heaven are few and far between, and not terribly appealing. Except for Tertullian's. He said that one of the pleasures of heaven was being able to look down at the suffering of those condemned to Hell – or at least, that was what Nietzsche claimed.

Tertullian made it clear that fun and pleasure must always include some element that Christian anthropology considered a chaotic passion. In this case, resentment: a mix of envy and wrath. And humans cannot understand a full life without fun and pleasure; as such, we cannot possibly comprehend a truly human life without some aspect of lust, gluttony, wrath, and sloth. Yet the sagest Christians demurred from going into details about what was attractive about the life to come: they weren't sure. And humanists have done the same thing. When they tried to imagine a perfectly ordered human life it was far from appealing.

One of the clearest examples is found in Jonathan Swift's book *Gulliver's Travels*. The protagonist, after visiting numerous kingdoms plagued by the typical defects of human societies – which the author exaggerates to satirical effect – finally arrives to the land of the Houyhnhnms, perfectly civilized horses who form the perfect society. After learning their language, Gulliver finds that the horses live without envy, rage, or any desire for domination; they all do their part without slacking and they all respect each other. The Houyhnhnms live alongside some disgusting ape creatures called Yahoos, who live outside of civilization. Unlike their masters, the Yahoos are violent, lustful, lazy, dirty and disgusting (the Yahoos, of course, are men, and show to what extent Swift, despite being a humanist, felt a strong disdain for the typical defects of humankind). The deeper question, however, is this one: the society of the Houyhnhnms, despite Swift's efforts to endow it with realism and attractiveness, is terrifically boring and devoid of the slightest vitality. One could even presume that the objective of the Houyhnhnms is to carry out a cadaveric life, a robotic life, a lifeless life.

Constructing a robotic, lifeless life in a perfectly ordered and civilized society also seems to be the basic idea of the post-humanist technological utopia. A society of manipulated zombies in which you cannot die, cannot grow ill and in which people can be modified to convert them into perfectly adapted and efficient beings (the first vice to go would undoubtedly have to be sloth): a robotic life, a risk-free life, a lifeless life.

It is highly symptomatic that no convincing utopia exists from the twentieth century, the century of technological explosion. Rather, what's proved more successful are the dystopias, beginning with *We* by Yevgeny Zamyatin (an interesting predecessor to Orwell's *1984*) and continuing with Huxley's classic *Brave New World*.

The fact that neither the ancient (Christian) nor the modern (humanist) reformers have been able to explain how human life would improve with the elimination of imperfections such as sloth, gluttony, lust, wrath, etc., proves – to our view – that this life is perfectly fine just the way it is, and in no need of reform.

IV – ANTHROPOLOGY OF SLOTH

Ancient Christianity saw man as a failed saint. He had to aspire to virtue and sanctity and could never quite pass muster. For humanists, man could ascend (neither original sin nor a God stood in his way) and had to ascend; he had to increase his power. Both anthropologies, that of the failed saint and that of the aspirant to godliness are, most certainly, erroneous. They both emerge from a wrongheaded concept of what human beings are.

A literary work that remains relevant despite dating back to the Spanish Golden Age is *Don Quixote*. In it, Cervantes manages to depict – through Don Quixote and Sancho Panza – the two faces of the human soul. We all want contradictory things; human nature means wanting contradictory things. We all have an idealistic side that wants life to be edifying, that wants life to be a heroic endeavour, that wants to offer it up for some cause, that needs to feel we are making sacrifices, that needs meaning and purpose. At the same time, we are all pragmatic and want what's good for us: we don't always act heroically (sometimes even poking fun at heroes) and what we want is to have a good time and be left alone. Christian anthropology deems this second facet of our soul as sinful and something to be repressed while humanists, obsessed with increasing human power, also vilify sloth. When presenting ourselves to others we usually conceal one of the two facets of our soul. We generally prefer to present ourselves as Don Quixotes and hide the second facet. Writers, professors, politicians, educators, judges, journalists, scientists, doctors, military and police officers, priests and monks and all others who, in some way, have the ability to shape society, tend to hide their own Sancho-Panzaness and accentuate their more epic Don Quixote side. They feel they must present themselves as responsible, serious people with concern for others. Those writers who promote sloth and unproductivity as a way of life, the Millers and the Bukowskis, pretend they've slain the aspirational, heroic side of themselves. Yet we don't quite believe them. Perhaps the characters in their novels have no ambitions, but the authors at least have the ambition of publishing and excelling in their literary art. As such, they aspire to some recognition and societal influence. Both characters, Don Quixote and

Sancho Panza, are part of us. We cannot escape that. Anyone who attempts to escape it is fooling themselves and going against human nature: both the ascetic who retreats to the desert and pretends he can leave Sancho Panza behind, and the imitator of Baudelaire who gets up at four in the afternoon only to start smoking joints and playing computer games, thinking they've banished their inner Quixote. Sooner or later, in both cases, the facet they've tried to supress will come back to take its revenge.

Sloth is an essential characteristic of human nature, as is the desire to overcome it. So we mustn't put forth an ideal of human beings in which sloth is suppressed. And we mustn't consider sloth as an impediment to reaching our true selves. Sloth is already who we truly are. In the end, humans are neither angel nor beast. They resemble angels in their ability to wish for and pursue higher things, and they resemble beasts in their occasional enjoyment of a good roll in the mud. And they should be happy to be able to do, and know how to do, both things. Pigs would probably be very surprised to see all of the things we do over the course of a normal day: they wouldn't understand even half of them. Pigs do not aspire to greater things because they lack our capabilities yet we shouldn't renounce our superior abilities just because pigs don't understand them. And it's possible that angels look at us with secret envy when we go out, get pissed and have a good time, or when we have a lie-in until noon instead of being the early bird who gets that worm. After all, that's something they can't do.

It's a curious thing to realise that because of our ingrained humanism, even today we stubbornly insist on engaging with this dilemma that juxtaposes pigs and angels. In 2017, Jordi Pigem still addresses it when analysing the problems of the modern world:

There are two paths, that of interiority and that of reification. There are two models, that of angels and that of robots. They are incompatible models, divergent paths. And one must choose.

The Catalan philosopher revives Pico della Mirandola's dilemma, merely substituting beasts for robots. His book is explicitly based on Christian humanism, among other traditions; it states that we are failed saints because we don't aspire fervently enough to 'salvation,' despite it being our true destiny. It is worth noting that Pigem considers human beings incomplete:

Hypertechnological and consumerist society tends to conceal a fundamental trait of human nature: our incompleteness [...]. Human completeness is not innate, but must be achieved along a long path, often filled with obstacles, that leads to what these traditions call [...] salvation or liberation (*nirvana*).

But the dilemma of angels or robots is false and unnecessarily depressing. Because our true vocation is not to be angels. Neither do we, when renouncing angelhood, automatically become robots. Nor is it clear that humans are incomplete, although many spiritual traditions have taught us to see ourselves that way. You can be a decent human being without having to aspire to become a 'spiritual' being. Being a decent human is already a good enough goal and certainly one that entails significant work to achieve.

From all this we can deduce that in human lives there is a time for all things (a time for the spirit, a time for the flesh) but that, above all, sloth and the other deadly sins are not always bad, and that a truly sage person will not aspire to completely suppress them.

V – SLOTH AND PAIN

Sloth is rather like pain, though usually much more pleasant. No one enjoys suffering, but everyone acknowledges that pain is useful. Without it, we wouldn't know when we are ill and need to recover before continuing on with our lives. Without pain, we wouldn't know when we are getting burned, or that some exquisite culinary delicacy is bad for us, or that we'd just broken an arm or a leg. Pain is always an exclusively internal sensation, but it can have external causes, such as when something attacks us, or due to some malfunctioning of our bodies, when something inside of us stops functioning properly. We too often make the mistake of believing that feeling sloth is always attributable to our imperfection; we believe that we feel lazy because we aren't good enough. This idea is absurd; it would be like saying we feel pain because we aren't good enough and that it would be better not to notice that we're getting a sunburn or have some internal injury. If we ignored our pain, our injury would only get worse, in fact, infinitely more serious: we would eventually die in unbearable agony. And we already know what happens when something is bad for us but doesn't cause us pain. Addictions, such as to tobacco or gambling, don't bring about pain until they are very far along and normally, when we want to react it is already too late. If instead of feeling real pain we had some theoretical, merely informative knowledge that something had ceased to function within us, we wouldn't bother to look for solutions with the urgency and intensity that pain demands of us.

Believing that sloth is always *only* bad can blind us to a common fact: that sloth is provoked by things that are actually harmful to us. Most of the time sloth, like pain, is a highly useful and adaptive defence mechanism. As with pain, sloth is an alarm signal that forces us to stop and take heed. But because of Christian or humanist prejudice, we tend to believe – very unfairly, very imprudently – that sloth is making a mistake, and we try to overcome it like a football player who continues playing through his pain because he doesn't want to miss an important match. It is admirable and we usually praise these sorts of decisions. But they are foolhardy.

We don't feel lazy about things that are true internal imperatives. Our footballer really wanted to continue playing, he didn't want to miss the match. But pain is the greatest imperative in existence. Modern hedonists understand this very well. They say that nature gave us two great moral teachers: pleasure and pain. We would amend this to three: pleasure, pain, and sloth.

Sloth reveals our true motivations. Sloth is an instrument of discernment. And, unlike the urgent message pain sends, sloth's message is more subtle, more philosophical: it informs us that what we were doing, or were set on doing before sloth reared its head, is not really something we wanted to do: it was an obligation of which we should be suspect. Almost always, the things we feel lazy about doing are obligations our Don Quixote has acquired, not with his own money, but with Sancho Panza's savings. And without Sancho Panza's permission, without his consent, without his participation.

VI – ACEDIA

Both the ancient Christians and the humanists knew it. They were aware of the virtue, of the potential for discernment that springs from sloth. But their own propaganda kept them from admitting to it.

Take the case of acedia. Acedia, or the Noonday Devil, is an old subject of Christian ascesis. In fact, it stems from the tradition of the first anchorites, the early Christians who went into the desert to publicly demonstrate their devotion to God. Invariably, it seems, after some months – or some years – of loyal solitary life, the temptation to give it all up and return to *civilian life* showed up with a vengeance. The devil would attack and tempt the believer when he had already travelled a good stretch of his self-imposed path to perfection. They called it the Noonday Devil because it never showed up right at the start, when one had first committed to that demanding way of life, and it rarely showed up when one had already spent most of their life living as a hermit: the devil attacked when the initial period had passed, just when the believer still had wiggle room to reconsider his life choices. The first symptoms of the devil's attack were feelings of emptiness, discouragement, and obviously, sloth. The anchorite no longer had any desire to continue with his extremely strict plan. He no longer had those feelings of spiritual consolation and voluptuousness during prayer; in fact, he didn't feel like praying at all, and his mind was distracted with unproductive memories of his past life and fantasies of what he could have been.

In a certain way, despite the centuries that separate them, the monk overcome by acedia was a victim of the same affliction, which they called spleen, suffered by the 19th century Modernists led by Baudelaire. The etymology is amusing: the spleen is a mysterious organ that can be life-threatening when it swells and bursts, but which can be surgically removed without the patient's life being affected much (if at all; it seems the liver can do the spleen's job). At some point in the history of Western medicine the spleen was deemed to be the origin of melancholic feelings. Because of the spleen, or the feelings that came from it, Baudelaire felt like a *jeune squelette*. His most programmatic poem – entitled 'Spleen (LXXVII)' – reveals some pain but also much, much self-pity:

> I'm like the king of a rainy country, rich
> but helpless, decrepit though still a young man
> who scorns his fawning tutors, wastes his time
> on dogs and other animals, and has no fun;
> nothing distracts him, neither hawk nor hound
> nor subjects starving at the palace gate.

When one chooses to see himself as a king surrounded by fawning tutors, one can't be feeling too bad. The prevailing emotion in an attack of spleen is ennui, metaphysical boredom. Realising that certain feelings are universal is less surprising than it seems at first glance; they occur in quite varied eras and circumstances – after all, what could a third-century monk in Asia Minor possibly have in common with a spoiled young 19th-century Parisian with a fondness for drugs and prostitution? Boredom, despair, acedia, we carry them in our very organs. Of course, one could have their spleen removed. But they probably wouldn't, in part because there are interesting revelations to be had in attacks of acedia.

Today we have another, more neutral, name for this same phenomenon, although it still retains a tinge of condescension and disdain: midlife crisis. The men and women of today are also faced with the *temptation* to reconsider their life choices, and the first symptom is a vague uneasiness and a very intense apathy, an inexplicable difficulty to accomplish everyday tasks that were once simple. Suddenly, they lose interest in their spouses. Suddenly, picking up the kids, making dinner, or tidying up the house, etc., seem like monumental undertakings.

The name change, however, is an improvement: we are no longer so convinced that this phenomenon is due to an attack by the devil, we are no longer so convinced that this crisis has to be a bad thing. We have learned to read between the lines and no longer have a Manichaean view of our existence (early Christianity – as paradoxical as it may sound – was deeply Manichaean). Today, we see the attack of the Noonday Devil as an attack of realism, which is what it is: only in midlife have we gathered enough information to know what life consists of.

And the best part of it is that, in situations like this, it is sloth that *leads the way*. A man or woman in the throes of a midlife crisis experiences deep laziness and great difficulty in continuing with his or her everyday life, which has become grey and boring. Now, wisely, they will allow themselves to be led by sloth in order to figure out what to do. Because what is more of a drag: continuing with life as it has been or going out in search of a new life? It would not be surprising if they were to decide to continue along their previously chosen path precisely because a drastic change, finding a new partner, a new job, a new house, a new family, *is even more of a drag* than continuing as before. The effort and the sacrifice it took to get to that point, even if that point is a painful crisis, weigh too heavily, and starting fresh would mean a new effort and a new sacrifice that aren't really worth the bother. If they decide to continue because they don't have the energy to change, they will be doing the right thing. If they still have a reserve of excitement about changing their lives, they will be doing the right thing to make the change. After all, everything requires much effort and the degree of laziness over one choice versus the other is the best method of discernment. Sloth at the idea of continuing has destroyed many struggling marriages, but sloth at the idea of making a change, sloth informed by experience, has also saved many. In the first case, Don Quixote would have won out; in the second, Sancho Panza. But there will have been a negotiation, and the wisest, most prudent judge that could preside over it is always sloth.

(A final coda before moving on to procrastination. An

example of these sorts of situations taken from fiction, and from real life. There is a novel by George Orwell, written in 1939, called *Coming Up for Air*, in which the protagonist – a man in a full-blown midlife crisis – admits that if his wife were unfaithful to him, he wouldn't feel jealousy or rage, but rather admiration. At a certain age, we no longer have the energy for certain adventures: thinking that his wife could still have the reserves of energy needed for an affair would be a pleasant surprise. That is precisely the reasoning of a conversation overheard at work: someone who admitted to being somewhat tempted toward infidelity but didn't follow through because of a laziness at having to plan, carry out, and, above all, hide the affair. How many times, and in how many different places, has that same conversation, with the same conclusion, been repeated?)

VII – PROCRASTINATION

Procrastination was explored in depth by Shakespeare in his play *Hamlet*. Young Hamlet is visited by the ghost of his father, the late King Hamlet, who explains that he did not die of natural causes but was murdered by his brother Claudius, who now sits on the Danish throne. The ghost charges his son to avenge his death. The prince, however, keeps putting it off. The play, in point of fact, revolves around the excuses the prince gives for not carrying out the mission he's been charged with – a strange plot, when in theory the protagonist of a play *should do things*. Hamlet, after the ghost's visit, declares that he will feign madness so he can more freely spy on the courtiers and confirm what the ghost has told him. One of the supporting characters, Polonius, on seeing Prince Hamlet's strange behaviour, exclaims *though this be madness, yet there is method in it*. This is precisely our theory: sloth is madness with method. Polonius says this because of Prince Hamlet's 'antic disposition'; we say it because of the virtue of discernment implicit in sloth and because Hamlet uses procrastination as a tool of discernment.

Shakespeare's tragedies are usually classified according to the dominant passion they explore. Thus, *Romeo and Juliet* is about love; *King Lear*, about rage; *Othello*, about jealousy; *Macbeth*, about ambition, and *Hamlet*, as we said... about sloth. The asymmetry with regards to the other passions is very obvious. Love, rage, jealousy and ambition have something honourable about them; they are dynamic passions, potentially destructive but laden with vitality and energy for action. Sloth deactivates all action.

This is precisely what Prince Hamlet complains about. His famous monologue, 'to be or not to be,' ends with a few magnificent verses on inaction that offer a very simple and profound key to interpreting the true nature of sloth:

> Thus conscience doth make cowards of us all,
> And thus, the native hue of resolution
> Is sicklied o'er with the pale cast of thought,
> And enterprises of great pith and moment
> With this regard their currents turn awry,
> And lose the name of action.

His constant postponement of his duty is rooted in the discovery of one's own finiteness. What the end of the monologue reveals is the connection between the impossibility of acting and the discovery of one's mortality. After meditating on suicide, and not daring to follow through because of the uncertainty of the afterlife, Hamlet states that it is conscience that robs our capacity for action. The idea makes particular sense when discussing suicide, as its direct consequence is death. But here, Hamlet links *all* action or enterprise with the most fatal of consequences, as if every action were a mortal reference, as if every truly free, conscious action must accept death in order to be carried out. What sloth reveals, according to this, is the existence of death itself. Not too shabby for a supposedly disreputable vice.

Once again, we find a parallel between sloth and pain. Pain also reveals our mortality. What remains to be discerned is whether this pain we feel, this laziness, is caused by something wrong inside of us or whether it is external. Humanist prejudice, of course, would say that Prince Hamlet's problem originates inside of him (remember: mankind is never good enough, not even for the humanists). His father's death makes Hamlet realise his own mortality, and his revenge killing of his uncle then becomes the demonstration of his acceptance of his own death. The play's plot indicates that Hamlet needs to accept his own death before carrying out his vengeance, and he does so in this short prose section:

We defy augury. There's a special providence in the fall of a sparrow. If it be now, 'tis not to come. If it be not to come, it will be now. If it be not now, yet it will come – the readiness is all. Since no man knows of aught he leaves, what is't to leave betimes? Let be.

And in the following scene, the final scene of the play, Claudius dies at the prince's hand. Thus, the play gives a heroic – titanic – idea of human existence: man's mission is to accept his own death and only then will he be free. It is a vision that was revived by the existentialists in the 20th century. Death's existence means that life is absurd and cruel, and man's mission is to triumph over it: like Sisyphus, man finds meaning in the carrying out of actions itself and, finally, is content to push enormous rocks up a steep mountain slope. In order to overcome sloth, man must accept death and meaninglessness.

For the existentialists, the man who has discovered his own mortality is slightly superior – in terms of living authentically – than the man who acts mechanically, who never has a problem with doing his daily tasks, who lives with apparent flow because he never questions anything. The second man who has no need for procrastination because no task presents a problem for him is very likely to be living an inauthentic life. Philosophically speaking, the slothful man has a deeper knowledge of his own, mortal condition. But the man trapped by anxiety and inaction is only halfway there. What he must do, according to this sort of humanists, is renounce and sacrifice himself. In this sense, existentialism is again a victory by Don Quixote over Sancho Panza. Existentialism is a tragic and heroic humanism: man is alone in the universe, in a universe devoid of meaning because of death. The existentialist hero is surrounded by mediocre people who are unaware of the intrinsic limitations of life itself, who turn their backs on death. Sloth and inaction revealed this mortal condition, but man had the duty to accept the meaninglessness and act anyway, taking the weight of the universe on his shoulders.

Herein lies the error and excess of the existentialists. Humans are not good enough, sloth is a symptom of their mortal condition, but eventually it must be overcome. For the existentialists, Hamlet had to kill Claudius even though that would mean his own death. Once again, this is Don Quixote acting unilaterally. For this sort of humanist, sloth, in the end, was a test to teach men to overcome: in the end, man needed to improve, to redeem himself through brave action despite the vacuum of meaning.

However, what this view of the human situation was forgetting is the fact that Hamlet's mission ended up destroying him and everyone around him. Perhaps Hamlet should have seriously considered the possibility that if an action is that costly, it means you shouldn't do it. Perhaps Hamlet and his family would have been better served by his allowing himself to be led by sloth.

VIII – SLOTH AND OBLIGATIONS

Sloth, in our view, is an instrument of discernment. Just like pain, it reveals our mortal condition. But its true function is to reveal the existence of fictitious obligations.

An obligation is fictitious when it is imposed by an idealised vision of ourselves, and without a real moral imperative. These imperatives are easily recognisable: do no harm, help those in need, treat others as you wish to be treated. But an idealised image of ourselves somehow slips in, complicating our lives to no end. It is no longer about allowing ourselves to be led by basic decency, but rather aspiring to more. When Don Quixote gets one of his ideas, Sancho Panza grumbles. And in those cases, the wisest thing is to listen to Sancho Panza. The only obligations we are truly obliged to fulfil are those that entail taking care of people; the only obligation is making sure others' needs are met, particularly those in our charge. We don't have the obligation to be the best people possible, but to be decent people, good enough people, each in our own way. We are not obliged to accept our own deaths with equanimity or heroism. We are not obliged to be saints, or to ascend to angel-like status. Rather, our obligation is to avoid people's starving to death or suffering unnecessarily. The rest is optional and, despite what Don Quixote, Jordi Pigem, the pope, or Raimon Panikkar want to believe, that doesn't make us better or worse. Because of our desire to fulfil an idealised image of ourselves, we do many stupid things over the course of our lives and, unfortunately, we sometimes don't do that which is a true obligation.

An obligation is fictitious when it entails work that does not lead to a truly necessary result. Jobs are actions we carry out in order to cover necessities. When it comes time to determine whether an obligation is real or fictitious and, as such, whether we should fight against our sloth or give ourselves over to it, it would be hard to find a more useful distinction than the one invented by David Graeber, between *shit jobs* and *bullshit jobs*.

A shit job is one that feels like an obligation but is actually necessary because, if it weren't done, it would lead to bigger problems. Shit jobs are those routine, annoying, repetitive jobs that are often ones we'd rather not do; but they are absolutely necessary, such as setting the table, loading the dishwasher, shaving, taking the bus to pick up the kids from school, helping them with their homework, walking the dog, taking out the rubbish, or (for teachers) grading exams. Accomplishing them provides very little in terms of prestige. None of them are very heroic. There are entire professions that fall into the shit job category: streetsweepers, cleaning ladies, restaurant waiting staff. Like all jobs in the primary sector, they are tasks that are absolutely necessary to all forms of social and political regimes. They are jobs that, in the past, were carried out by slaves. In our daily lives there are always quite a few moments when a shit job has to be done but they're real obligations because they are invariably related to taking care of people and dealing with absolutely basic necessities. We often postpone them as much as possible but we eventually end up doing them, because they're necessary.

On the other hand, a bullshit job is one that in no way deals with a necessity, one that helps absolutely no one. Those sorts of jobs, clearly, have no real content and do not need to be done. Feeling sloth about doing them is natural and the correct thing would be to listen to that sloth and not do them. Unfortunately, bullshit jobs have proliferated greatly. Given that human needs are much less sophisticated than we tend to believe and that, apparently, everyone needs to go to work every morning, most jobs today fall into the bullshit category. Industry produces countless goods that do not meet any basic need; there are tons of service jobs that offer no service (the entire financial sector, according to Graeber) except for the service of maintaining the system. The objective utility of jobs is always arguable. But bullshit jobs share a common feature: those doing them know they are pointless and, therefore, they feel very lazy about doing them.

The only reason they do these sorts of jobs is because they are well-paid (sometimes, in direct relation to their degree of uselessness). The only benefit that others derive from these jobs is that the system continues functioning. As soon as one discovers that these types of jobs are taking over their life, they must immediately quit, without looking back. Those who understand the nature of these jobs feel overwhelmingly uninspired by them, and that overwhelming feeling of sloth is the first symptom that sets the discernment process into motion. It is one of the clearest cases of sloth as our best guide. Quitting a paying job will only lead us into poverty, but poverty is better than a life taken over by useless tasks; if everyone quit their bullshit jobs, the system would collapse, but one wonders to what point it is worthwhile maintaining a system capable of generating such jobs. This sort of jobs are fictitious jobs (they don't fulfil any need) and, as such, we are not obliged to do them.

But we must insist on this point: beyond bullshit jobs (which are a trap we usually fall into by deceitful means), sloth vaccinates us against an idealised image of ourselves, from which a large number of fictitious obligations derive. Especially when we strive to better ourselves. The sloth we feel about going to the gym, or dieting, or eating better. Or learning a new language. The sloth we feel about following new trends of moral perfectionism: clean eating or veganism, etc. The sloth we feel about having to keep up with the latest in everything; about having to promote ourselves on social media, about having to take sides in political controversies. None of that contributes a substantial improvement to our lives, but rather ends up feeding our neurosis and our vanity. Meanwhile, no one doesn't feed their children out of sloth. If they aren't feeding them, it's for other reasons.

IX – SLOTH AND THE MIDDLE GROUND

The example of the married couple who stay together rather than deal with the hassle of divorcing is a perfect demonstration of human nature. One could certainly consider the survival of a dysfunctional marriage due to the laziness of the couple as terrifically sad, a pathetic example of human incapacity to act in the service of truly higher motivations. One could say that a person led by sloth is a coward and that those who break with what's holding them back and abandon what hurts them, even at a cost, are acting with admirable bravery. One could say that those who are guided by inertia and the path of least resistance, those who remain in their comfort zone, are making a mistake. This is false. Those who remain in a marriage out of passivity are fulfilling an absolutely universal and absolutely basic moral law: the law that says we must keep our promises. The fact that they do so out of sloth takes the gleam off their decision, making it rather less presentable. But, in the end, that decision also conforms to an ideal, albeit an ideal that is subtler, less showy, yet equally honourable and worthy of admiration: they are keeping their promise humbly, with the humility of the weak.

Humans, as we stated earlier, are beings situated in a middle ground. We should be content with our lot, between the angels and the beasts. Fulfilling a promise out of sloth demonstrates the greatest virtues of our middle condition; in fact, it shows that in that middle ground we can carry out decent acts with less than angelic motivations. After all, that is humankind's true destiny and the source of our dignity: we are able to do good things without having to feign entirely pure motivations. In the case of humans, when their less than perfect motivations result in a higher good, they are carrying out the highest good of which they are capable – a good that will never be angelical. They are fulfilling their most authentic calling and their true nature, which is not angelic. It is the nature of beings who are as much angel as they are animal, beings who are situated in the middle ground of that hierarchy.

There is no law that makes less than elevated motivations always result in good. At no point have we said that following sloth's lead will always guide us to a moral good. There is no *invisible hand* that converts mediocre things into good ones. All we are saying is that when people do the right thing, they generally do it with a variety of motivations, both good and bad, both base and elevated. Luckily, or unluckily, pure good will is beyond the grasp of humans because we are a mix of angel and beast, and innately impure. Mostly, rather than attempting to do good, we spend our time trying to avoid doing too much bad.

Given this middle condition, the choices that are in human reach are always more about diverting the deficiencies of everyday life toward something good than about choosing between good and evil. Regular folk are not heroic, or at least not consciously. Sloth is not so much a vice of human nature, but an inherent characteristic that can be used for good, like all the other characteristics of the human condition, including the brightest and most prestigious. The imperfections of everyday life are our natural terrain, our element. Losing our patience with them is clearly ridiculous and stupid; working in conjunction with them is clearly wise. Our task is not to suppress them, because we shouldn't strive to suppress an aspect of our nature. Our task is to make them fruitful, take advantage of the possibilities they offer us. Good that is done for base, negative reasons, is the natural human good. It satisfies both our inner Don Quixote and our inner Sancho Panza, our angel and our Yahoo. And it is in this spirit that we conclude this brief essay, with some advice on how to make the most of sloth. The diligent maximise their tendencies to increase their virtue. We sloths can do that as well.

Sloth is the pathway to rest and a contemplative life. A contemplative life is incompatible with both production and consumption. The capitalist system teaches us that our free time is for consuming, or that our free time must be productive. However, given the conditions imposed by our economic system, consumption is nothing more than a version of work: when we consume, we are working for others, we are working for others just like when we're at our jobs. And when we aspire to productive leisure, we are removing the very essence of leisure. If our sloth keeps us from both working and consuming, we are on the path to contemplation and we must continue along it, joyfully and guilt-free.

Sloth allows us to go home and stay home, physically and spiritually. Action forces us to expend our energies outwards. Sloth, the desire to do nothing, opens up space within us. Sloth in its fullest expression is comparable to the greatest richness. The true slacker no longer aspires to anything and, therefore, already has it all. Pascal said that all of man's problems derive from his inability to stay locked in his room. This is precisely what the slacker aspires to, and what slacking offers him. Sloth is what keeps us locked inside our inner rooms. Who can say whether the slothful no longer need anything, who can say whether the slothful already have it all and are staying in their rooms to enjoy it, or whether we should heed Pascal, who neither commits evil nor falls prey to it?

And it is when we settle down into our inner rooms, out of sloth, that our truly luxurious lives begin. Luxury is that which we enjoy precisely because we don't need it, and also because, to a greater or lesser extent, it is something exclusive, that only a few enjoy. Luxury, as such, is identical to gratuitousness and secrecy. Luxury is pleasure detached from necessity; it is hidden, private pleasure. Therefore, luxury should not be associated with consumption. Luxury is actually the ability to live without producing and without consuming. Both production and consumption force us out of our rooms and our homes, they make us expend our energies externally. Both production and consumption oblige us to interact with others, losing privacy and secrecy. Both production and consumption imply seeking out the approval of others. Luxury is being able to escape interacting with others. And when sloth keeps us from both producing and consuming, we find ourselves in a territory superior to need: the territory of luxury.

On the other hand, we normally associate human plenitude with situations of public success, with situations of reward for work and effort. Yet true plenitude is a private achievement that has no motives and goes unnoticed: it disappears when made public and is, in fact, hard to communicate at all.

To put it another way: we usually understand human plenitude as something linked to passion and bursts of vitality. We understand plenitude as ecstasy, as expansion, as an increase in power. We underestimate calm, dispassionate plenitude, which stems from knowing how to stay home. Sloth neutralises passion, but passion has always had very good press in the West. Saints are always passionate people, as are geniuses – the saints of the humanists. Which is why sloth and half-heartedness have always been looked down upon. But a true capacity for contemplation is incompatible with passion. Authentically contemplative people aren't *seekers*, what they do is closer to allowing themselves to be found. They don't sacrifice themselves but learn to sacrifice their passions.

When we are caught up in sloth, our usual passions fade away. A prejudice we've inherited from our culture makes us feel we must chase after them and recover them. Don Quixote represents the passion of production; Sancho Panza represents the passion of consumption. Sloth gets a bad rap because a superficial glance leads to it being interpreted as the triumph of Sancho Panza over Don Quixote. But what we are discussing here goes far beyond that. True sloth also cancels out the passions of Sancho Panza. This true sloth is the only path to our inner rooms.

In any case, we certainly don't need to live constantly searching out contemplation. Humans are motley beings, for whom permanent states do not exist. There is a time for all things in human life, yet we undoubtedly have the capacity for contemplation. Curiously, sloth is a doorway into that introspection that we would be wise to open.

We must learn to be slothful. We must learn to procrastinate. There is a sloth tinged with anxiety, a sloth that does not allow one to rest. This sloth lies at the opposite extreme of the sloth we invoke now. Anxiety around procrastination is what Don Quixote complains of when he is submitted to Sancho Panza's authority. However, a good procrastinator is one who has learned careful discernment. The good procrastinator is not anxious. He knows that if what he is postponing is truly a necessary duty, he will end up doing it. He knows that if what he supposedly has to do is actually a fictitious obligation, he will end up not doing it and be happy to be freed of the commitment.

Ultimately, sloth is one of the elements of our human nature, and one that must be factored into our prescriptions for the art of living. In the end, since it is not at all clear that our objective should be to become angels, there is no need to renounce sloth or banish it.

GLUTTONY

ADRIÀ PUJOL

Glotonia procura ladronici, e descortesia,
e luxúria, e vergonya.
Ramon Llull, *Llibre dels mil proverbis*

INTRODUCTION

Evil did not exist before human life awakened here on Earth. And evil will continue to throb in our hearts until human life here on Earth is snuffed out. However, that is not to say that we invented evil. It means that our ancestors could feel its throbbing because that which we can't perceive, that which we cannot *represent*, we cannot battle, exalt, conjure, or even tolerate. Whether humankind was created to battle evil or whether we were the evil seed is an altogether different question. Although it seems most likely we weren't activated for any higher calling other than to leave behind some fleeting testimony of beauty, pain, or things of that calibre.

We awoke. We decided we were the centre of the universe, or a winning lottery ticket, and we perceived evil. Gradually we began to ponder it, suffer it and reproduce it. More than one precocious mind tried to keep it at bay with flimsy rituals and schematic paintings, but it wasn't until the appearance of a minimally articulated language, some 70,000 years ago now, that we put a name to evil. And in doing so, we stipulated a hierarchy, some sort of thermometer for measuring malignancy. And with the appearance of writing, a mere 6,500 years ago, we fleshed out all of its characteristics. Since then, in every land and in every period, every priest, thinker and leader has made their own list, reflected in laws and rosaries. And that's as far as our progress has reached. We continue to pontificate on evil, amid paganisms buried deep in the dark recesses of our minds, ancient religions in their death throes, and new secular dogmas, media prophets and doom-merchants abound. We live among naysayers and enthusiasts, and the chaos is considerable. We certainly have a lot of opinions about good and evil.

On the other hand, nothing lasts forever, and some doctrines erode as quickly as beaches. For example, the evolution – which is to say, the perception – of sin has changed considerably. We'll go into this in more depth further on, but the concept of the seven deadly sins was not set in stone in the Bible. In the 4th century, we had the classification of temptations and bad thoughts put forth by the monk and ascetic Evagrius Ponticus, who included gluttony alongside drunkenness, fornication, greed, pain or sadness, wrath, sloth, vainglory and pride. Almost parallel to this we have the reflections of John Cassian, a priest and father of the Church in the 4th and 5th centuries, who deemed the pair made up of gluttony and fornication as the origin of all the other sins.

Classified in order of decreasing seriousness, the sins were considered the most ignoble transgressions of the soul. Yet some nestled inside the belly of others, and theological analysis wrestled with a hodgepodge of similar terms, so this meant the list wasn't formalised for another few centuries. It turns out that it isn't easy to categorise evil. It was Pope Gregory the Great, in the 6th and 7th centuries, who fixed the traditional sins, dissolving pain and sadness into sloth, vainglory into pride, swapping out fornication for lust, and adding in envy. And they became the seven capital sins in this order: lust, wrath, pride, envy, greed, sloth and with gluttony bringing up the rear. But, again, nothing lasts forever. In the 13th century, St Thomas Aquinas shifted it up. Gluttony moved into third place, after pride and greed. And, because humans are drawn to sadly pendular classifications, the theologists invented seven virtues: the cardinal virtues of human origin – prudence, justice, strength, and temperance – and the theological virtues of divine origin – faith, hope and charity.

Depending on the time period and the social climate, certain sins are seen in a worse light than others. As it currently stands, the scale of severity is not what it was in St Thomas' day, when Christianity topped the charts. Today, for example, unlike the Early Middle Ages, the sin of gluttony has many fans cropping up everywhere and, despite that, it's considered a lesser offence, a bearable vice. There are several different reasons for that. The main one is that we've democratised leisure, bingeing, our access to social benefits, the media and the energy we trade for comfort and, as a result, we've gained weight. And it turns out that, of the seven sins, the only one that can be seen at first glance is gluttony. Philosopher Francesca Rigotti explains that the first time she went to the United States she was shocked to see so many overweight people, so many shops filled with gigantic clothes. She also says that years later the phenomenon had spread to other parts of the globe: rolls of fat on display in the public square and a growing fondness for collective excess. The consumption of sugary drinks is off the charts, as if there were no tomorrow. Coca-Cola and Santa Claus dressed in red arrived in Europe with the Marshall Plan.

It is in this sense that Rigotti sets gluttony apart from the rest of the sins, because it be intuited. The others aren't as obvious, whether we are their victims or their perpetrators. When strolling down the street we can't pick out the greedy or the wrathful. We have no way of knowing if our neighbours often lapse into pride or envy. And perhaps we might think one of them seems lazy or lustful, but such judgments would be prejudgments. Not even when looking inside ourselves are we brave enough to accept that we have these flaws and so, generally, we turn a blind eye. The human capacity for self-indulgence is impressive. On the other hand, the sin of gluttony, inscribed on the soul and therefore impossible to hide like the others, also becomes flesh. Borrowing the concept from a WHO report, Rigotti speaks of global obesity or *globesity*.

Now, with the 21st century underway, all signs point to the worldwide number of gluttons only rising. To put it another way, it seems that gluttony is already making its way off the list of the seven traditional sins. Freed from any and all guilt, bingers are legion and doctors speak of an inherited disease or unhealthy habits. On the other hand, activists blame capitalism, and those who profit fight to wrest gluttony from archaic belief systems. In 2003, some French restaurant owners, gourmets and journalists made a formal request of Pope John Paul II, which the following year was published with the title: *Supplique au Pape pour enlever la gourmandise de la liste des péchés capitaux*: they asked him to substitute *gourmandise* (the canonical term for gluttony in French) with *gloutonnerie*. They didn't succeed, but – all snickering aside – the subject is not a trivial one. These days, a gourmand is someone who loves to eat but maintains a balanced, if somewhat quasi-aristocratic, relationship to food. Gluttons, however, are lost to insatiable appetites. At the same time, it is absurd to continue to view gluttony as an offence to God, when everyone clearly knows that the glutton's sin is really more of a mutilation. Double self-harm, both physical and social. Cardiovascular risk and side-eye, translatable into more expenses (taxes) for everyone and a poor group image, basically a tribal failure. Fatness is no picnic: it is purported to be depressing and, to top it off, it engenders distrust; the pot-bellied are the living image of a lack of control. Penance for today's gluttons entails rejection by distant relatives and self-rejection when looking into the mirror, without the aid of any hope for redemption in the world beyond.

We both scold and absolve each other among ourselves and

the punitive aspect impregnating all religions has waned in its zeal to repress gluttony. It's not for a lack of pulpits telling parables about the bad fate of gluttons, it's the audience who aren't listening anymore. On the other hand, there is a growing interest in other sorts of stories where gluttony is a distinguishing facet of evil. In the realm of fiction, we have numerous memorable villains of ample proportions who are fan favourites. For example, Kingpin (Stan Lee and John Romita, 1967), the portly crime lord in the Marvel universe, and Jabba the Hutt (Toby Philpott, 1983), the lascivious fleshy slug of *Star Wars*. The tough-as-nails mobsters in New York City, and other agents of evil that abound in contemporary fiction, seem proud of their nervous tics and their glandular disorders, or at least not embarrassed: their moral and physical deformities go hand in hand. Gluttony and obesity have a big role in this. Sinners fill their bellies and loll around and, sooner or later, they explode, reminiscent of the carnivalesque world of Rabelais and many other Renaissance writers: they made literature out of the last medieval worldview, trimmed it of guilt and warnings, and started us down the path of secularisation.

The profession of moral enforcement is not as popular as it once was, but the reward/punishment binary still keeps us on our toes. It must be that we have some need for it. The world's a crazy place, we tell ourselves, and now that we are less accepting of moral lessons and our souls are more controlled by economics than religion, we still enjoy the age-old stories. They don't solve the problems of incongruence and injustice, but they make them easier to take. We love to see others sin, not caring whether they're fictional sinners or whether they receive their just desserts *as God intended*. In the film *Seven* (David Fincher, 1995), a veteran detective and a rookie with anger issues hunt a serial killer who preaches: 'an eye for an eye.' In fact, he applies it and eliminates one sinner for each of the deadly sins – in common parlance, giving them *a taste of their own medicine*. The murderer serves up the glutton with a double punishment: forcing him to cut off a pound of his own flesh and then eat it, and then force-feeding him until he bursts. This punishment may seem over-the-top but, according to Xavier Theros, it is in keeping with medieval ideas, which were dominated by a tendency to mock everything and everyone. Gluttony is a deadly sin: related to pleasure and indebted to the stomach, it is of the flesh and settles in the flesh. As such, the killer in *Seven* stuffs his victim's belly and also makes him slice the outside of his body. At the end of the film, the rookie detective loses control and murders the murderer, the message being that evil will continue to haunt the world through sinners.

But let us return to real gluttony. In today's world it is both victim and guilty party. Its sufferers are enslaved to their weak wills – as shown in *Super Size Me*, the 2004 documentary by Morgan Spurlock that satirises the noxious effects of fast food and treats obesity as an evil endemic to wealthy societies, where gluttons spend above their means – and makes them look bad in the eyes of others who do take care of their appearance: a divine virtue in contemporary society. Gluttony has shifted from being an offence against God to a social sin. Except for certain days when feasting and lack of control are accepted and even encouraged (Christmas, Mardi Gras, hen and stag parties, weekends, celebrations with friends), and leaving off those for whom it comes with their work territory (F.C. Barcelona bigwigs' sumptuous dinners, truck drivers' heavy meals), unbridled gluttony is usually considered to be in poor taste (British all-inclusive package holidays to Salou, the proletarian frenzies on Sundays at the mall). Apart from that, there is much room for a variety of judgments (or not); everyone can decide for themselves whether a huge traditional roast of *calçots* served with romesco sauce is excessive, or a cultural imperative to improve the species.

In the Middle Ages they made a distinction between sins committed in the community, such as gluttony, wrath and lust, from those that only effected hermits and anchorites. Today gluttony needn't be practiced in groups: when we can spend our Saturday nights at home alone with a pizza and some calorific soft drinks. But in medieval times it was already considered a social sin and, furthermore, a sin of the rich. As such, sometimes the upper classes concealed it beneath their unwritten prerogative to ostentation. Eating and drinking were class markers: the banquet, the amount of meat (a luxury item), pastries and liqueurs. Today, however, the tables have turned, and a fatty, sauce-laden meal is no longer a symbol of power or distinction, not even in an economic sense. Now the rich can afford balanced diets with expensive, healthy ingredients, and invest quite a lot of money (and consequently, time) to maintaining a gorgeous glow that comes from being good-looking and physically fit.

From this perspective, the only aspect of the sin of gluttony that remains from the Middle Ages to our day, and which affects rich and poor alike, is not *edacitas* (the insatiable desire for food and drink) but *ebrietas* (insatiable desire for intoxicating beverages), as pointed out by Le Goff and Truong. The former included desserts, haute cuisine and fine liquor. The latter, however, could be anything from box wine to trendy cocktails. Gluttons have always sinned with alcohol, formerly in palaces and taverns, and today in neighbourhood bars and exclusive nightclubs. The only difference is that alcohol gluttony has mutated into an illness, shifted from voluntary vice to hereditary misfortune, from a sin of the rich to a sin across class lines, from individual depravity to social trend. Marshall Berman defines modernity as the era of a contradictory unity of disunity. We have socialised the virtues, but also the vices.

I – SIN, SICKNESS OR SYSTEM?

At the turn of the century, the World Health Organisation (WHO) began to warn us about the growing crisis of global obesity. There were no longer any barriers, or limits of age or gender, to being overweight. What is most interesting is that the WHO points to a morbid condition, in other words a sickness that is nearly pandemic, when the roots of the word *obesity* tell another story altogether: it comes from the Latin *ob* (on account of) plus *esum* (the passive participle of the verb *edo-edere*, to eat). While doctors are working hard to find a scientific response to the fattening of the human race (metabolisms and environmental factors), the etymology is respectfully reasonable: fat is not nature but nurture. Poor eating habits can start early. Formula feeding wreaks havoc with ingestive self-regulation and industrial baked goods in childhood are a diving board into the pool of future adiposity. If we add to that picture *incorrect* lifestyles (sedentarism, driving short distances, ordering in), obese adults will soon become sick, walking mosaics of wounds as their obesity leads to diabetes, hypertension and cancers.

When gluttony was a deadly sin, it also produced other minor sins. And, from medieval monks to today's taxpayers, only a correct lifestyle (without mood-altering substances, without junk food, and with some exercise) will give us the proper recipe for not committing the sin of gluttony. In other words, what was asked of the monk, and is asked of today's obese people, is self-restraint. That they fight against temptations. However, nowadays food and drink are relatively cheap and easy to come by, so fasting and the spirit of renunciation have fallen by the wayside. We are, after all, only human.

The ancient calendars were based on routine stretches alternating with special days and weeks, in which fasts and restrictions were punctuated by periodic feasts maintained by uses and customs: organising life in such a way that made it easier to appreciate a special meal or exceptional activities like dancing, getting drunk, acting the fool, or performing sexual acrobatics. The organisation of the almanac is a reflection of pre-industrial periods. Calendars still order earthly life, even though they are now used more for work than for ritual; yet there has been a sea change in uses and customs.

In the 13th century, Thomas Aquinas spoke of temperance in his *Summa Theologica*, the most influential work of medieval theology, which revolves around the distinction between needs and desires. To be honest, do we gobble down food according to our biological mandates or do we open the fridge for other, more temperamental reasons? Aquinas already saw, then, that when we can sate it without problems, excessive hunger is not a moral failing but a personal inclination that requires prudence; a perfectly achievable effort of restraint. Gluttony – he says – is a deadly sin, because if we don't control our bellies and the adjacent sensory pleasures, we debase ourselves and become fools inured to basic virtues. And the saint drives it home: greedily snacking on exquisite delicacies between meals is clearly related to enjoyment, but being happy is not such a serious sin if happiness is reached through order, reason and a love of God. On the other hand, from chaos we fall into excessive loquacity, leading us down a vulgar path, becoming cretins who embrace lasciviousness and impurity. Seven centuries later, the anthropologist Mary Douglas and the sociologist Pierre Bourdieu proved that gluttony has more to do with what is available to us and the social milieu into which we are born, grow up or join, than with a lack of love for God; and, depending on which way the wind is blowing, it's not about a lack of respect for one's fellow man, either.

The idea that the biggest piece of meat is for the head of the family harkens back to the caves. In any case, it's never been a simple task to recommend or even impose prudence, generosity and balance. When the punishment was supported by the idea of guilt and backed by divine authority, it was easier for people to moderate their habits or purge, even if only in the name of a tribute to God or in the hopes of a reward, generally good fortune or health associated with divine grace. But we have been through many centuries of secularisation, and the social sciences, trash television, the internet and medicine have created an entirely different moral order. Gluttons are victims of their surroundings. Character is a lottery that depends on one's family, along with cultural and social factors. Genes are a whim of evolution. And individual responsibility is watered down in the social ether which, on the other hand, is what we impose on ourselves through our habits. Gluttons are innocent, kidnapped by consumer society, neglected people who neglect themselves in the endless string of social causes and effects. It's everyone's fault, independent of whether this idea is good, bad or a pipe dream. And, therefore, any possible penitence will also be communal. There is nothing left of the individual act of contrition because the conditions that allowed it to exist have vanished in the smoke of centuries of atheism. Obviously, gluttons can go on a diet, join a local gym, or sign up for hypnosis for self-control, but these things will never be propelled by the extraordinary force of pointed guilt and secret confession. They are sick, not sinners, and we've all contributed to making them that way. And if they get past it, we'll applaud, and if they don't, we'll continue to pity them – the mask that rejection all too often wears.

While gluttony has gone global and become the subject of many remedies, the severe fasting that once served as its counterpoint has switched sides. It no longer counts among the virtues and today is seen as another manifestation of the same illness, an illness of psychological origin, of not being able to determine desirable limits. Anorexia, symbolically and by adopting the form of a disorder, has picked up the baton of brutal saintly penitence. For example, 16th century saint Charles Borromeo practiced long, rigourous abstinences, including lifelong celibacy. He was so famous for depriving himself of food and sleep that Pope Gregory XIII ordered him to be more moderate in his fasting. Borromeo looked horrific after subsisting for an entire Lent on dried figs. The saint told the Pope that he had learned much from the experience, that he believed himself capable of carrying out his duties in that state (he was a bishop) and that he preferred to die for the Catholic Church than to live outside of it. The Pope allowed him to continue and Borromeo died at the age of forty-six.

As can be gleaned from the feats of the saints in hagiographies, austerity and celibacy diminish sensuality and crystallise spirituality, smoothing the path to God, but it was understood and forgiven if they accepted small donations, or occasionally ate a cupcake, or touched themselves in the privacy of their chambers. But today, while receiving public approval, the austere or sexually apathetic (or merely sensible) are considered – in late capitalism – little more than losers. On the other hand, in the Middle Ages, rather extreme fasting was also seen as a triumph over the temptations of the flesh and served to set an example, as an arrow to jam into the abdominal bullseye of the immoderate. Harsh fasting made you holier, gluttony just the reverse.

Despite the fact that, in our era, those who practice prolonged abstinence from eating are put into the same 'sick' bag as gluttons, we are always more clement with anorexics than with overeaters. Because the former show a willpower of which the latter can only dream. And that links them to the admiration for Numantian renunciation of the body that Christian theology professed for the anorexic saints (see Hinojosa, 2009). We'll delve more into this later, but what hasn't changed much is the opinion that women, when they sin, sin doubly. Montaigne, in his 16th-century *Essais*, said that: 'it is much easier to accuse the one sex than to excuse the other.' When women shamelessly gain weight, when they fornicate left, right and centre without feeling guilty about it, and when they declare their devotion to some activity that could become a vice, the tribe regards them in a worse light than men who do exactly the same things. That is also why female redemption *seems more epic*. History, however, has been around for a long time. James of Voragine gathered, from 6th century sources, the torments that Radegunda (Thuringia 518 – Poitiers 587, second wife of the Merovingian king Chlotar I) imposed upon herself. When her husband killed her brother, Radegunda left him and devoted herself to monastic life. She also made a barefoot pilgrimage and founded a hospice for lepers. But what has made her a legend is that, for example, she would wrap her entire body in chains during Lenten fasting and, when she took them off, her skin would stick to them, leaving a trail of purulent wounds.

That said, what symbolic muddle remains within what we now call illnesses or heroic feats, and what we once considered sins or virtues? We've already seen that the glutton is still between a rock and a hard place. Once considered sinners and now considered lacking in willpower, it doesn't seem they'll be offered merit badges anytime soon. The glutton is not on a first name basis with a single virtue and, to top it all off, seems to be the modern-day reincarnation of the giant Gargantua, the paradigmatic sinner. Gargantua is proud, thinking himself superior. And he's overwhelmingly greedy, obsessed with filling his gullet. Gargantua is also lustful: it goes without saying how common the transubstantiation of meaning is between morbid flesh and a pornographic appetite for filthy, greasy sex. And he dies of envy because he always wants more and, if possible, more than his neighbour has. And he's wrathful, in proportion to his physical size and his psychic disorder. And, of course, Gargantua and the gluttons are slothful slackers. Here, again, we see the range of sensations provoked by the obese, whether we consider them sick or greedy. On the other hand, the anorexics are not considered mortal sinners, because excessive fasting can easily be brandished for a just cause. Hunger strikers are always good folk, or that's what people say. There is no evil person, no sinner, who goes on a hunger strike. And if a reprehensible person were to go on one, it would be because they were mortified by the actions of even more reprehensible people.

To fully understand the space currently occupied by gluttony, the shift it has made from sin to sickness, and how it has gone from the realm of a few to the majority, we would do well to revisit Montaigne, the sceptic. He affirms that we can repudiate our personal inclinations and condemn them publicly, either hypocritically or sincerely. We can even beg God to forgive us and make us good, but – no way, no how – that cannot be called *repentance*, meaning the basis of all redemption. Because we always find – he continues – something more perfect than us, a superior model of behaviour, even in the smallest of actions. And if each time we have to repent for who and how we are – he concludes – if we ask for penance every time, the end of the world would be an unfathomable ocean of desolation and guilt. It seems as if he is speaking of the standard character of the late 20th and early 21st Centuries. And here we find the key: ever since the Renaissance we have gradually become more and more convinced that sins are not blunders against God, but rather between us. The cruelty of some toward others, declares Montaigne.

It is in this frame of mind that we struggle to link ancient ethics of mortification (prevalent in grafted Christian culture) with capitalism's ethics of satisfaction. If an obese person's main sacrifice is having to go to the gym, that can't be considered a severe penitence by any stretch of the imagination.

So how is it possible that gluttony has such a good reputation? The popular philosopher Fernando Savater wrote that the sins designated by the Catholic Church are still the engine driving our contemporary economy. Without greed there would be no accumulation of wealth. And without gluttony there would be neither Carme Ruscalleda nor McDonald's. But then what has become of the virtues and the whole religious system of exemplars, penances and the renunciations of the saints who championed rectitude? Although perhaps a stretch, one might argue that celebrities (and their highly publicised lives) have substituted the lives of the saints and other protagonists of moral tales. *Saints and celebrities: a history of iconography.* While it is true that these sorts of substitutions, when one attempts to look at them archeologically, are more slippery than greased ghosts, it is clear that contemporary models of rectitude are no longer found in pulpits or in the books deemed sacred. No: the models are usually derived from the mass media. And they must be incarnated by *real* characters, because the titillation of realism reigns in a world of sceptics such as ours. As ridiculous as it may sound, think about it: athletes, actors, singers, politicians, media therapists, social leaders: the prototypes of the virtuous and the sinner travel through fibre optic lines, but begin and end in flesh and blood people.

The bestselling book by the celebrity who's overcome an addiction, the self-help plague, self-sacrificing or libertine princesses, prime ministers who combine fatherhood and work or who perpetuate other patriarchal god models. Good-natured or directly 'Fascist-lite' leaders, public figures today are the beacons of collective behaviour, whether we like how it reflects on us or not. Which is why the sensationalistic press mocks celebrities who inaugurate bikini season with more cellulite than glamour. The excesses of a retired footballer, the sad skeletal weight loss of an actress at a low point, magazines and television admonish, the public corroborates, and the world keeps on spinning. And, if the celebrities manage to *resuscitate* (emerging from sloth or an addiction to underage Asian prostitutes, if they ask for forgiveness for their drug use and donate to fifteen charities, if Hillary Clinton makes amends for her husband in public over the Monica Lewinsky case), spectators are moved and perhaps even absolve them – or martyrize them for evermore. On the flip side of this double function the saints have passed down to celebrities is their iconographic function.

But at this point it is still unclear what thread joins the functioning of the economy and the agents of evil. Because – Savater continues – it's okay that private vices become public virtues (*voilà* capitalism), but only up to a certain point. Those who step over the line and eat and drink more than their share will eventually be gobbling down what corresponds to those disadvantaged by the system. So, who or what do we have in place to keep evil at bay if its vehicles and bureaucrats (sins and sinners) are precisely those who maintain the functioning of the reigning capitalism system of constant, instantaneous, growing and highly contagious gratification?

We have scientists (doctors, biologists) who fight to stave off the dystopian future depicted in the film *WALL-E* (Andrew Stanton, 2008), when humans have fled an inhospitable Earth and live stuffed, obese and aided by robots in drifting spaceships. We have willing politicians and a financial system that periodically have to admit that access to unbridled consumption has its limits. We have ecologists and philanthropists. The occasional philosopher recycled into a star and the occasional star recycled into a philosopher who, with third-rate metaphors and cranking out the tears, warn us of the perils of voraciousness. And it must be said that we still have a vast network of mutual aid, heirs to the Christian charity that so often reaches the angles of existence that the government has left for dead. And we also have humour, malady of the ill, because in the name of total freedom of speech there isn't a single spark of morality that isn't automatically scorned by some joke.

The clergy are used to being the butts of jokes, since forever. Author Francine Prose explains that in contemporary Rome there is a popular bit of advice for tourists that says: 'if you happen to be near the Vatican at lunchtime and see a group of Jesuits or Dominicans, follow them and eat at the same restaurant.' Anticlerical humour that mixes the devout cynicism of the gluttonous clergy with a tinge of admiration for how large they live. But it's only a joke, like another one that says that: 'if you see trucks parked outside a restaurant, the food there must be first rate.' On the other hand, humour on the internet and in the media, the offshoot of this extremely modern shaming of each other that we engage in, makes it nearly impossible to find the measuring stick, the midpoint on the scale that weighs gluttons and moderates. Contemporary humour always leaves scorched earth in its wake, but it isn't a completely bad ally in our search for a solution: humour keeps the scammers at bay, even though it can't always distinguish them from the intrepid.

According to the sociologist and jurist Max Weber, it went like this: hardcore Protestantism placed responsibility back in the hands of the individual (eradicating the indefinite, blind, Catholic contract with God) and led him to believe that success on earth was a passport into heaven, and that trend lasted at least three centuries. Now that it's waned, the West finds itself nearing a new change in the moral order. The remains of Protestant ethics, after the poorly understood prescription of personal success and austerity, has left us with a panorama of gluttons, white-collar criminals and tourists looking for their next selfie to show off their expensive, remote destinations. Despite not being able to predict if that change will happen, atop the ruins of extravagant waste, an *aesthetic shift* has made its way through the sinner's fleshy rolls. Who knows whether it's just the latest turn of the capitalist screw, merely glimpsed in these pages, but we cannot ignore the first cries of a new proposal for collective redemption.

Earthly life takes up much more space than spiritual life. Even in countries where most of the population are devout believers, daily life – professional, political, economic and leisure time – has greater weight and, insult to injury, is profane: it is on the *religious holiday* of rest that we eat our weekly ice cream. Those who aspire to earthly plenitude, in other words those who are secularised in substance, pagan asceticism or Christian mortification, both leave them indifferent. The *oh so* Mediterranean ideas of shame and honour have lost their sting and we have freed ourselves from all moral meddling. But since it is clear that we will destroy our bodies and minds if we continue along this modern path, our collective concern is focussed on this worrisome eventuality. The warning comes in a therapeutic and ecumenical guise, but above all an aesthetic one. The body, the body.

We begin with the presumption that we are imperfect, that we are prone to small mistakes and, despite that, that we are good people, because we aren't harming anyone else. We've shaken off the Christian thinking that says that human nature has been evil since the original sin. We sidelined all hope in divine compassion and we've placed all our trust in doctors, politicians and industrial engineers. We are secular and kind-hearted and have only a few cravings that, after all, we deserve to satisfy. Evil comes from outside of us, from society, from capitalism, from history, from the neighbouring country. There is no personal blame and, at most, there remains some collective sin which, in any case, can be attributed to the institutions that represent us: the system. Immune to guilt, detached from any personal responsibility towards others or a job well done, we delegate. If my gluttony costs the system money, let the system fix it for me, because it is what's made me dissolute and licentious. I am aware that my mobile phone was put together by enslaved Chinese workers, built with materials mined by enslaved Congolese workers, controlled by weapons sold by my country, and I already know that the phone will only last a few months and that the landfills of electronic waste are ruining the environment for humans on the other side of the planet but, hey, I don't know, I voted for a green candidate and I just inherited this world I live in. I know it's unsustainable that I stuff my face with chocolate spread that deforests the other hemisphere but, really, they should look for some alternatives! I'm just a poor, harmless glutton who loves everyone.

If we are bad, it cannot be said that divine redemption or twinges of guilt are particularly successful at combatting that. If, however, we are good, and that is the general feeling, but just beset by a string of pathologies, the race against the clock to cure them seems like it's not working terribly well either. The doctors who treat the body and soul are breaking their backs to get us, in body and mind, on to the track of a healthy, happy life, but the queues are endlessly long. The horizon looks pretty bleak. Meanwhile, various doctrines of salvation are emerging. Aesthetics attempts, in the name of love and respect for others and ourselves, to return responsibility to the individual. To return people to the centre of the universe, but sheltered by the promise of a different universe, reminiscent of the one we found when we first awoke. Beginning with the body, with the balance of the body in harmony with the head, it wants to eradicate gluttony, but not by blaming the glutton or by marking him as a potential patient, but by inviting him to open his eyes. The basic message would be to consume responsibly and take care of his body, in solidarity and health.

Despite the tendency to veer toward virtuosity, we have to admit that it's very incipient. In theory, it has already been proven that excess (which begins with the individual and ends in the group) has taken on the dimensions of a biblical plague. But, in practice, it's a gargantuan task to implement collective temperance as a solution. The market has taken the message of moderation and, paradoxically, put it up for sale. Humour is scathing with the environmentalists who fly in airplanes and treat themselves to a weekly Scottish fillet. The state fines the dissident who installs solar panels without permission. Those who preach other lifestyles are put on the system's payroll. Gluttony continues to blot out the sun. The gyms are filled with people sweating like pigs while across the street crowds gobble down croissants and chips at cafés.

II – ORIGINS OF THE SIN OF GLUTTONY

We may or may not be believers, more or less devout or not in the slightest, and yet it is still unsurprising that at some point in our lives we feel the calling of transcendence, even if we leave the itch unscratched: when a loved one dies; when we feel we've been touched by Lady Luck. However, everyone – atheists and the pious, heathens and punks, the baptised and the apostate

– has heard of the system of vices and sins. It is imbedded in the messages we send and receive and is a system of rehashed Christianity that has made its way firmly into our cultural baggage around good and evil. These words by Ramon Llull (8th-9th centuries) from his *Libre de la primera e segona intenció*, would be seconded by any contemporary father:

'GLUTTONY, son, is the sin of superfluous eating and drinking; this be a vice of disordered will due to absence of temperance unloved by will; and this vice, son, be not created by null intention, but rather be accidentally come to destroy the intent for which temperance is created.'

However, the system of vices was not forged in year one of our era. It was distilled from ancient Eastern doctrines of astrology, hermeticism and gnostic speculation. The series of seven deadly sins is what remains of the astral voyage of the soul according to the convergence of the gnostic doctrine with early Christianity. At the time, it was believed that the individual soul emanates from God and travels down the seven or eight planetary spheres. It receives some positive traits on each sphere and is incarnated, on Earth, in a newborn's body. After death, the soul makes the opposite trip back, returning all the elements received on each sphere and again merges with God and lives happily ever after in the great beyond. The expression *being in seventh heaven* is a vestige of this idea.

In the words of the mythologist Mircea Eliade, the first ones to incorporate sin into the Christian tradition were the writers of the Patristic era, in other words, during the time between primitive Christianity (from the crucifixion of Jesus to the First Council of Nicaea in 325) to the twilight of the 8th century. Along the way, the Christian apologists linked the evil spirits of Gnosticism with the demons of classical antiquity and the Jewish religious tradition. In short, the idea of sin predates Christianity and the problem was already the same: the origin of evil and the need to rein it in.

In Christianity, evil is the negation of divine will, reduced – to cut to the chase – to human noncompliance with the commandments and the works of mercy. For Jews, on the other hand, everything is more manageable: if God created everything, he also created the possibility of evil. But in the Hellenistic period, evil was considered to be outside of God, alien, neither created nor caused by any relationship to him. In any case, there were evil spirits, enemies of men, the inhabitants of the seven or eight stars from which they wreaked havoc. In more precise words, the sins reached us in the form of spirits, of celestial gusts that penetrated humans through the five openings or senses and settled into their souls to corrupt them. One or two sins at the door to each of the senses (sight, smell, touch, taste, hearing), which are precisely the tools humanity has for relating to the world. Gluttony, in particular, could enter through any of the senses, and that meant it was one of the most commented upon and condemned vices.

We can imagine the religious disputes of early Christianity being highly interesting, because they sparked much speculation and, therefore, achieved prodigious heights of creativity. The *theorists* worked long and hard to establish doctrine, often through the reformulation of previous tales. Some Christian thinkers took a fragment of the Gospel of Luke (8:2), written around the year 80, in which Jesus goes preaching from village to village accompanied by women who'd been freed from demons and cured of illnesses, including Mary: 'called Magdalene, out of whom went seven devils.' It was Gregory the Great in the 8th century whose homily linked those seven demons with the cardinal sins, although he also, somewhat naively, drew a connection with Revelations 13:1, written in the 1st century by an unknown author, in which the Antichrist sends: 'a beast rising up out of the sea, having seven heads and ten horns.' It was all a bit of a stretch, but the passion was definitely there.

The idea of the planets having a pull on humans, for better or for worse – still visible today in horoscopes – is an inheritance from classical antiquity. In the mid-4th century, the Latin grammarian Maurus Servius Honoratus wrote a book of commentary on Virgil's *Aeneid* (1 BCE) that reviews the traits of the planet-Gods: the proud Sun, greedy Saturn, gluttonous Jupiter, angry Mars, lusty Venus, envious Mercury, and the melancholy sloth of the Moon. Character flaws marked by the heavens that were already considered vices or sins among Virgil's contemporaries. In Book I of the *Epistles*, addressed to the son of a nouveau-riche Roman, Horace (1 BCE) suggests he seek out only the necessary, avoiding excesses and shunning pleasures. Horace presents a string of vices based on his reading of *The Iliad* and *The Odyssey*, a collection that reads like a psychic act of plagiarism of the later Christian list of sins. Noteworthy in Horace's collection are sloth and gluttony, associated with *the love of wine*. In the first epistle, addressed to his friend Maecenas, Horace takes moral points from the *Aeneid* and sings the praises of hedonism tempered by moderation. In any case, his is a doctrine that reflects the battle between Stoic and Epicurean philosophies, widespread in classical antiquity. Christianity had no qualms about appropriating it to extend its popular reach.

But while earlier we said that today gluttony is considered an illness, in classical antiquity the vices were already seen similarly, in the sense that sinners didn't sin merely out of a lack of willpower or self-control, but because their (autonomous, contingent) bodies, and the firmament also had their own agency. The *theory of the four humours* is attributed to Hippocrates, a

Greek physician who lived in the 5th and 6th centuries before the common era. In those times, humour had no relationship to people acting silly or laughing at others' ineptitudes. Hippocrates said that good health depended on maintaining a balance of bodily humours in connection with the four elements that made up the universe.

Phlegm was associated with water, the yellow bile with fire, blood with the air, and black bile with the earth. Four elements that were also combined with different degrees of dryness or dampness. The theory of the four humours grew with the later addition of the Aristotelian framework and the association of the bodily fluids with the seasons and the stars. One's personality could be inferred by one's dominant humour [...] If we listened to a certain sort of music, we were lymphatic (phlegmatic, calm), hepatic (choleric, hot-headed), sanguine (contented, amorous), or nervous (melancholic, romantic).

Four standard personalities, vulnerable to being poisoned by a handful of vices. Four types susceptible to falling into the hands of evil spirits which, seen through the light of Christianity, turned into sins. What Hippocrates saw as more or less indomitable inclinations, Thomas Aquinas understands as perversions and offences toward God. Gluttony leads a troop made up of unseemly joy, scurrility, uncleanness, loquaciousness, dullness of mind, and lasciviousness. Here we see that gluttony is a *capital* sin because it is the captain of an army of soldier sins. And it is *capital*, basically, because its potential as a vice is exacerbated by voluntary acts against Our Lord, the true Captain.

The sins were soon divided into two categories: the deadly sins, that had to be punished with the extermination of the soul (Dante chooses annihilation for sinners in Hell), and the venial sins, which were eventually forgivable and could be set straight with harsh – but not eternal – penitence. In *The Divine Comedy*, the difference between these two types of evil was clearly marked. The evil dispositions or inclinations could be atoned for in the seven levels of Purgatory. But the serious sinner, who has broken one or more of the Ten Commandments, will rot in Hell, punished not for the base sin but for the results obtained from it. As for gluttony, eating for survival is not sinful, and the occasional lustful eagerness of the greedy guts is a redeemable sin, according to some a *pecatta minuta*. However, when it becomes chronic it is a deadly sin.

Yet the sin of gluttony is strange. It hangs on the abuse of two permissible things: eating; and enjoying oneself within reason. What's most curious is that it has no strictly contrary virtue. Broadly, sloth has strength; lust, the wisdom of maturity; wrath has knowledge, and pride can be reduced by fear – in each of these cases the sin is more clearly defined than the remedy. But gluttony can only be lessened by temperance, a vague virtue whose beginning and end are hard to pinpoint. This peculiarity is perhaps due to the fact that Christian morality presents the opposites in terms of a struggle between sins and virtues, in accordance with the spirit of Paul the Apostle's letter to the Ephesians (1st century):

Put on the full armour of God, so that you can take your stand against the Devil's schemes. For our struggle is not against flesh and blood, but against the rulers, against the authorities, against the powers of this dark world and against the spiritual forces of evil in the heavenly realms. (Eph. 6:11-12).

Notice here the astrological origin of the sins, and also notice the smattering of Christian testosterone that affects the later treatments. The virtues have never been given an equally bellicose treatment, neither in terms of doctrine nor iconography. The sins are at war for men's souls. And they all come in female guise. The virtues are also feminine in the Romance languages, but they don't come bearing arms. And the first sin is gluttony. Tempted by Eve tempted by the Devil, Adam tastes the fruit of the tree of the knowledge of good and evil. The first sin is a capital one: it opens up Pandora's box and sows the earth with evil, guilt and pain.

In the 5th century, John Cassian wrote twelve manuals for the proper functioning of monasteries. In those pages, the sins alternately appear as seven and eight, like the spheres an ascending soul must climb on its path to salvation: a process that is so reminiscent of Dante's Purgatory. After Gregory the Great in the 8th century, the sins remained fixed as seven, so the doctrine would match up with the most widespread symbolic model of human nature: a sum of the three powers of the soul (heart, will and mind) and the four elements of the body (air, earth, water and fire). Seven planets, seven colours, seven notes, seven winds, seven sins: we won't start in with the amateur numerology now, but this is the number that ordered our cosmos; it is the lucky number. And in this ancient classification, gluttony was considered the worst sin. Cassian speaks of *gastrimargia* (eagerness to fill one's belly) in order to explain this chaotic anxiety and the eager desire suffered by Adam and Eve. We speak of *gastromaquia* (the battle of the belly) and we opt for a juvenile blend of hunger and curiosity, that of teenagers chained to the sensualism of their time of life. But it is essential to point out the relationship between gluttony and the expulsion from Paradise, the Gordian knot of the system of sins, until the arrival of Augustine of Hippo in the 4th-5th centuries who placed pride at the top of the hierarchy of sins.

This shift was not in vain. Adam, the glutton, swapped God's love for the pleasures of pabulum, and it's all a demonic woman's fault. From then on, human bodies will reflect that most basic sinfulness and, as such, be susceptible to reproach, control and punishment. Dante places those who commit the sin of lust in a circle above gluttons, because gluttony is unleashed first and leads to a raging of the nether regions. One of the most skilful writers of medieval theory, the monk John Climacus (6th – 7th Centuries), attributes all the subsequent sins to the demon who settles in the belly. He says that after having eaten all of Egypt and having drunk all the water in the Nile, the belly demon and the spirit of fornication join forces to make the glutton imagine himself a cosmic *playa*. John Climacus wrote *The Ladder of Divine Ascent* (in Greek, *E climax Theías anódu*), thirty steps or chapters that advise and point the human soul on the path to salvation, which was why he was called 'John of the Ladder.' The basic concept here - as noted by Esteban - is that once gluttony and lust come together, they form the perfect expression of diabolical embodiment, the incarnation of evil, and this idea continues to hold sway today.

III – GLUTTONY AND WOMEN

Gluttony is a man's sin. It's been depicted as masculine quite frequently, often with moral connotations and always with aberrant physical dimensions - as pointed out by Vigarello. From the moment the male was placed in the world in order to dominate it by battling against other males and against misfortune, taking a bite out of the world has always been his assignment. All muscle and power, the hero is called to win, but runs the risk of devoting all his energy to pleasure: he may forget about his mission, and that is when gluttony comes into play. A fat hero is a fallen hero. Tempted by gluttony after sacking, raping and subduing (after winning in legitimate representation of his role), the bellicose state of the male remains permanent, on guard against temptations except when – well-fed and having drunk his fill – he rests inside a female who helps him to find that balance or, at least, to drain off his excess energy.

That is the basic cultural perception, and a real drag for the delicate, modest and retiring male. It forces the male to be brave, magnanimous and fertile, and if he manages to reach that peak it is when he finds himself most vulnerable to gluttony – and the correlative lust of a tentacular female. Then he may seem an immoral greedy guts, riddled with avarice, syphilitic, sickly pale, irresponsible, a dominator devoid of virtue and, yet, with immense power.

In his 1987 novel *The Broom of the System*, David Foster Wallace creates a memorable character, Norman Bombardini, an obese man who is both an incarnation of the archetype we've just described and philosophically sophisticated. Owner of a building and a company that bear his fatty last name, Bombardini isn't satisfied with his social and economic success because he is lagging in another male prerogative, sexual success. His wife has left him and he falls in love with a young woman *contra natura*, but cannot win her heart. Sad, but also haughty, he decides to gain as much weight as he possibly can. Like a clinically depressed Gargantua, he wants to swallow the universe, fill it entirely, become coextensive with it, because he fears a contextual world-view that is full yet personally empty. And, in a metaphor for late capitalism that fails to provide the archetypical winner – in this case, the businessman – with a meaningful life, nothing satisfies his hunger.

The tragicomic condition of the obese man (he cannot control himself and he is the butt of jokes) is ideal for discussing the human condition, because it is so paradigmatic: order and adventure. Gluttons are constantly satirised in art, irrespective of whether it's high- or low-brow. We see it in comics: Obelix is a big-hearted well-padded glutton, naïve, obsessed with wild boars and Romans. And we see it in the theatre: Falstaff, Shakespeare's fight-picking, drunken buffoon (vulnerable to *great aesthetic aversion*, according to Fernando Díaz-Plaja). The figure of the overeater also makes an appearance in popular traditions, with Santa Claus, a jolly old man whose round little belly shakes when he laughs like a bowlful of jelly, and with the Carnival King, the ravenous jester who never meets a good end. And we see it in painting as well: from Bosch's *Allegory of Intemperance* in the 15th century, which depicts a complete bacchanal, to the patriarchal portraits of the bourgeoisie (in which bellies are proportional to power), and it has a modern incarnation in the well-known paintings and sculptures by Fernando Botero that, despite the artist always speaking about the dignity of the soul, are received by the public with smirks and mocking comments.

The male enslaved (or compelled) by gluttony is also common in the most popular video games, for example Pac-Man (Toru Iwatani, 1985) and Super Mario Brothers (Shigeru Miyamoto, 1983), two cases where the objective is to gobble down or gather the highest possible amount of food, coins or anything that can be hoarded. This psychopathic accumulation has become the engine of the digital entertainment industry, inspiring a wide variety of video games with male protagonists designed around ingesting or stockpiling excessively (be it victims, jewels, steaks), which has already led to control and addiction problems in some players. In fact, in 2018 the WHO included 'gaming disorder,' of the mental kind in its 11th International Statistical Classification of Diseases and Related Health Problems. The insatiable *gotta catch 'em all* that drives some video games can lead to unhealthy behaviour and, obviously, the obesity of the sedentary lives of screen-lovers.

In every era of literature and in cinema there are also gluttons to loathe and laugh at. Often they are stock characters of priests, bankers, or kings, and we see fat jokes in such diverse settings as *Don Quixote*, *Laurel & Hardy*, and films starring Terence Hill. Ignatius J. Reilly, the disturbed fat man in the 1980 novel *A Confederacy of Dunces* by John Kennedy Toole, and Homer Simpson, each in his own way, are a pair of charming gluttons, and we forgive them their moments of imbecility in the name of their ineptitude and social maladaptation, which in the end is their earthly condemnation.

On the other hand, if we search out female sinners, we are unlikely to find many representations of those possessed by or given over to gluttony. Seen through male eyes (the prevailing gaze in art), women have been vilified more for their (supposedly) innate tendencies toward envy, sloth, greed and their own variant of gluttony, which is sometimes lust and other times excessive prattling on. The distinctive feature of the male glutton – his adiposity – does not usually have the same connotation in women. Figurative art has employed female obesity in terms that are more aesthetic than moral. Depending on the prevailing beauty canon – and sexual or social, maternal or supernatural powers – there have been eras in which a fat woman was the living image of candidness, of joy or of procreation – and the promise that, as beast of burden and birthing and nursing mother, she would make the grade – but gluttony and, often, lust haven't been as closely linked to female plumpness.

And when a woman with rolls has been depicted in a seductive light, these voluptuous women haven't been taken further than pejorative caricature or a tool for male sexual initiation. Literature has rarely created a tandem of women and the weight that denotes gluttony, opting instead to link extra female pounds with a carefree disregard for convention or a life on the margins.

We have the buxom tobacconist of *Amarcord* (the 1973 film by Federico Fellini) and the zaftig prostitute in *Boule de Suif* – alternately translated as Dumpling, Butterball, Ball of Fat, or Ball of Lard – an 1880 novella by Guy de Maupassant; in the end, both women are brutalist, Freudian depictions of sexuality. While *La niña gorda* [*The Fat Girl*], a 1917 newspaper serial by Santiago Rusiñol, does include a satire of gluttony, in this case it is the gluttony of those around a poor girl who merely eats, grows bigger and cries; she is displayed like a zoo animal for the profit of others.

In the cave paintings and ritual objects of the Palaeolithic and Neolithic, it is common to find women with pendulous breasts, generous rumps and prominent bellies. The Venus figures of old are embodiments of fertility. Rubens, as pointed out by John Berger, painted obese women from the perspective of the prestige of health. And more recently, the market (including the pornography market) came up with the word 'curvy' to designate the fat woman who is nonetheless desirable. Does all this mean that there aren't any female gluttons? Javier Gurruchaga and the Orquesta Mondragón sang the praises of the well-upholstered woman in jocular erotic terms in the 1987 song *Ellos las prefieren gordas* [*They Like Their Ladies Big*], dismissing or sidelining the possible view of overeating as illness. Seen from another perspective, we only find obese women when art recreates atmospheres of carousing and revelry. When they appear, they are linked to a lightening of sexual mores or, at least, to a somewhat pastoral vibe. Because real women live, eat and exist behind shutters, latticework, closed doors, in private spaces. Rivera shows that, in the Middle Ages, women's cloistered condition – their role associated with caretaking, procreation and housekeeping – exempted them from being accused of such a public sin as gluttony. Furthermore, since before Aristotle, the supposed relationship of women to food and drink has been viewed differently from men's. By their very nature, women eat less, better control their temptations toward excess, are smaller physically, and have fewer opportunities to go into overdrive – a package that makes them less susceptible to gluttony. *By their very nature*: here we see the crux of the linking, still prevalent today, of (male and female) ways of operating with an indemonstrable natural inclination. This has led to, eventually and symbolically, women being relegated to using their mouths for two things, neither of which is overeating: either to satisfy men or, above all, to talk a blue streak (supposedly).

The evil of gluttony takes hold inside women not as swollen flesh, but by turning them into sibylline chatterboxes, gossips, carriers of words that cloud men's hearts and minds. It sounds like original sin, this tempting men with whispered words. In that sense it is interesting how anthropologist Manuel Delgado partially associates the male, Latin anticlericalism of the 20th century with the role of devout women who return home after mass (to the bastion of the impious – *by his very nature* – man), bringing with them the priest's words. Men controlled by men via women, something that emerges from the murky cultural depths of the past. And while being garrulous can be considered a mode of gluttony, it doesn't make you fat and doesn't leave a visible trace. What's more: you cannot speak when your mouth is full.

IV – VERBORRHOEA AND GLUTTONY, IN CONCLUSION

In a dialogue written by Plato (427-347 BCE), Socrates and the poet Phaedrus philosophise after lunch. Instead of giving in to the drowsiness brought on by a full belly and napping, they talk.

Socrates says that abandon is the triumph of desire over reason and that it has many faces: for example, overeating. Plato also addressed gluttony in another dialogue, *Gorgias*, and like in *Phaedrus*, the cousin of culinary gluttony is rhetorical gluttony. Victuals and drink befog the mind, bringing blood to the stomach. And that unleashes rhetoric, lazy thinking that also uses the mouth to sin. It creates illusions; it is blustering: rhetoric is cerebral gluttony. Fatuous speeches and Pantagruelian banquets are linked, for example, in the moment of the feast when we chime glasses to indicate that the ridiculously eulogistic and inebriated toast is about to begin.

With no clear path, the belly full and the blood poisoned by drink, it is hard to think in an elegant manner, but that is temporary as it lasts only as long as we are digesting. Then, however, rhetoric crops up, unworkable if it attempts to find reasons with guarantees. Plato forswears both practices, the culinary and the rhetorical dependency, because they are stultifying, yet he doesn't deny that they can be used for one's own benefit. Because obviously one must eat and one must converse. The anthropologist Claude Lévi-Strauss explained the symbolic relationship between *eating* and *knowing*. A stew or a theory, both are cooked elements. Cooking and thinking are structurally similar activities. Raw food is for animals, just as raw thinking doesn't contribute knowledge. Coarse foodstuffs (like game meat, for example) require meticulous, elaborate and experienced cooking in order to become fine cuisine (*spezzatino di cinghiale*), knowing the ultimate truth of things also entails a process of stewing, marinating, seasoning... the metaphors could go on ad infinitum. And the mouth, the tasting orifice, also explains what one is thinking or has thought. As such, the mouth is multifunctional, and is the entrance and exit point for gluttony, excess, verbosity, or the uncontrolled vomiting of words. Taking a bite out of the world is a way to get to know it. Explaining the world is regurgitating it. And beyond all of these symbolic loans, gluttony plagues both the overeater and those greedy for seasoned words, those addicted to baroque (but empty) speeches: this is why popular expressions such as *running off one's mouth* are used to describe the braggart, the bore, the know-it-all, the mediocre, the moralist, the weisenheimer. There are word gluttons, witlings, the malapert; they are insufferable. It's no coincidence that they are usually fat. They eat, drink and run off at the mouth with the same impertinence, through the same hole, through the same sin. They commit perjury while polishing off a chicken drumstick. They judge left and right after gulping down their nth cocktail. We are what we eat and what we say; and what we don't gobble down and what we keep to ourselves, if we are trying to be virtuous.

The Greco-Roman banquet had two parts: the time for eating and the time for drinking and talking, the *symposion* (from *syn*, 'together with,' and *pòsis*, 'drink'). One came after the other, as if it were the logical continuation; Dante did not put overeaters and chatterboxes together in Purgatory. We do, however, because head and body cannot be recklessly disassociated. If the belly can and must be purged, then the brain must as well. And since we are aware that less is more, we'll cut off the flow of words here. Often virtue merely means enjoying everything, but not letting it show. The gym and the scalpel conceal gluttony. And the democratisation of pulpits created by social media allows everyone to be a pontificator, a prophet, champion prattlers, unable to shut their traps. And, that said, we'll stop here for the sake of temperance.

LUST

ANNA PUNSODA

I – THE VAST CHASM

Twenty-five years ago, somewhere in Lleida, a discreet husband, strict father and diligent taxpayer left his wife for a Russian woman thirty years his junior. The entire town could talk of nothing else. Since the adults were discussing it at home, I took the opportunity to ask what was going on. My grandfather replied colourfully: 'Look, kid, when they come knocking downstairs, there's nobody home upstairs.' I didn't understand the expression, and his pointing to his groin to indicate downstairs and his forehead to indicate upstairs didn't help.

When they come knocking downstairs, there's nobody home upstairs. The cliché that sexual desire gets the best of even the most level-headed men runs through the whole history of thought and explains why lust is so feared. It is not the most frowned-upon sin, because secretly we can all understand and forgive it, but it is definitely the most feared, as reflected by its many admonitory appearances in literature. Lust strikes such fear mostly because it endangers the family structure, which is the building block of political communities. And because, beyond this public aspect, lust can sometimes seem to overtake us like demonic possession.

The whole region took sides after the man abandoned his family, some siding with the poor husband, mostly men wary of being enraptured themselves, and others in favour of burning the man and his young lover in the town square; this second group included many women wary of being left for young Russians. To me it seemed like a complicated affair, because it turned out the poor husband was rich and influential, and the Russian, while a powerful enchantress, didn't have a pot to piss in.

When I got to university, I came across a text by Eugenio Trías that shed some light on the subject. In his *Tratado de la pasión*, Trías distinguishes between power and control and maintains that nowhere is the difference so clearly seen than in love. In any relationship, the person who is not in love has control over the other and can have their way with them. The ones in love, in contrast, feel an increased sense of self, and of their abilities and possibilities (*puissance*), while remaining in the hands of a greater power (*pouvoir*).

Clearly, the poor husband must have been experiencing *puissance* because, as twisted and dull witted as he was, he was convinced the young woman was in love with him. And it is also clear that the young woman had him under her thumb and was using her control over him to compensate for a lack of power. It is because of this obvious structural imbalance that I must refute the main premise of this essay: I maintain that lust is not a sin, but rather a luxury that only men have enjoyed for many centuries. From Delilah to *Manon Lescaut*, if only focussing on the iconic *femmes fatale*, we find that they are merely projections, spectres of men who ruined their lives based on a supposed seduction. And I say supposed, because if you reread the Book of Judges or the work of Abbé Prévost you won't find anything – not a single thing – about any Machiavellian strategy to seduce the men. In fact, there is no female strategy of any kind. The women are merely observed and desired by the narrators. Manon Lescaut, the inspiration for more operas than any other literary character in the history of music, does not speak a single word over the course of the novel that bears her name. Lust has always been about male desire, explained by men, and merely provoked by women.

Tout est pardonné, because I agree with Virginie Despentes when she says that women's bodies have belonged to men to offset the fact that men's bodies belonged to industry in times of peace and to the state in times of war. But I am interested in both men and women's desire, which is different and has taken me years to understand. And I am interested in the desire of the modern subject, understood as a self-aware, self-possessed psychic apparatus. As such, I will primarily discuss modern and contemporary works.

Despite the fact that history speaks to us of victims and executioners, lust doesn't make a distinction between the injured parties. It impacts men and women, but also the young and the old, the wise and the foolish. Surely, you've seen somewhere an image of an older man on all fours with a long-haired young woman riding on his back through a forest: Aristotle and Phyllis. She takes revenge on Aristotle by seducing him after the philosopher advised Alexander the Great to break up with her to keep him from being distracted. Seeing his teacher carrying his former lover around on his back, Alexander is enraged and Aristotle is said to have told him: 'If thus it happened to me, an old man most wise, that I was deceived by a woman, you can see that I taught you well, that it could happen to you, a young man.'

Desire is the chasm into which great projects fall and flounder. Empires, marriages, religious vocations, artistic geniuses, political careers. Desire is what best calls into question the modern individual. What creates a crack in the reasoning that we consider the foundation of a free, autonomous self, able to keep alienating passions at arm's length. And yet, it is also the miraculous chasm where what we'd given up for dead is reborn.

In a world completely controlled by technology, we must defend the right to let some things get out of hand. I defend the luxury, for men and women, to get lost between each other's inner thighs with as much dignity as possible. The luxury for men to be so foolish as to lose their heads over a nice rack. And the luxury for women to be diabolical creatures who use their bodies to take revenge or to access spaces they couldn't otherwise. And, throughout the essay, for men and women to be understood as open, communicating spaces.

II – THE AUTONOMY OF DESIRE

Nowhere do desire and affection mix as intensely as when women experience their first loves. We need look no further than the paradigmatic novels of the 19th and 20th centuries. We've been conditioned by works such as *Jane Eyre*, by Charlotte Brontë, and *Aloma*, by Mercè Rodoreda: two novels of first love, narrated in the first person, with orphaned girls as the protagonists.

Jane Eyre arrives at Thornfield Hall after a horrific childhood and adolescence. She grew up in a home where she was abused and then in a boarding school where she experiences hunger and her friends die. When she meets Mr Rochester, she has yet to have been with any man. Aloma's story is similar. She doesn't suffer as many tribulations, but when Robert arrives in Barcelona, she had only just left home. For Aloma, that house was her entire world, and Robert moves into the room across from hers. He places himself, literally, in the middle of her world.

Despite both being complete innocents, Jane and Aloma are not blind. In fact, Jane is very clear on what she expects from Mr Rochester. When he asks her just that question, she replies:

I suppose your love will effervesce in six months, or less. I have observed in books written by men, that period assigned as the farthest to which a husband's ardour extends. Yet, after all, as a friend and companion, I hope never to become quite distasteful to my dear master.

Aloma also, from the very first few pages, expresses her suspicion that Robert might have a secret family in the Americas and be only interested in her as a distraction. Despite her suspicions, despite her distrust, despite being clear on what you can expect from a man when you belong to a lower class than he, both women confuse the awakening of desire with falling in love. It could be said that they were programmed to confuse those two things. The case of the male characters is different, as illustrated by the popularity of brothels as a means of sexual initiation prior to marriage. You merely need to pick up *Private Life*, where Josep Maria de Sagarra tells us at length about the most intense moment in a man's life, that moment when as a virgin boy he first steps into a bordello.

Over the years, that confusion of desire and love in female literary characters will wane. This can be sensed already in *Fanny*, a novel by Carles Soldevila that caused a great scandal when published in 1929. While it is a lesser novel compared with *Aloma*, the psychology of its female protagonist is ahead of its time and makes explicit subjects that Rodoreda only hints at.

Fanny is a déclassé young woman from Barcelona's bourgeoisie who finds herself working as a scantily clad showgirl at a theatre on the Avinguda Paral·lel. She is twenty-three and has no regrets about her fall in society. We could say she is a liberated woman, pleased with her economic independence and happy to be free of the prejudices associated with the middle class. She is proud of her liberation:

As soon as a man starts to make love to me, a feeling inside me wins out over all others: my desire to make it clear I won't be led up the garden path.

Fanny wants to put paid to the paradigm of the naïve girl and, above all, she wants to make that abundantly clear. But this war against innocence leaves her always on the defensive and makes it very difficult for her to understand her own feelings. That is precisely what enslaves her. What she wants or doesn't want is of no use to her:

Though my steps seem to suggest it, I am not in love, not in the slightest. It's more like deep down in my soul there is something willing me to be, and pushing me in that direction.

When Fanny meets Jordi, a middle-class young man who sees something different in her and wants to save her from the show-girl life, she unconsciously ends up fulfilling each and every one of the rituals of falling in love. Everything she does to distance herself or break it off only binds her to him more tightly. And precisely on the night when everything seems the bleakest (because she's rumoured to have syphilis, Jordi flees, and she chases after him to explain that it's baseless) is when she loses her virginity and ends up getting engaged.

Fanny ends up confusing desire and love, but she goes to great pains to avoid it, making those efforts explicit. Over the last thirty years of female protagonists, we've seen these two impulses gradually separate, until they are finally independent of each other, as in *Permafrost* by Eva Baltasar: on the one hand, desire gains autonomy. On the other, more and more voices rise up to condemn this passionate love.

What does it mean for desire to be autonomous? It means that it's no longer tied to emotion, and that leads us into a quandary. Contemporary sexologists have devoted much time and energy to measuring the amount of blood flow to the genitals experienced by men and women when looking at sexual scenes. Afterward, they asked them whether they felt desire while watching. The results are unambiguous: in the case of men there is a sixty-five per cent correlation between the degree of penile erection and the degree of excitement they report experiencing. In the case of women, the correlation between genital desire and mental desire is less than twenty-five per cent.

In other words, I might get wet watching some orangutans fuck, but that doesn't mean that I'm feeling aroused. Women's desire is in their brains, which is why no one has been able to invent a female Viagra, because it's not just a matter of dilating the penile blood vessels. So, when contemporary literature separates desire and affection, when it presents women who see a nice ass and feel compelled to chase after it, what it is doing is converting us into men, and basic ones at that. It remains to be seen whether that will be useful to us in gaining access to power.

We must also consider where that leaves affection now that it's been separated from desire. It is often said that passionate love has subjugated single women and wives by distracting them with domestic ideals while men took on the world, and other women. It was a nebulous love, imbued with a vaguely conscious desire, that promised a world of fulfilment and pleasure projected onto a man. Let's take a look at what this drug is and if there is any aspect of it we can rescue without it ending too poorly.

III – THE STRUCTURE OF LOVE

We'll begin with the legend of *Tristan and Isolde*, a tale which best embodies our link to the chivalric tradition and is the foundation of an inherited sensibility. According to Denis de Rougemont, what this legend strives to illustrate is a conflict between the code of chivalry and the existing feudal laws of the time, which understood marriage in a purely practical way. Getting married was only useful for annexing lands through dowries or inheritances and it caused all sorts of conflicts. It was in those low points of marital history that the idea of passionate love emerged, in opposition to what husbands were offering.

There are two clichés I want to highlight from the romance of *Tristan and Isolde*, myth of myths, European canto to adultery that has circulated in various versions since the 12th century and has filtered into both literary and popular culture: the idea that passion and marriage are incompatible; and the importance of obstacles in love. These two old chestnuts take on various nuances depending on the concerns of each time period, but they can still be found even in the most idiotic Netflix shows.

Let's take a closer look at the legend. We'll see that it is filled with opportunities for the lovers to flee and live in peace, but every time either one or the other puts up some obstacle. And while it is true that their endless separations and re-encounters are what create the progression of the story, this is not just a literary device. The link between obstacle and passion is very deeply rooted. When the obstacle is exterior, for example Isolde's husband, Tristan overcomes it with great valour, and as such affirms life. When he has exhausted all the exterior obstacles, then the interior ones begin to appear, which he can only overcome by conquering himself.

And what drives it all? Where does that compulsion come from, for the first great lovers to separate themselves from what they desire? Some personal preference for misfortune? From a contemporary perspective we might think that it was a childish way to avoid the prosaicness of the time and its commitments. But that would mean we were applying psychology to heroes who lived long before the psyche as we now know it was invented. Throughout the entire legend, however, we see that there is something that demands to come before Tristan and Isolde's wellbeing and happiness. Their passion places them beyond good and evil and, more than loving each other, they love the very act of loving.

Behind their fondness for suffering, their excitement at living on the edge, there is a clear religious inspired instinct for seeking out death, and not just any death but a purifying one. Passion, love of love itself, is a means to that death. As Rougemont says: the lovers seek out what hurts them in order to access a true life, accessible only through death. Tristan and Isolde are both narcissists who use each other for their impulses because pain, and particularly painful love, is seen, in the West, as a path to knowledge.

When, centuries later, Stendhal writes his now classic treatise *On Love*, he dubs this type of love as passionate love. As opposed to physical, courtly or vain loves, this is the only love that he defends, despite it having already lost all mystical meaning. Stendhal's love is a human – painfully human – love, without the web of esoteric filters, symbolic obstacles, and metaphysical loyalties. Only the Romantics retained part of the religious background that passionate love deserves; only Wagner, with his simplification of the legend and his impactful union of music and text, will bring Tristan and Isolde back together in ecstatic death.

Let's discuss this. Was this beleaguered mystical love – that degenerated over eight centuries in five-hundred-page novels – a female narcotic? Of course. Love has always been the most successful mechanism for exalting us, even more than religion and obviously much more than art, to which only a minority had access. That is true beyond a shadow of a doubt. Although there is something that marks a difference between various loves, it being the nature of their obstacles and how we're able to benefit from them. I propose we look at the obstacles that arise in each love story: we will see that the meaning of that love depends on the quality of these obstacles, and the effect they have on our consciousness.

Let's look at Jane Eyre. The external obstacle is Rochester's first marriage, but the internal obstacle is Jane's rigid morality and constant awareness of the gap between their social conditions. For Aloma, the external obstacle is Robert's lover in the Americas while the internal obstacles are Aloma's pride and her not wanting to be loved out of pity, which leads her to hide her pregnancy. Charlotte Brontë doesn't bring the lovers together until Mr Rochester is a blind, one-handed widower, and Jane has received an inheritance and finally believes herself worthy of that marriage. In the case of Aloma, Rodoreda cleverly obscures from the reader which obstacle holds more weight in their separation. We will never know what would have happened if Aloma had told Robert the truth before bidding him farewell at the port. In both novels, the internal obstacles are so well thought out and well-reasoned by the heroines that love not only doesn't alienate the young women, but it expands their consciousness and gives them depth. While falling in love was a narcotic, losing love was the most efficient path to growth – and perhaps the only one, as the authors well knew.

Following in the footsteps of Tristan, we find Julien Sorel. Stendhal also introduced some formulaic ideas about marriage that were later ironically adopted by the dandies. 'The boredom of married life certainly kills love, if love has preceded marriage,' he wrote (in Burton Raffel's translation). This idea has had so much traction that even today we associate passion with adultery. Why? It is always easier to be exalted by a new body than a familiar one, especially when your bad conscience has led you to delay the encounter with the new body, heightening your desire and tinging it with your anticipatory imaginings. It takes a certain wisdom – one that I don't believe our literature offers us – to bind us to the present and the body we already know.

The philosopher Marta Segarra points to a magnificent etymological meaning of *desire* that illuminates all these complications. She tells us that the *de-* was a privative prefix and that the *sidus-sideris* referred to the stars. So, to desire meant to stop looking at the stars. To desire would be to confirm the absence of something. This confirmation of absence is a feeling of desire that has gradually faded, and now the prevailing idea is that of trying to gain something. I am convinced that every time someone falls in love in an over-the-top way, there is a prior void; and that confirming the presence of that void, taking a good look at it, understanding it, getting used to the absence of something unknown, is the best defence against alienation.

Passionate love has subjugated women because at some point we believed, or were led to believe, that our own personal voids that we're born with can be filled by men. Men have aspired to fill them with influence, power and recognition. Desire as a contemplation of an absence – a lack that varies with each person and that they must solve for themselves – is much more fertile than longing to be possessed. The former expands our consciousness, which is useful in and of itself. The latter, besides leaving a vast trail of corpses, creates anxiety, which in turn feeds more passion, in a never-ending loop. Let's have a look at a specific case.

IV – DESIRE AND MENTAL COLONISATION

Supposedly, falling in love makes you a better person. That's probably true of people who are more or less balanced: men and women who feel desires of a reasonable intensity and who have the mental resources to keep them in check. They experience an increase in energy, a sharper attention, a more flexible will. If they are somewhat intelligent, even their poetic abilities emerge more expressive. But ecstatic love, mixed with unbridled sexual desire, colonises the mind. Then, as Ortega y Gasset maintained, the person in love becomes someone whose attention is paralyzed.

Of all the infinite objects in the world, they can only see that one object of their affection, which looms larger and larger in their mind's eye.

Let us take, for example, *Letter from an Unknown Woman*, by Stefan Zweig, a famous tale of desperate love. Zweig's lovely writing and the intensity of the story make it difficult to analyse, but the effort is worth it because it is filled with revealing tricks. First of all, there's the title, which tells us that it is a letter. We associate the epistolary genre with veracity, as the author of *The Sorrows of Young Werther* and that mysterious Portuguese nun knew full well.

We also know that it is a letter from an unknown woman, and that anonymity contrasts with the story's opening line: 'When R., the famous novelist, returned to Vienna early in the morning…' He is a famous novelist and she is an unknown woman sending him a letter with no signature or return address. This opposition does not refer merely to contrast in their public relevance. Like any good woman desperately in love, she knows his every movement; she tracks his schedules and his friendships. He is always foremost in her mind. He is what is most important, most real in her life. Absolutely everything else is on the back burner, everything except for him.

The novelist, on the other hand, doesn't even recognize her as the same person on the three occasions when they are together: as a thirteen-year-old girl, a teenager of eighteen, and a woman of twenty-nine. This discrepancy in how largely they each loom in the consciousness of the other is the story's main subject. And because he does not know her, she will forever be 'the unknown woman.'

The first thing the unknown woman explains in her letter is that her son died the previous night and that she is sitting beside his body as she writes the letter we are reading. She also tells him that by the time he receives this letter, she will be dead, not having been able to survive such pain. I can't think of an opening that creates more of a bond between protagonist and reader than this one. The way she portrays herself, and her always self-sacrificing love without demands on him, underpin this bond.

When the unknown woman was a young teen she lived right opposite the novelist in the same apartment building, and her love for him was mere idealisation. It isn't until she and her mother move to another city that her love becomes carnal. She explains that change to him thus:

I loved you from that second on. I know that women have often said those words to you, spoilt as you are. But believe me, no one ever loved you as slavishly, with such dog-like devotion, as the creature I was then and have always remained, for there is nothing on earth like the love of a child that passes unnoticed in the dark because she has no hope: her love is so submissive, so much a servant's love, passionate and lying in wait, in a way that the avid yet unconsciously demanding love of a grown woman can never be. Only lonely children can keep a passion entirely to themselves; others talk about their feelings in company, wear them away in intimacy with friends, they have heard and read a great deal about love, and know that it is a common fate. They play with it as if it were a toy, they show it off like boys smoking their first cigarette. But as for me, I had no one I could take into my confidence, I was not taught or warned by anyone, I was inexperienced and naive; I flung myself into my fate as if into an abyss. Everything growing and emerging in me knew of nothing but you, the dream of you was my familiar friend. My father had died long ago, my mother was a stranger to me in her eternal sad depression, her anxious pensioner's worries […]

The void inside this girl existed before the novelist showed up. And in her case, we also have the opportunity to see how this void functions in relation to love and memory. The unknown woman moves away between the ages of sixteen and eighteen, and during that time she never leaves the house; all she does is replay every memory of the writer as if her mind were a theatre. She relives the memories hundreds and hundreds of times, and they become engraved into her mind. When popular wisdom says that after a breakup you should travel and distract yourself, it's basically so that new images enter your mind to ensure you don't remain stuck in a hermetic mental loop.

The story of the unknown woman is also the story of a body discovering itself. When she turns eighteen and her senses are awakened, she wants nothing more than to make love to the novelist. He is a cultured man; she could have chosen to educate herself in the hopes of forging a more lasting love, or at least a friendship. But what her body demands is to bed him. And Zweig deals us another harsh blow with that as well. She was a virgin and he beds her oblivious to that fact, and without giving the matter any importance. She writes to him:

But how could you guess that, beloved, when I offered no resistance, showed no bashful hesitancy, so that you could have no idea of my secret love for you? It would certainly have alarmed you, for you love only what is light and playful, weightless, you are afraid of intervening in someone else's life. You want to give of yourself to everyone, to the world, but you do not want sacrificial victims. […] I am not blaming you, I love you as the man you are, hot-blooded and forgetful, ardent and inconstant, I love you just as you always were and as you still are.

They share the same sexual act, even though for her it encapsulates all her desire and love, while for him it is merely a desire with no past or future. And yet everyone would deem his night more lustful than hers, because cliché separates lust from love.

As readers we are dealt the harshest blow from the lovers'

third encounter. We know that the unknown woman fell pregnant by him but that she hasn't revealed that fact, not wishing him to feel bound to her by pity. We know that, in order to feed and clothe her son, she becomes a luxury concubine. We know that she refuses countless marriage proposals from barons in case the novelist one day realises and seeks her out. But when they meet for the third time in a café in Vienna, he again fails to recognise her. The novelist asks her to spend the night with him and the next morning, before he leaves, he stuffs banknotes in her muff. The humiliation we feel as readers of this passage is immense because it pinches the nerve of many prejudices. The unknown woman explains it thus:

In bliss, I accepted your expert caresses and saw that your passion draws no distinction between someone you really love and a woman selling herself [...] I have never felt such concentration on the moment of the act of love in any other man, such an outburst and reflection of his deepest being – although then, of course, it was to be extinguished in endless, almost inhuman oblivion.

If it can be bought, it is not passion. That is what the cliché tells us, partly in order to make us believe that we all have something to offer that money can't buy. The novelist's inability to distinguish sincere passion from paid passion is due to his Don Juan nature, which is said to be common among artists. There are those who are able to give everything in the moment and then completely forget it in the next. This is the essence of Don-Juanism, which works particularly well with girls like this unknown woman: virgin orphans with no sense of their own wellbeing. Twenty-nine years tossed on the trash heap. Without any awareness of the void, without working through the pain, falling in love does not make you a better person, not by a long shot. It is merely mental colonisation.

V – THE HYMEN FRAUD AND THE THRUSTS

If there is anyone who's skilfully played with all the clichés about femininity, it's Madonna. But *Like a Virgin*, with its video of the bride who wanders through Venice until a man in a lion mask spreads her out on a bed, would be unthinkable without a long tradition of myths about 'deflowering' and a long collective scam about the hymen. The hymen isn't a thin veil covering the hole but rather a thick membrane we have at the walls of the vagina. The entire vagina is flexible, but if we aren't wet enough, it could tear, and it would be that membrane tearing. Since the hymen scars without leaving any visible marks, there is no difference between a virgin vulva and an experienced one. That's why *Fanny Hill*, which returns again and again to the concept of 'deflowering,' is such an interesting case.

Fanny Hill: Memoir of a Woman of Pleasure, by John Cleland, published in 1749, is considered the first great pornographic novel in Western history. Also told in the form of a letter, we find ourselves with another orphan girl from the sticks who arrives in London with little knowledge of the wider world. We follow her story for three years, during which time she loses her virginity ten times. Or at least she tries to. The first time is at the house of Mrs Brown, a madame who will fatten her up and give her baths and dresses so she can sell her to the highest bidder. This is how the virgin girl describes the first 'gentleman':

Imagine to yourself, a man rather past threescore, short and ill-made, with a yellow cadaverous hue, great goggle eyes, that stared as if he was strangled; an out-mouth from two more properly tusks than teeth, livid lips, and breath like a Jake's: then he had a peculiar ghastliness in his grin, that made him perfectly frightful, if not dangerous to women with child; yet, made as he was thus in mock of man, he was so blind to his own staring deformities, as to think himself born to please, and that no woman could see him with impunity: in consequence of which idea, he had lavished great sums on such wretches as could gain upon themselves to pretend love to his person, whilst to those who had not art or patience to dissemble the horror it inspired, he behaved even brutally. Impotence, more than necessity, made him seek in variety, the provocative that was wanting to raise him to the pitch of enjoyment, which he too often saw himself baulked of, by the failure of his powers: and this always threw him into a fit of rage, which he wreaked, as far as he durst, on the innocent objects of his fit of momentary desire.

It proved impossible. Neither the wine, nor the hours a colleague had devoted to her clitoris in an attempt to excite her, had done any good. When Fanny sees the monstrous brute, she squeezes her thighs together tightly and it is her 'thighs and linen' that end up receiving the 'effusion.' The monster beats her up and returns her to the madame with the accusation that she has: 'left her maidenhead with some hobnail in the country.' In that glorious moment the law of the pendulum will take hold and Fanny, still impacted by the ugliness and brutality, throws herself into the arms of the first kind and handsome man she meets: Charles. He is moved by Fanny's offer of 'that jewel, which can never be twice lost,' and he falls head over heels for her. The young man is sent away by his father, but his love stands the test of time, despite all of Fanny's bordellos and bizarre fornication. For example, with Mr H, a good lad, brother of a lord, and a virgin himself, whom she partially describes in this way:

Curious then, and eager to unfold so alarming a mystery, playing, as it were, with his buttons, which were bursting ripe from the active force within, those of his waistband and fore-flap flew open at a touch, when out IT started; and now, disengaged from the shirt, I saw, with wonder and surprise, what? not the play thing of a boy, not the weapon of a man, but a

Maypole, of so enormous a standard, that had proportions been observed, it must have belonged to a young giant. [...] When our mutual trance was a little over, and the young fellow had withdrawn that delicious stretcher, with which he had most plentifully drowned all thoughts of revenge, in the sense of actual pleasure, the widened wounded passage refunded a stream of pearly liquids, which flowed down my thighs, mixed with streaks of blood, the marks of the ravage of that monstrous machine of his, which had now triumphed over a kind of second maidenhead. I stole, however, my handkerchief to those parts, and wiped them as dry as I could, whilst he was re-adjusting and buttoning up.

Fanny will always be a resilient soul. She describes the scene with a mix of horror and delight until young Mr H finally, with 'a home-made thrust sheaths it up to the guard.' Then a miracle occurs, one which will repeat throughout the novel: when he comes inside of her, she, with no further need of any rubbing or simultaneous gesture, merely from the stiffness and splattering of his sword, comes at the same time with shrieks and tears of joy. Such are the powers of the tool, which naturally needs someone to wield it.

This tool has its correlative: the female canal. The conservation of this blessed tightness is the very fount of pleasure for men, affirms Fanny, who is: 'favoured [...] by nature with all the narrowness of stricture in that part.' As such, she is able to pass as a virgin as many times as she needs to, which will be quite a few, because when she lands in another brothel, she becomes aware of a sacred rule of the profession that forces her to present herself as a virgin the first night she works there. That is how she ends up losing her virginity, being made a woman – as if she'd been a geranium up until then – a number of other times.

The first time will be with Mr Norbert, the heir to a large fortune and a small penis that leads to some scenes of high comedy.

Fanny tells us how his 'machine, which was one of those sizes that slip in and out without being minded, kept pretty stiffly bearing against that part, which the shutting my thighs barred access to.' This comedy around making Norbert believe that his tiny member can pop her cherry, and the supposed tearing of Fanny's hymen which she feigns with red paint, is the only moment of revenge that she allows us in the entire story. Don't misunderstand me: it's not that a small penis deserves to be the object of ridicule, but the source of your pride is where you are vulnerable to humiliation, and that was the site of all male pride – which makes even less sense when the women were supposed to keep their thighs tightly closed at all times.

The fact that the novel is authored by a man is glaringly obvious: the penis is the object of all greedy eyes; coitus is presented as a series of thrusts (the longer and wider the battering ram, the better) that are all that is needed to bring women to orgasm. We see a fixation on vaginal tightness, which as women we discover when we give birth and face the threat of the 'husband stitch': that extra postpartum suture you may get if you aren't attentive, designed to make sure you are nice and tight down there.

The judgment towards men is very benevolent; in fact, it uses the cliché of their foolishness: 'There is, in short, in the men, when once they are caught, by the eye especially, a fund of cullibility that their lordly wisdom little dreams of, and in virtue of which the most sagacious of them are seen so often our dupes.'

Yet judgment towards women is very severe: 'It will add, too, one more example to thousands, in confirmation of the maxim, that women get once out of compass, there are no lengths of licentiousness, that they are not capable of running.' Despite being considered the first great pornographic novel, it is a very moralistic book: while sex between women is seen as entertainment, sodomy is described in terrible terms. And Fanny's 'deflowering' is focused entirely on penetration by a man. The fact that she masturbated herself and was masturbated by another woman is given no importance. Sex is synonymous with a battering ram intent on breaking a transparent veil that doesn't exist.

The reasons those men want to deflower Fanny are exactly those described by anthropology and explored by psychoanalysis. They all include the exclusive rights a man would acquire over the woman he has deflowered and her sexual servitude toward him. Being the first to set foot on a new continent. There is also the thrill of risk-taking: it is assumed that deflowering entails the peril of arousing a young woman's hostility, and they all try to stick their penises into Fanny without hurting her too much. There is no attempt to teach her, or satisfy her curiosity, or give her pleasure, as there would be with Casanova, or as there was with Fanny when she deflowers the lad with the large penis. There is a fixation with entering a closed space and tearing a hymen, making of it a rite of passage and elevating it to the realm of myth.

VI – THE GENIAL INSTINCT AND THE MACHINE MAN

Another man Fanny meets at the bordello is Barville, a young man: 'under the tyranny of a cruel taste: that of an ardent desire, not only of being unmercifully whipped himself, but of whipping others.' The madame has no compunction about making the introduction, convinced that pleasure is always the: 'universal port of destination, and every wind that blew thither a good one, provided it blew nobody any harm.'

John Cleland explains that the passion for sadomasochism

is generally a recourse of older men, who are forced to resort to it in order to stimulate circulation and thereby resurrect their 'flagging shrivelly parts.' Whereas such cases in handsome young men like Barville were few and far between, and always owing to an innate predisposition. Barville can only have erections after he's been whipped, and the lashing is merely a means to an end. There is no pleasure in his use of force, and in all the sex he has with Fanny there are no excessive eccentricities. In fact, throughout the book the author condemns a sex act as basic as anal intercourse: between men because he believes it to be feminising, and between men and women because he says it will destroy their anatomical passage.

This was written in 1749, three years after the birth in France of Donatien-Alphonse-François de Sade, who would revert Cleland's objection and take it to a more macabre extreme. More macabre because there were no shades of Grey or Redtube videos where a fifteen-year-old girl eggs on a syphilitic man to repeatedly rape her mother and then wants to sew up her vulva like a zipper to make sure the disease can fester. We remind you that Sade's hero Dolmancé would refuse to penetrate anything but an anus. The only law he respects is the inverse of Fanny Hill's lovers: he never penetrates a woman vaginally.

The philosopher Marcel Hénaff has a very good book where he discusses the contributions the Marquis de Sade has made to our concept of the body and of sex. He says that Don Juan still wanted to seduce and could still hesitate beneath another's gaze. That, despite everything, Don Juan continued to be nostalgic for courtly love. On the other hand, industrial and technological rationalism eliminated the hypothesis of the soul and turned desire into something new. Sade would invent a new body for the libertine, a body subjected to a process of geometrisation and chopping up. The body would become a group of organs with no internal unity, merely a series of cogs and measured quantities.

An avid reader of La Mettrie, Sade turned the libertine body into an automaton in search of pleasure. As such, the body becomes a device that, once set into motion, is no longer master of its movements, because its movements only obey the internal logic of its anatomy. Considered a machine, it is forgiven all psychology in its relations with others. For the libertine, the other is first and foremost a structure of organs that can connect with his or her own.

According to Hénaff: 'saturation is to the libertine body what depth is to the lyric body.' And, certainly, we need only pick up the most introductory of Sade's books, *Philosophy in the Bedroom*, to see the effect provoked by the excess, the accumulation, the torrent of organs, bodies, copulation. It's all holes that need filling, and complicated group positions. And while the descriptions of places and people are general and clichéd, the descriptions of organs and of sex are very detailed. So much so that when you've finished imagining the described group scene, any hint of arousal has dissipated.

There is a case I'd like to discuss from the month Fanny Hill spends in the last bordello because it illustrates this process well. It turns out that near the brothel there is a young flower vendor of limited intelligence:

[…] he was not only a perfect changeling, or idiot, but stammered so that there was no understanding even those sounds his half-dozen animal ideas, at most, prompted him to utter.

The most curious of the women in the cathouse wanted to see whether, as was believed in that day, nature had compensated his complete lack of intellectual endowment with an oversized cock. Between the two girls they lead him into a bedroom, arouse him and finally strip him naked. The description of the idiot's attributes is definitely worth a read, but what I want to highlight here is the following: when he gets going, there is no human way to stop him. He mounts her and rides, rides, rides. The girl starts to shriek from the pain of his immense tool, but: 'his whole frame agitated with a raging ungovernable impetuosity: all sensibly betraying the formidable fierceness with which the genial instinct acted upon him.'

Seeing that she couldn't reason with the idiot, the girl decides to participate in the coitus and, once the first waves of pain pass, she finds she is completely beside herself: 'she was now as mere a machine as much wrought on, and had her motions as little at her own command, as the natural himself.' They both lose control of their bodies and when they've finished they are only anxious to be rid of each other. The girl will not dance with that partner again, despite his having the largest penis she's ever known, and the idiot will only retain a faint recollection of what happened between them.

Ortega y Gasset distinguishes between 'sexual instinct' and 'sexual love.' According to him, in sexual instinct, desire precedes its object. We feel desire even before meeting the person we want to satisfy it and we don't differentiate much between the available options. Although he also says that sexual instinct is rarely seen in isolation, because all instinct is usually accompanied by higher manifestations of an emotional, or even spiritual, nature.

Perhaps we will never see pure instinct in action, says Ortega. But the description that John Cleland offers us in the scene with the idiot in *Fanny Hill* is exactly that. And this 'genial instinct' – *genial* in its original sense of 'pertaining to marriage rites' – confirms what Marcel Hénaff says about Sade's libertines. They are autonomous machinery that, once set into motion, do not respond to being begged to stop and is not responsible for its actions. We are only rescued from the possible implications of that by the hypothesis of the soul, which true libertines and idiots lack.

VII – THE HEIRESS WITH THIGHS OF STEEL

It's not easy to find libertines in Twentieth Century Catalan literature. Or even lustful characters. We've already mentioned Fanny, the declassé bourgeois girl who ends up as a showgirl on the Paral·lel. She herself speaks ironically of her condition: 'It's always easier for a girl named Fanny to end up dancing in a revue than one named Montserrat or Carmeta.'

Then she goes on to say that, among the other dancers there is more than one Carmeta, but her comment works because since then (1929, when Carles Soldevila wrote the book) it's become established as true. The image she paints of Jordi also holds up, that bourgeois young man who woos her against his parents' wishes, until he's told the rumour that Fanny has syphilis and he runs off without looking back. 'There are too many Jordis in Catalonia,' she complains. But why can't a Montserrat make a living off her sensual body or a Jordi depart from what's expected of him?

In 1959, in a tribute to Víctor Català on her ninetieth birthday, Sebastià Estradé and Joaquim Carbó edited a volume of short stories by Catalan writers of the time. Salvador Espriu decided that the stories should address the seven deadly sins and Mercè Rodoreda was assigned lust. That gave rise to 'Negrita Rum,' which shines a light on this matter.

In brief: five journeymen have taken refuge from the rain in a bar in Sant Gervasi and they are chatting with the owner, Bartomeu. One of them is trying to sell some shoes that his wife bought for their eldest son in too small a size. A mysterious stranger comes in and sits alone at the bar. With his eyes fixed on a bottle of Negrita rum, he orders – in quick succession – three glasses of manzanilla sherry.

The five journeymen talk about Bartomeu's wife, Lisette, who is keeping vigil over a neighbour who died early that morning. The men insinuate that she was having an affair with the deceased man and that now she's having one with his son, despite the fact that she also seems to be involved with his brother. When Lisette arrives at the bar, soaked from tip to tail, in tight clothes and smelling of rain, she flirts with a couple of the journeymen and the mysterious stranger, who oversteps his bounds when he touches her thigh and breast. Bartomeu sends the man packing, and his wife to the kitchen. The shoes remain unsold and the journeymen and the stranger scatter out into the neighbourhood, beneath the pouring rain.

To begin with, Rodoreda chooses a French woman to personify lust, a woman who is in vast contrast to the Catalan ones in the story. There is Cinta, the dim-witted wife who buys her son's shoes for him – by tracing his feet onto a piece of paper – because he's too lazy to go to the shop himself. 'My wife practically chews his food for him,' says her husband. There's also Margarida, the baker's wife, who doesn't dare refuse Lisette's request to put the shoes up for sale in the window. Later, it will be the baker who has to come to the bar to renege on the arrangement. 'You know how Margarida is: she wants to make everybody happy, and if she sees someone in need, she'd give 'em the shirt off her back; she'd give away everything she has and then some.'

Lisette is neither a doormat of a mother nor a spineless pushover. She is brazen and efficient. She and Bartomeu met during the exodus into exile in France, on a bridge being bombed by German dive planes. She speaks an incomprehensible but amusing mix of Catalan, Spanish and French, which is why her husband complains that he can't have deep conversations with her. And, at the same time, he says that he's happier and happier with her every day. Lust, Mercè Rodoreda is telling us, is a kind of language in and of itself. In fact, and this isn't Rodoreda talking but me, you don't know whether you can have a lot of deep conversations with someone until the honeymoon period is over. And that will always be harder to figure out when you don't share a native language.

Rodoreda is constantly drawing parallels between women and shoes. 'The minute merchandise leaves the store, it's already lost more than half its value,' says one man. 'Shoes that are too small make you walk like a partridge,' says another. There is also a constant parallelism between humans and snakes. One of the journeymen breeds snakes on his balcony and brags about being the first person able to get them to procreate in captivity, instead of just refusing to eat and wasting away. Rodoreda tells us that Lisette, contrary to the Biblical text, is actually fond of the creatures.

In 1959 Mercè Rodoreda is asked for a story about lust and this is what she writes. A scene in a working-class bar in Sant Gervasi where a stranger comes in and drools over rum but orders sherry. A scene where everything is too tight, too constrained: the shoes, the cages where the snakes live in such close quarters that they refuse to procreate. A scene where Catalan men walk like partridges and Catalan women are real dimwits. Where there is only a single lustful and free light, and it comes from France.

Something similar happens in *Bearn*, the novel by Llorenç Villalonga, written in the same period as 'Negrita Rum.' While Rodoreda tells us of the scant lustfulness of the average Catalan, Villalonga tells us of the tortured lustfulness of an aristocracy in decline. Don Toni, marquis of the imaginary Bearn, leaves his wife Maria Antònia in Mallorca and runs off to Paris with young Xima. In France, drunk on youth and pleasure, he squanders a great fortune. When he's old, he paces regretfully around his Mallorcan castles in trousers and wig, and confesses to the family priest for his former lust. Or, if we take his wife and lover as symbols, what he laments is not having been able to defend his bloodline and lands and having allowed himself to be dazzled by the hedonism of the big city.

Lust is also historic and is linked to cities and countries. Again, it was Stendhal in *On Love* who spoke of lust in those terms. This book was published in 1882, shortly before the arrival of The Hundred Thousand Sons of St Louis and the return of absolutism in Spain. He never mentions Catalonia, and when he speaks of Spain it is primarily to comment on the voluptuousness of the Andalusian women, which he attributes to their Moorish roots and the atmosphere of porticoed gardens surrounded with orange trees and a fountain at the centre. 'I consider the Spanish people the living representatives of the Middle Ages.'

However, if we take what he says about Paris and compare it with the image portrayed by Rodoreda and Villalonga a century later, we see how the tables turn. According to Stendhal, since the French are merely creatures of vanity and physical desires, their women:

[...] are less active, less energetic, less feared and, what's more, less loved and less powerful, than Spanish and Italian women. A woman is powerful only according to the degree of unhappiness she can inflict as punishment on her lover. Where men have nothing but vanity, every woman is useful, but none is indispensable. It is success in winning a woman's love, not in keeping it, which flatters a man. When men have only physical desires, they go to prostitutes, and that is why the prostitutes of France are charming and those of Spain the very reverse.

Throughout Stendhal's text, women behave depending on the virtues their male counterparts value, but men behave depending on the wishes of nations. As such, of the United States he tells us that Americans do not know how to enjoy physical pleasures, partly due to the influence of Protestantism, and partly because they do not have a government that affords them safety and tranquillity. The great passions, writes the Frenchman, are a luxury of Europe.

The relationships between sexuality and gender or between sexuality and religion are more obvious. But its relationship with phenomena such as emigration and minority assimilation is also important. This is the basis of the repression of Catalan heiresses during the 20th century, with their thighs of steel for working and for birthing, and their scant ardour. When Philip Roth published *Portnoy's Complaint*, the American Jewish community went for his jugular. And yet, by airing the dirty laundry in those homes, he shed light on the impact that the process of Jewish assimilation into American society had on individual and collective psychology (which are very difficult to differentiate).

'My wang was all I really had that I could call my own,' explains Alexander Portnoy to his psychoanalyst. Faced with a suffocating mother obsessed with her son's health (whom she introduces as Albert Einstein the second, hoping he will deliver her from her frustrations with her second-class status in America), his wang was the only space of freedom that he had. The guilt that produces in Portnoy explains his tortured sexuality, which deserves a closer look.

VIII – LUST AND DISORDER

Alexander Portnoy's father is a soulless man who lets everyone use him as a doormat and suffers from chronic constipation. Which is why Alexander's mother is in charge of everything. 'Filling the patriarchal vacuum!' says their son. Philip Roth offers us a rollicking example of psychical impotence as described by Freud.

Alexander fails to properly unite the two currents that make up healthy adult erotic behaviour: the affectionate and the sensual. Once the affectionate current has been developed within the family nucleus, he is unable to seek out sensual objects outside of it. As always occurs when the ties between mother and son are suffocating, and whenever there is a context of great religious or cultural repression, the libido disassociates from reality and bombards us with the images of the first affectionate erotic objects. Like any other neurotic, Alexander is incapable of choosing an erotic object in which the affectionate and the sensual converge. So when he loves he does not desire and when he desires he does not love. And so, in order to desire, he must debase the erotic object.

Juliette, one of Sade's most famous characters, says that apathy does not kill desire, but rather intensifies it because it creates a vacuum around it. Is that true? I don't believe so. Among my broken friends there are sex addicts and those who abstain. In order to have a reasonable and pleasurable relationship with sex you have to be okay, and that's not discussed enough. We talk about how when we are feeling low or anxious, we lose our appetite for food. We also talk about how boredom, that heavy feeling of immense sloth, is one of the first symptoms of depression. There is a whole branch of popular wisdom that links mood and hunger, mood and motivation, but there isn't as much that talks about our inner landscape in regard to sexual desire.

I maintain that sexual desire is an excellent thermometer for our mental health because it reveals our energy levels. We've already mentioned that, in women, there is little relationship between genital arousal and desire, which is basically located in our brains. When my daughter was born, I fell into a deep dark hole and the first thing I lost during that postpartum depression was my sexual desire. Of course, those early months of sleep deprivation couldn't have helped. And, of course, the emotional prehistory stirred up by the new bond must have been a factor. But suddenly we were no longer a woman and a man. We were now a family.

My breasts, which from Ancient Greece to Redtube are presented erotically, were constantly taken over by a tiny person whose nourishment depended entirely on me. Combining the roles of mother and woman was a challenge, and I felt split. Then I remembered a theory Marta Segarra discusses in *Politics of Desire*, where the Biblical paradigms of Eve and Mary – the desired woman and the mother – are contrasted. The maternal woman is respected but not desired. There was something inside me that was saying (timidly, because I usually turn a deaf ear to my body) that a good mother shouldn't be prancing around with no knickers on.

I had always rejected the feminist idea from the seventies that said everything personal is political and must be treated as such, and so I didn't have any bibliography to rely on. While an intuitive woman, or at least as a reader, can distinguish a cad from an honourable man, or a marriage that will last forever from one that will soon grow tedious, there isn't enough popular wisdom or fictional material about motherhood and how it alters your desire. Relinquishing your lustiness, as in my case, is a cry for help. This mental disorder ruins your sexuality, the same way that sex without any affection leads us to insanity, as any clandestine lover in a hopeless love story knows.

Jeanette Winterson has a novel called *The Passion* that is a very good example of the latter. It takes place in Venice occupied by Napoleon's men because, according to the protagonist, an occupied city is a hedonistic city for those who've abandoned themselves to pleasure. A young woman who works in a casino falls hard for a lady who comes there to gamble. It seems the desire is mutual, but then she finds out the lady is married. They see each other for a while on the down low, until the young woman ends up feeling so desperate about their not being able to share a life together that she leaves the country.

I spent the weeks that followed in a hectic stupor. Is there such a thing? There is. It is the condition that most resembles a particular kind of mental disorder. I have seen ones like me in San Servolo. It manifests itself as a compulsion to be forever doing something, however meaningless. The body must move but the mind is blank. [...] With this feeling inside, with this wild love that threatens, what safe places might there be? Where do you store gunpowder? How do you sleep at night again? [...] Somewhere between the swamp and the mountains. Somewhere between fear and sex. Somewhere between God and the Devil passion is and the way there is sudden and the way back is worse.

IX – A COMPLICATED LUXURY

The way back is worse. There is something that inflames the brain, which needs a particular body and won't be soothed by any other drug. Sex works as a reward: if you experience pleasure, you repeat; if there's pleasure that drives you mad, you repeat madly. And it's like that for everyone. The old canard that men are more lustful than women, and therefore need more sex over more years of their lives, comes from a certain vision of desire as a strictly spontaneous impulse, without memory or motives or learning. This is the dominant vision of desire because men's orgasms are more automatic, not because women are less lustful.

This is an example of how biology and myths become muddled together. If women's desire was as automatic as men's, if it weren't almost entirely located in the brain, literature would not be filled with Jane Eyres and Alomas who confuse first desire with falling in love. If there were not a thinner membrane in the vagina, the myth of virginity would not have stuck and Fanny Hill and her endless deflowerings would not exist. We could even go so far as to say that if there weren't such guilt and such a need for punishment, if domination and submission in bed had no social traction, no one would be aroused by sadomasochism (and Sade would have fallen into oblivion, like so many pornographic authors of his century).

Private life and political life also get muddled up, as do personal and collective psychology. Which is the source of the comments Mercè Rodoreda and Llorenç Villalonga make about the French, and the source of the repression of their Catalan heroines who, because their subjugation is two or threefold, have more difficulties with eroticism than the women of other nations. This is also the source of Alexander Portnoy's madness, of the pressure to be both a proper Jew and a worthwhile American. Lust is a luxury, but complicated, because it is run through with power and control.

We've all heard stories of castrating mothers or wives, mothers-in-law who mistreat their son's spouses, women who scheme against women over suitors or crumbs of flattery. Control has been women's domain, because control needs more psychological resources and is best plotted in smaller places, such as private spaces where women often have more sway. But the terrain of power, which is what determines the course of history, has belonged to men for centuries. Which is why Oscar Wilde ironically stated that women always hold all the winning cards but can't ever win a game.

Is there any way for women and men to relate to each other without engaging in these power struggles? I don't believe so. Even in a theoretical egalitarian state, where power no longer determines relationships, there would still be relationships of control and, as such, slaves of love. We mate, we even marry and procreate convinced that we are armour-plated against any inclement emotion threatening that love. One day we realise that's false, and many of our beliefs collapse. Then, despite having years of maturity on our side, we have no choice but to coexist honourably with the vulnerability.

Aloma is not Mercè Rodoreda's most interesting character, but there is something about her that makes her very special to me. The day Robert leaves, he enters her room to say goodbye. He tells her that he loved her and that he had her too close. And she, who over seven months has learned perfectly how everyone's desire works according to their gaping voids and circumstances, thinks that she also loved him, because she knows absolutely nothing about love. 'She, in his place, knowing life the way he must know it, would have respected her.'

I think that there is an obligation in the partner who has lived more, toward the one who has lived less. We all have the duty to think of the consequences our desire will have on its object, whether they are too close or not. And, at the same time, this moral minimum crumbles as soon as desire is known or believed to be reciprocal. Here everyone becomes defenceless, be they Aristotle, Aloma, or a mad farmer from Lleida. If that weren't the case, there wouldn't be so many marriages, genius artists and political careers that got lost in that crevasse.

If a Big Brother could actually control everything, either through technology, the market, or the threat of Hell or military terror, there would still be a marginal space for the subversion implicit in desire. This is both fortunate and unfortunate.

Fortunate because it is the reaffirming path that life finds to escape any suffocation; this is what makes it such a good thermometer of our health and energy. And unfortunate, because the ways in which desire is complicated by power and control mean that it is easily abused. Conceiving of sexual tensions that still protect the weak is a duty toward your partner and toward history. Doing so without killing desire is a duty toward life, art and the grace of the world.

WRATH

RAÜL GARRIGASAIT

I – REVOLT

My lips tremble, my veins throb, my face contorts. My gaze turns sharp as a knife and suddenly I'm shouting in a harsh voice. I don't know where this unexpected power comes from, but it seems determined to make someone pay. This energy lashes out at parents and children, strangers and friends, even objects. It feels purely physical, but there's something else behind it: an idea, a judgment, a feeling I've been insulted or witnessed an injustice; perhaps it was all set off by a thought. It could linger, becoming an unvoiced grudge that eats away at me, or it could vanish quickly, leaving behind just a memory: I've made a fool of myself, or I've messed up, or I've fulfilled my duty.

If you aren't an angel or a robot, this has also happened to you. Wrath is the most vehement of passions: it's like a revolt of all our physical and moral potential. It takes shape where biology, convictions, and learned culture intersect. It's unclear if this is the revolt of a single individual or the whole inherited legacy of their forebears, if it's me or something that comes from somewhere else, high above or long ago. Wrath has a deep, far-reaching history and, apparently, a magnificent future. Christian tradition deems it a mortal sin, but the Bible attributes it to divinity itself. Ancient philosophers reflected long and hard on it, and Greek literature devoted its first epic poem to it. In each of these moments there are bits and pieces of our own furious selves. The past has made wrath what it is today, a phenomenon with many layers.

As such, if we want to understand anything about wrath, we must look back into the past. And not only to satisfy our antiquarian's curiosity: by exploring history, we can discover holes in the box of unconscious clichés we inhabit, or simply different ways of living. Looking back is also looking forward. Let's begin.

II – THE FIRST PASSION IN EUROPE

It all started with some proud, sensitive men who were waging war in Troy. All of them, particularly the strongest ones, particularly the most admired ones, had that which the Greeks called a great *thymos*, a word that is difficult to translate. *Thymos* was life, strength, desire; but above all it was the source of all vital impulses. The finest warriors had to have great vigour and momentum, and entered combat driven by a destructive fury that would bring them either glory or death. Death entailed exhaling their *thymos* through their mouths and becoming an inert body, without impulses. Either they were men who used their wrath to triumph on the battlefield or they were corpses: this was the disjunctive choice they faced. Sometimes, the word *thymos* also meant 'wrath.' The best warriors had to know how to cultivate this fury within them. Achilles, the best of the Achaeans, was the most irascible of them all. When asked to control his *thymos*, he clung even harder to his passion, eventually paying dearly for it because *thymos* was an ambivalent power which led to both the highest glory and the most extreme desolation. And though aware of this, the heroes were unable to renounce it. The fifteen thousand verses of *The Iliad*, harsh and filled with a beauty that made the war even harsher, revolve around this problematic life the heroes led, this tension that made them admirable, fearsome and miserable. Thus begins written literature in Europe.

Recklessness, fury, rage, anger, rancour, indignation: the Greek of *The Iliad* has words for all of these things, words that appear again and again in almost every scene, and which never cover the same semantic field as our words for them. 'Sing, goddess, of the accursed wrath of Achilles!' begins the poet, announcing the subject of the thousands of hexameters that follow. Here, at the very start of the verse – and the poem, and

Greek literature – the original says *mênis*, a solemn word that is usually only applied to the gods; Achilles is the only mortal overcome by *mênis*, and that in itself elevates him above the others. Only a great hero deserves a poem like *The Iliad*, but the poem itself begins with a reminder that this hero's passion leads to destruction. His accursed wrath brought 'sufferings by the thousands' to the Achaeans and sent numerous heroes to Hades, leaving corpses at the mercy of dogs and birds. For the Greeks, and perhaps for every culture, the most terrifying image of them all is that of unburied, rotting cadavers being devoured by animals. Achilles, overcome by wrath, abandons the battle and allows his fellow soldiers to drop like flies. Not only that, but there are so many corpses laying on the battlefield that the animals eat them. This is a breakdown of life's most basic principle: respect for the dead. In Greece, a cadaver that isn't buried or burned is a monstrous aberration that shatters the relationship between gods and mortals; it is an impurity contaminating and condemning the entire community, as shown in Sophocles' *Antigone*.

What is this *mênis* wrath that echoes in the first verse of *The Iliad*? It isn't a burst of anger that flares up in a moment and disappears without a trace. The ancient commentators paraphrased it as lasting resentment or persistent irritation. So, let's look at what sparked the conflict: Agamemnon, the leader of the Achaeans who've come to destroy Troy, is offended by having to give up a concubine he captured as a prize of war. To compensate for the insult to his honour, he takes Briseis, Achilles' concubine. These captives are women, but what matters most to Agamemnon is that they are also spoils of war, booty that forms the basis of their honour as warriors, and as such their glory. The heroic code states that excellence must always be rewarded, so the most courageous soldiers have the right to the

117

best spoils. It is this principle which gives meaning to war. The fatigue, the suffering, the bloodshed, all of that is justified because the efforts are never in vain: the finest warriors will have more spoils and more honour and, once dead, the poets will celebrate them for generations. It is those two certainties that keep the soldiers going. Yet it is Agamemnon, their leader and ostensibly the highest guardian of this heroic code, who actually breaks it and humiliates Achilles. The problem is not that Agamemnon is more powerful, but that he abuses his position of power and violates the unwritten law that legitimises the hierarchy. When he sees his booty threatened, Achilles considers drawing his sword and killing Agamemnon then and there, but the goddess Athena, visible only to him, comes down from Olympus, grabs him by the hair and stops him. So Achilles' first reaction is one of anger, but that is not *mênis*. That predictable, fleeting flare of rage is not worthy of becoming the subject of one of the most extraordinary poems ever written.

Mênis wrath is a much more twisted and devastating emotion. Achilles accepts Agamemnon's authority. He knows he cannot stop him from taking Briseis, his captive of lovely cheeks, and the material reward for his honour. But he is not resigned; he calls him a drunk and a coward and a useless king, and he makes a solemn oath: one day the Achaeans will miss Achilles, when they are dying en masse at the hand of Hector of Troy, and Agamemnon will tear his *thymos* in anguish over not having honoured the greatest of the Achaeans. Achilles refuses to take part in the war, remaining in his tent even as the Trojans are rounding up and annihilating the Achaeans. He stays on the sidelines for as long as it takes for Agamemnon to finally humble himself and beg him to return, because without Achilles the Achaeans are lost. Now it is not a flare-up or fit of rage, but patient resentment determined to make Agamemnon pay for his arrogance, even at the cost of his comrades' lives. That is *mênis* wrath: the emotional basis of a sinister plan for revenge, designed to bring suffering in order to restore the world's balance.

The mechanism is implacable. Achilles is offended because Agamemnon has abused his power and infringed on the warriors' code; as a result, he himself departs from the code. His *mênis* wrath bursts onto the scene because of a specific offence, but it collapses the entire system of principles that sustains the community of warriors. Achilles goes so far as to say that war no longer makes sense, because the distinction between a courageous, strong warrior and a coward in the rear-guard has been blurred. He proclaims that he wants to return home, even though his presence is essential to the victory, even though it would mean all of his comrades' blood being shed in vain. War is meaningless, I'm going home, I'd rather die of old age and in obscurity than young and glorious. Only an idiot would remain in Troy, says Achilles, led by his *mênis*, to his fellow soldiers.

This wrath shakes the foundations of their shared presuppositions. The offended warrior distances himself from the others and destroys their prejudices, suddenly seeing the world from a different perspective. Once he's been dishonoured, if that's how the game is played, he wants no part of it. Up until then his life had been too governed by the laws of war and he had allowed himself to fall into heroic naiveté; his wrath frees him from the web of honour and glory. First conclusion: wrath is the strongest and surest way to say no.

But Achilles did not go home. His heroic spirit would not allow him to truly accept the idea of dying as an anonymous old man. His very plan, his determination to make Agamemnon pay for offending him, forces him to remain near Troy. He can't help but follow the war's development with interest. After all, the anti-war speeches he makes are only a way to hurt Agamemnon.

While it seems he's abandoned the principles of the hero's code, he cannot desert the leader who has insulted him. He continues to be subject to the economy of honour and dishonour that rules soldiers' lives. The vengeful nature of his *mênis* prevents him from categorically saying no.

And here is where tragedy ensues, because in his state of *mênis* he makes a miscalculation. Achilles, who is practically a teenager, has an older friend, Patroclus, who gave him advice growing up, and is now his squire. Out of loyalty, Patroclus has withdrawn from battle with Achilles but cannot bear the sight of his comrades dropping like flies. He begs Achilles to allow him to return to combat and beat back the Trojans, and when Achilles consents, Patroclus puts on his friend's armour to scare their enemies even more. Patroclus advances furiously, reaching the very gates of Troy, and manages to kill Hector's charioteer with a hurled rock. Spurred on by the blood, he continues fighting until he is stopped by the actions of a god and two mortals: Apollo knocks his helmet off, young Euphorbus wounds him in the back, and Hector runs him through with a spear.

When Achilles learns of this, they have to restrain his hands to keep him from slitting his own neck: he has just discovered the true nature of *mênis* wrath. His withdrawal from battle and his plan to humiliate Agamemnon in retaliation for the insult, has led to the death of his friend and the loss of his armour. Now, Achilles exhorts everyone to put the past behind them and control their wrath. Agamemnon admits that he was blinded by divine forces and returns Briseis along with a mountain of valuable gifts, and Achilles states that the conflict would not have happened if the gods hadn't wanted to harm them. This is not a way to minimise their human errors but rather to comment on them. Achilles and Agamemnon make peace with each other, and the *mênis* wrath dissipates.

Achilles had been stubborn in his refusal and declared the warrior code obsolete, but he now finds himself more chained to the circle of bellicose violence than ever before. Nothing could justify his remaining in his tent now. Despite knowing, as his goddess mother Thetis told him, that his fate is to die young if he does not desist from war, he must emerge with an unprecedented destructive fury to take his revenge on Hector. When he goes out to avenge his friend, he goes to die in the name of future glory, to become the protagonist of poems yet to be written. His desire for revenge, for death, for honour and for glory: they all come together in that moment. And Achilles gets the extraordinary strength he needs from a new wrath – not the slow, calculating *mênis* but the burst of fury called *kholos*. It is *kholos* that will lead him to kill Hector and drag his body around in an attempt to disfigure it, and also to slit the throats of twelve Trojan boys at the pyre for his dead friend. Nothing can stop him. Second conclusion: wrath imbues us with more strength than any other passion.

The Iliad revolves around these two forms of wrath, embodied by Achilles stubbornly withdrawing to his tent, before then destroying everything like a madman.

The *mênis* wrath was paralyzing; in his tent, Achilles played the zither and brooded incessantly over his pain. All the hierarchal relationships that had seemed obvious to him were revealed to be false. His *mênis* placed him at a certain distance from the world: a perspective that makes us see things as smaller, yet isn't enough distance for us to forget everything and start a new life.

While *mênis* wrath allowed him to retreat and calculate and even get depressed, *kholos* wrath is all action and violence: it seeks out physical contact and blood, enjoys mutilating corpses and killing innocents. It is a force that acts of its own volition, without reason or memory. When the warrior becomes enraged, he is beside himself because his whole self is the flying spear, the slicing sword, the feet pursuing the enemy. When Achilles sees his new armour, crafted by a god, his heart fills with *kholos* and his eyes flame.

The Iliad explores these two extremes: the destructive no of the *mênis* wrath and the equally destructive yes of the *kholos* wrath. But neither of these are nihilistic actions. Wrath, in all its forms, emerges from an intense concern about something, from an identification with someone, or from a specific way of understanding the world. Achilles explodes because his most basic principles are shaken, and because they kill his most beloved friend. His wrath wants to restore balance to the world through suffering. It is his love for what he has lost that compels him to bring pain to the earth. Third conclusion: wrath would not exist without intense love, deep concern, or a clear vision of the world.

In *The Iliad* we see this impulse in men, but there are also women in Greek mythology who seem to be archetypal representations of wrath. We find them on the margins, as if best kept at a prudent distance. One of the best-known examples is Medea, a foreigner and witch who kills her children when her husband betrays her. But there is another, even more exceptional case that borders on the absurd: the monstrous Medusa, her head covered in a tangle of twisted snakes, fangs as large as a boar's, bronze hands and gold wings and eyes that turn anyone who looks upon her to stone. Living on the extremes of the known world, as if keeping watch between civilisation and destruction, she embodies a fury trapped inside itself, pure alterity, with no insult required for her to explode.

Between *The Iliad* and these myths, two extreme dangers are depicted: a resentment that clings to the past and broods over an offence until eventually rotting all in its wake, and a rage that can no longer even recall its origin.

The poem itself offers us a vision of the way out of wrath. In the end, a still devastated, raged-filled Achilles stays up all night before tying Hector's body to his chariot and dragging it three times around Patroclus' burial mound every morning. After twelve days, the gods have had enough. Priam, Hector's father and King of Troy, enters the Achaean camp by night, protected by Zeus. Priam grabs Achilles by the knees in a sign of entreaty and kisses his hands, the very hands that killed his sons. He asks him to think of his own elderly father and to return Hector's cadaver to him. And then they cry together, each for their own reasons, but also in mutual understanding: one for his dead son, the other for his old father and his fallen friend. Finally, Achilles lets go of his wrath, returns the body to Priam and grants him as many days of truce as he requests. *The Iliad*'s fifteen thousand verses on wrath end with one of the most memorable scenes of mercy ever composed. A fourth conclusion: crying with someone, seeing your own and the other's grief side by side stops wrath.

Yet it is worth noting that this mercy only comes at the very end, when each side's suffering has been balanced and there is nothing left to destroy.

III – CRUSHING THE BEAST

Acting as a medium for the muse, the poet of *The Iliad* wastes no time moralising: he depicts the actual clashes, the passions that seize the mortals, and the terrible consequences. But the ancients soon began to elaborate moral theories about wrath. Heraclitus warned that it is difficult to fight *thymos*, our inner impulsiveness that can dominate the soul. In the first centuries of Greek history the idea emerged of a vertical hierarchy within man. At the top was reason, thought and the psyche; at the bottom were impulses and bad habits. The first ethics established a duel within human beings between the superior and the inferior within. Ancient philosophy was that duel: through a succession of exercises, it aspired to subjugate the lower impulses and elevate life towards purity.

This vision of the individual is analogous to the political community. Reason had to dominate the lower impulses just as an aristocratic government forced the unruly masses to submit. In both cases, the clarity of order was found in the enduring power from above while the unpredictable elements below were a muddle of confusion. No passionate revolution had the right to tumble the rule of reason. Vertical ethics, vertical politics. The fight against the passions was reason battling chaos.

The Stoic philosophers took part in this battle. They imagined an aristocracy of the spirit free from passions. Their ideal sage possessed an unflappable cold intelligence that never grew irritated, fell in love, or got depressed. They saw the passions as impurities that sullied the individual, jolts causing us lose our self-control. For the philosopher to be his best self, he had to be free of them. Once he had suppressed his passions, his individual reason aligned itself with universal reason.

Lowest on the hierarchy was wrath, the greatest threat to the dominion of clarity. In the most famous treatise on the matter, *On Anger*, the Roman Stoic Seneca deemed this passion the most 'foul and frenzied.' The angry individual turns ugly, his physical deformity reflecting the deformity of his soul. His inflamed eyes, red face, trembling lips, his bellowing, the beating of fists and stomping of feet, all these signs of a 'deformed and bloated' man make his wrath impossible to hide. Unlike more easily concealed vices, wrath is an evident manifestation of a lack of self-control and, since the discovery of vertical ethics, losing control of oneself has been the worst thing that could happen to any aspiring sage.

The strangest aspect of anger, however, is that it cannot be said to be a passion completely detached from reason or justice. Seneca defined it as a desire to punish an offence we've suffered, or as the arousal of the soul towards exacting deliberate punishment, describing it in a series of three movements. The first is a mere involuntary reaction in the face of a threat or insult. The second implies a judgment: it introduces the idea that one must exact vengeance because one has been offended. The third movement is utter chaos: it wants punishment, come what may, despite reason and usefulness; it is a blind, destructive impulse to exact justice. The problem is not the desire for revenge in and of itself, but rather that this desire inverts the inner hierarchy: furious impulses overtake control of reason. Wrath is like a revolution that is sparked by a lovely ideal and ends in a bloodbath.

At the heart of this theory is the conviction that the aroused state is not natural. For Seneca, human beings are born gentle and have an innate desire to help and be around others. Eliminating wrath means returning to the natural human state, yet any trace of fury can drag you back down the slope of vice. As such, Seneca considers it easier to suppress pernicious passions than to maintain control over them. Since wrath is a composite passion that 'passes through the soul' or, in other words, relies on the intervention of judgment, the remedy is to intervene in the very moment when the idea of taking revenge first forms. That way access is barred to the third movement, the chaotic fury that demands an eye for an eye at any cost.

Ancient vertical ethics came up with all sorts of mental exercises so as to intervene at the right moment to smother bursts of anger. They are ideas that later influenced Christian literature and, in turn, self-help books. I will summarize them here and readers can decide for themselves if they are useful or not.

The first remedy is delay: when the offence is explained, we must turn a deaf ear and question it; we must defend the absent offending party and not partake in suspicion and conjecture. The second is to relativise: the vast majority of our problems – Seneca mostly focuses on slaves who don't serve well – are insignificant and undeserving of our exasperation. The third remedy is that we must remember that it is lunacy to become irritated with inanimate objects and beings such as children whose reason is undeveloped, as they do not intentionally offend us. The fourth: we must remember that no one is free of guilt, that we've made as many mistakes as others, and that we are no better than anyone else. When our anger flares up against someone, we must tell ourselves: 'I too have done that' and remind ourselves that the earth is filled with pain and repugnance, that it is a 'pestilent domicile' and the pain we encounter is both inevitable and predictable. And, finally, fifth: we have to put ourselves in the other's place and try to understand their limitations and hardships. Think that if they have been rude or not served us as we might have wished, it could be because they have suffered injustices that have caused them to lose their natural human sweetness.

But perhaps the most efficient remedies are those that flatter us: when we begin to boil with indignation, we should think that great souls pay little mind to offence. Like a powerful beast, we must be indifferent to the barking of little dogs. We might also think of the prestige of forgiveness and clemency as it is the weak who become aggrieved and that retreating from wrath is the act of a winner.

Finally, we can appeal to our sense of aesthetics. When we gaze into the mirror to contemplate the ugliness of our rage-contorted faces, we appear as hellish monsters like Medusa with her snakes and her petrifying gaze. No other passion disfigures us to that extent. By abstaining from wrath, we are embracing beauty.

Through the repeated use of such meditations, the Stoics

aspired to make their souls as independent and hard as a rock. Once everything had been examined and relativised, what remained was a completely self-possessed being, free from fear and deception and pride, a minimal, whole self requiring nothing more than the sensation of being unflappable, a morsel of universal reason surrounded by a hunk of flesh. It is unclear what compelled this passionless self to go on living; indeed, the Stoics always defended the legitimacy of suicide.

Is the impetuous desire for retribution, an eye for an eye, ever justified? For Seneca, the problem is not the sanction in and of itself, but the lack of reflection and self-control. A punishment might be useful, but it must be 'serene and reasonable.' Seneca never questions that 'characters depraved by vice' can be corrected 'by punishment of body and soul.' If it has a 'salubrious effect,' then nothing is too harsh for him; he even deems capital punishment acceptable if death is a benefit to the wrongdoer and the community. The wise judge does not feel pleasure upon sending a man to the gallows as his verdict is not meant to satisfy a rampant desire for revenge. When the judge submits someone to such public dishonour it is meant as an example that will serve as a 'lesson to all.' Having weighed up the pros and cons, the judge's sentence is one of cold calculation. It is precisely because he maintains the natural inner hierarchy, with reason leading from above, that the punishment will be more effective than an angry reaction.

But is there any possible advantage to the strength produced by wrath? There are some who have said that both hotheadedness and the spur of rage are necessary in war. The Homeric heroes would be nothing without their *thymos*, and that momentary loss of control that caused them to enjoy spilling their enemies' blood. Seneca shakes his head: a warrior's courage never needs vice as a spur. Nothing savage and out of control will make a soldier stronger.

But is there no possible way of using this insurrection in a positive way? Isn't wrath necessary against aggressors? Seneca again says no: it is precisely in a war where impulses must be obedient and moderate. But then he is presented with specific images. The barbarians, so hale and hearty, so unflagging. Is their wrath not useful against the Romans? No, repeats Seneca. Reason is stronger than irritation; we must act as the hunter serenely awaiting the beast as those who are most inflamed rashly deliver themselves into the hands of their adversaries; wrath is the ruin of itself. But then the philosopher recalls the Germanic people and his theory seems to come apart at the seams. The Germanic barbarians are courageous, ardent, bellicose, tireless; they employed wrath to banish the Romans from their lands and seemingly owe their freedom to it. And here it is that Seneca makes a reflection that reveals to what extent the inner hierarchy of reason and passion mirrors an outer political hierarchy. Look at the Romans, he says: they stop, they delay, they set aside their resentment and thirst for revenge, they calculate slowly, they are cautious. And it is thanks to that character – devoid of wrath – that they've built an empire. Germanic ferocity will never achieve anything even close.

And here, despite his stoicism, Seneca admits to an important point: wrath could have a defensive utility, to expel an invasive force and maintain one's freedom, but it is not useful for building an extensive, complex military supremacy, which is something that requires serene reasoning.

When German nationalism appeared around 1800, some writers were fascinated by the image of the furious Germanic character. The Prussian playwright Heinrich von Kleist considered it ideal for defending freedom in the face of dehumanising bureaucracy and French invaders. He imagined German soldiers fighting against Napoleon with the savage wrath of the ancient Germanic peoples and dreamed of enemy corpses piled up so high as to divert the course of the Rhine. Readers would be forgiven for thinking that that exaltation of impulsive violence must have led straight to National Socialism. But the Nazis in fact learned Seneca's lesson: the extermination camps are not an angry fist banging on a table, but the result of cold, meticulous calculation based on science and bureaucracy. Eradication in the most efficient way. The Nazis practiced Stoic unflappability. Had they not, they would not have been able to create a broad system of annihilation in which those involved collaborated with such discipline. Seneca said it long ago: punishment that stems from reason is more effective than punishment that stems from wrath.

And given the destructive madness of reason, might not the wrath that leads us to lose control over ourselves be, paradoxically, a more reasonable reaction? Is there not also a noble sentiment in wrath? Can it not be a sublime manifestation of our moral indignation? Can it not be the strongest and surest way to say no to the barbarities of cold calculation?

Ancient philosophy itself expressed doubts of this sort. Aristotle did not admire the callous who feel nothing nor suffer over anything. He believed that overlooking affronts to one's self or one's family and friends was a vile, lowly act and, as is common to his ethics, believed there was a middle ground between apathy and unbridled ire: a good rage that flares up for the correct reasons, against deserving persons, in the proper way and at the right moment. The problem is that, beyond the abstract, it is very difficult to locate this middle ground. As Aristotle himself acknowledged, no general criteria can be established here: our verdict will always be dependent on the particulars of the situation. But there remains an even greater difficulty. Wrath is an explosive emotion that overpowers us in an instant: when its disruptive fury rages through us, its own verdict already

established, what is the likelihood that it will listen if we set out
to reason with it about finding a middle ground?

IV – THE PASSION AT WORLD'S END

It is a scene that has obsessed Christian imagination for centuries. The world will tremble and turn to ash, and God will
appear as a judge; a trumpet will raise the dead and call them to
stand before His throne. At that moment, the Most High will
pull out a book containing all our defects and all our desires, all
the evil thoughts we've ever had, all our moments of affliction
and regret, the names of every person we have failed. And with
this universal book God will judge the world. Fearsome Majesty,
Judge of vengeance, He will bring to light all that is hidden.
God will divide humanity: to the right are those who will be
saved, to the left those condemned to the flames. The writhing
accused plead for mercy from eternal hellfire. For centuries that
is how Christianity has imagined the day of Final Judgment that,
according to Saint Paul, will come like a thief in the night, like
the labour pains of a pregnant woman. The most famous hymn
about that day, attributed to Thomas of Celano, disciple of Saint
Francis of Assisi, calls it 'Dies irae,' the day of wrath.

It is an absolute, singular wrath that makes the definitive
selection and its extreme nature makes it a useful tool when
trying to understand this passion. In God, power, knowledge and
justice coincide and, as Ramon Llull maintained, in the divine
substance these three principles convert into each other because
they form a single essence. Divine justice, absolute power and
total knowledge are applied, deployed, and materialise at the
same time. In the supreme being, justice is clearly manifested as a
form of power, as is knowledge. And wrath is the revolt of justice

and power and knowledge against everything incongruous with that, against all degradation and turmoil; in short, it is a revolt by divine reason against the chaos of the earth.

We see warnings and manifestations of that wrath from the very beginning of the Bible. In paradise, when the snake seduces woman, and woman and man infringe the divine order to desist from eating from the tree of knowledge, God becomes furious and condemns the snake to slither on its belly and for man and woman to live with pain. It is a God jealously guarding His position who tells Himself: 'Man has become like one of us,' and for that He banishes them from Eden.

Soon, however, other divine faces are revealed. God parts the waters of the Red Sea with a great wind, allowing the Israelites to cross, before drowning the Egyptian army pursuing them. Then Moses sings a song to celebrate the Lord's victory; he exalts Him as a great warrior and proclaims: 'In majestic triumph You overthrow your foes; Your anger blazes out and burns them up like straw.' Here we see a desert warrior god facing off against the Egyptian official gods, a god who looks favourably on the surprising victory of the underdogs. His wrath is an impassioned violent defence of the oppressed.

When the Israelites corrupt the law, trample the weak, ruin the farmers, abuse women and profane the name of the Lord, Yahweh rises up in fury against them and sends an enemy army to destroy them. 'There will be wailing in all the streets and cries of anguish in every public square. The farmers will be summoned to weep and the mourners to wail,' He has the prophet Amos say. That will be the 'day of the Lord.' According to another prophet, Zephaniah: 'that day will be a day of wrath, a day of distress and anguish, a day of trouble and ruin, a day of darkness and gloom, a day of clouds and blackness.' When Israel is destroyed and its inhabitants deported, it is thanks to the idea of divine wrath that everything makes sense. Because that wrath proclaims that misfortune is not gratuitous or random but rather the price an individual or community must sooner or later pay for travelling down the path of decline. But for the prophets, wrath also has another meaning: Yahweh only mercilessly annihilates Israel because he has an intimate relationship with its people and worries more about them than about any other.

And this feature is not exclusive to the God of the prophets or the Old Testament. Jesus also becomes enraged with the rabbis whose hearts are hardened from so much worshipping of the written precepts and he drives out the merchants who are sullying the temple. Despite the later Christian tradition of considering wrath a sin, it seems clear that it is also a divine attribute and that some extraordinary characters make use of it. But the absolute wrath – composed of justice, power, and knowledge – of the fearsome day of the Lord is seen only in representations of God. In humans we already find it broken into various partial and problematic forms.

The first partial form is the exclusive linking of wrath and power at the risk of losing out on justice and knowledge.

For the Stoic philosophers, wrath was worthy of study because it represented the opposite of wisdom. They saw man as an animal capable of rationally restraining himself, and self-control as an essential trait of the philosopher. *Ataraxia*, the tranquillity of the sage, was a state invulnerable to passions, be they one's own or others.' As such, wrath was a bad blunder: the angered man loses self-control, ceases to be superior to himself, and is left at the mercy of a violent passion. Getting angry means losing authority over one's self, while repressing wrath is a sign of power both over oneself and the world.

Fits of rage, however, are a typical feature of the powerful: God, executives, governors. An interesting case is the former president of the United States, Donald Trump. In his all-caps and exclamation point filled tweets we saw a truly rage-filled man. One of his most spectacular moments was on the 23rd July 2018, when he addressed the Iranian president, Hassan Rouhani, with these exact words:

NEVER, EVER THREATEN THE UNITED STATES AGAIN OR YOU WILL SUFFER CONSEQUENCES THE LIKES OF WHICH FEW THROUGHOUT HISTORY HAVE EVER SUFFERED BEFORE. WE ARE NO LONGER A COUNTRY THAT WILL STAND FOR YOUR DEMENTED WORDS OF VIOLENCE & DEATH. BE CAUTIOUS!

The capitals are shouts and fists banging on the table evoking images of atomic bombs and massacres. Two months later he tweeted: 'Despite requests, I have no plans to meet Iranian President Hassan Rouhani. Maybe someday in the future. I am sure he is an absolutely lovely man!' Tweets like this lead us to believe we are getting a glimpse of the real man: capricious, fickle, devoid of self-control; an irascible Donald Trump who is later surprisingly calm and friendly yet merely two seconds away from exploding with rage again. This feeling is strange: after all, nothing must go through more filters than the public messages of the President of the United States. The success of Trump's tweets is also due to the impression that they're totally unfiltered, that there is no solid reflection behind them, that they've come straight out of his mobile phone in a moment of true fury. And this fury warns us that such a man is dangerous and should frighten us.

We might wonder if these tweets are the real anger of a specific man; we do know for certain that their dramatic staging of wrath is a strategy of power. Few things convey so forcefully the idea of vast control than seeing how someone can ignore filters, precautions and social conventions. The executive raises his voice, personally attacks an underling, bangs his fist on the desk, intimidates, threatens wordlessly. Wrath reinforces his superiority. There are those who've made an art of these sorts of stagings; management and leadership schools teach how to use this most effectively. We might even say that power needs the ostentatiousness of wrath to display itself, as Saint Paul insinuated in one of his gloomier thoughts: God the potter created defective vessels that deserved wrath – evil men – so He could punish them and show His full glory, which He will pour into the 'vessels of mercy,' the good Christians.

When wrath and power come together, it can result in a dangerous intoxication. The Stoics loved to tell a cautionary tale which said that a tyrannical ruler in Magna Graecia had a philosopher (who'd conspired against him) arrested and tortured so he would reveal the names of his accomplices. The prisoner named all the friends and adulators of the ruler. Enraged, the tyrant had them killed one after the other before asking the sage if there were any others. 'Just you,' responded the philosopher. The paranoias of the powerful can always be used against them.

Wrath as an effective strategy of power is not within everyone's reach. One of the risks of angry reactions is that you can be pigeonholed into a stereotype. The most typical one is the hysterical woman or, even more pejoratively, the hysterical mother. As we can see in Homer, wrath has been closely tied to masculinity from the beginning; it's as if women couldn't get angry or didn't need to be taken seriously when they did. The stereotype of the hysterical mother plays to that idea: she's lost sight of what's important, no need to pay her any mind, we can even poke a bit of fun at her. The stereotype deactivates the strength of her wrath and mocks her concern. This mechanism reveals that even getting angry is a kind of privilege: we do not recognise everyone's right to do so. A god, a Homeric hero, an executive: in those cases wrath is a part of their very essence, helping them to deploy their strength and power. A woman, a subordinate, a beggar: when they get angry, people often look at them with disdain or indifference.

Effective wrath does not allow itself to be thus pigeonholed. It can be a true art, shaping the predictable reaction into something altogether different. For example, shifting the desire to shout into some other response such as a slow, tense, fury-laden word. Wrath's strength is too great to renounce. And repressing wrath is dangerous and counterproductive because it comes out of a truly deep concern, out of an intense relationship that affects us profoundly; repressing that is like amputating our relationship with the world. But in order for this concern to be fully expressed, in order for us to be able to get angry and have our anger recognised as such, we must avoid the danger of being mocked or – if we are – intensify our wrath to intimidate and nip the mocking in the bud.

The danger of stereotyping also threatens powerful, cantankerous men. If an executive gets angry too often, he will eventually be seen as not being quite right in the head, despite his subordinates fearing him. His indignation will soon be seen as neurosis, more pitiful than intimidating, and those working under him will soon learn that his display of yelling and pounding on the desk is his usual reaction; it might scare them, but each time they will be less affected by it, and one day they will even stand up to him, because no one wants to be subservient to someone who is unbalanced.

The enraged God of Moses defended the oppressed against the Pharoah's armies and so just as wrath can be an instrument of the powerful, in the exodus from Egypt it was revealed to be a passion that looked kindly upon the subaltern. Though it could be deduced from their theory, this is the possibility the Stoics didn't want to recognise: if wrath has a moment that requires a moral judgment of an offence suffered or witnessed, it means that it is not a fundamentally simple chaotic passion, but rather a noble feeling of justice. In the face of a cruel world, the irascible person vindicates a just order and their indignation is a revolt of their sense of justice against an abuse of power.

In his broad-ranging philosophical study *Rage and Time*, Peter Sloterdijk described modernity as a period in which rigorously hierarchical revolutionary organisations accumulated and directed rage toward unprecedentedly extensive political actions. Today it seems that a similar political emotion prevails, but it is scattered and stripped of utopian faith. It is the wrath of those who feel scammed by the enlightened rhetoric of nation-states, by the cynical use of the myths of progress and state neutrality, and who've come to the conclusion that institutions serve only the dominant social or national group. As such, this wrath is actually the breakdown of modern promises of justice and freedom, blowing up against the state as a mere device of power and repression. The revolts we see on the streets around much of the world, the contemporary days of wrath with fire and violence, bring the fury that Moses' God brought upon the oppressors down to earth. Burning garbage dumpsters is imitating God, but with the instruments of human impotence.

The enlightened rhetoric of the state rearms itself against these flare-ups of indignation. The large media outlets transmit the idea of civilisation as a form of pacification, that those acting violently are primitive beings and that there are things that no longer happen or should no longer happen in our societies. And wrath appears as a burst of animality or barbarism that we should have evolved past.

In this we also see how wrath is deeply rooted in our world. In part, the rejection of this passion comes from the view on violence that has extended throughout modernised countries. With the expansion of state machinery, everyone has tacitly assumed that the only legitimate violence belongs to the state. Outside of this monopoly, the state itself demands we condemn all forms of violence, the mass media amplifies this message, and we citizens internalise it and repeat it all the while feeling that we are contributing to humanity's progress. We come to truly believe that all violence that isn't exercised by the state is immoral. This illusion is the total and utter triumph of the machinery of the state. And I use the word illusion because it clearly doesn't align with anyone's personal experience: if you saw your child, your mother, your brother or sister in danger, would you not use necessary violence to save them? If there were no other choice and we weren't paralysed by fear, we would never consider it immoral to exert violence in such a situation. Some – the most heroic among us – would even use violent force to defend a stranger. It could be said that this violence is moral because it doesn't come into conflict with the state, that it is moral because of its legality, and because it is defensive and doesn't contradict the state monopoly on violence. But, in truth, if a police officer commits an unjustified aggression, then the violence used to stop that aggression, despite its illegality, would be considered moral by any reasonable person, setting aside any considerations of prudence and strategy. If we innocently accept that the only legitimate violence is that which is wielded by the state, we leave ourselves totally vulnerable to authoritarianism. Flashes of rage reveal this truth to our eyes.

Yet we must acknowledge that all violence is traumatic. Even the violence we wield ourselves and believe to be moral. A tense individual with a penetrating stare and all their strength directed toward another person, the pain of the aggressor and of the victim: it all leaves a deep scar; it creates a strange feeling of dislocation, of timelessness. There are aggressions that provoke amnesia in both the attacker and the victim, yet leave them both tormented, and fits of rage are disturbing in part because they remind us of that. And they remind us even when it doesn't go as far as real violence: just the act of raising our voice or our hand, or even the simple wish to do so, is enough to give us a sense of the traumatic nature of violence. Wrath leads us to simulated aggression much more often than to actual aggression, even when we don't use one of the Stoic exercises. It is the body's warning that teaches us about how the world works.

Fits of wrath are among Yahweh's anthropomorphic traits. One of the Hebrew words for that reaction, *'af*, primarily means 'nose'; when God gets enraged, he forcefully exhales from his nose. Another word, *za'am*, evokes the foam that comes from His mouth. This behaviour is not particularly in keeping with the divinity philosophers and theologists usually imagine. At one point, even Ramon Llull questions whether God can get angry. If the substantial glory where all divine attributes lie is an infinite kindness, how can it splutter with rage? According to the enlightened Mallorcan, wrath distorts all the faculties of the soul and moves all blood to the heart. It is an obscured, muddled state in which memory becomes oblivion, understanding becomes ignorance, and good intentions become irritated rage. In this passion the faculties of the soul are upended, emptied, and at the same time dominated by a strange force. Yet in God, the eternal principles (goodness, greatness, duration, power, wisdom, etc.) can always convert into each other through some sort of peaceful, metaphysical dance. As such, Llull writes that nothing and no-one could be further from wrath than 'He who is glory and glorious.'

Seen in that light, the strength of wrath is a human weakness. In no other situation is that so clearly illustrated as in the saddest wrath of all: that against innocents. A father asks his son, as sweetly as he can, to put on his shoes. The boy gets distracted by a crumpled piece of paper. The father looks at his watch: it's a quarter to nine, the boy will be late for school and the father to his very important meeting. Put on your shoes, he orders. He takes a deep breath. The boy picks up a dirty twig he sees on the street and starts to scratch at its bark. His father repeats the order. He repeats it two, three more times. He ends up repeating it ten or twenty times, always gently, but finally with a sweetness that is almost a desperate begging. And when the father loses his temper and shouts at the boy, maybe even shakes him, and the child gets scared, his eyes dampen, and he puts on his shoes right away. Anger was more convincing than patience; yet after his outburst, the father feels cruel and helpless.

In this variant of wrath, justice no longer plays a part. While the child is away with the fairies, the father sees his work commitment or convention endangered. The boy does nothing unfair or cause any intentional harm and is nothing more than an obstacle in the path between the father and his goal. There is no clash between justice and evil, but rather an adult's organisation of life against a child's distraction. This wrath is a revolt of social norms against innocence and that is why the father feels guilty: even if only on a deeper level, he sees a conflict between his adult responsibilities and his son's ability to waste time, and it's as if he's thrown a grenade into the innocent peace of childhood. With every outburst, the father pushes his son further into the adult world (as, after all, is his duty), but he also kills a small part of his childhood. Wrath, ever quick to bring a truth to the surface, reveals this basic moment in the experience of raising a child.

When faced with innocence, we can't help but suspect some abyss. When a conviction or a simple expectation transforms into irritated yelling, wrath lays bare our adult pretensions. Is there any point to them? Are these efforts we make useless against this power that is stronger than ideas? Is it possible that these outbursts prove we are nothing more than a strange mass of nerves and blood and bones that revolts before we have a chance to adorn it with words and reasons? Wrath, especially wrath that comes out of frustration at innocence, often leaves us with that feeling of helplessness and absurdity.

There is a period where this aspect of wrath is well represented. In medieval Catalan and Occitan, the word *ira* usually meant sadness, dejection; it could even mean something similar to depression. In Ramon Llull's poetry, the word is associated with melancholy, affliction, crying and grief. In his prose we read: 'Ire is a sudden movement of will linked with sadness' and 'ire is sad passion' and 'ire is a habit that begets sadness and passion against deliberating to do good or avoid evil' and, as such, he says that the irate man does everything 'by chance,' randomly, without articulating any meaning. Despite its initial sudden movement, most prevalent in this painful ire is a helplessness akin to suicidal ideation. 'The irate,' writes Llull, 'are more dead than alive.' This points to the paralysing effect of the most profound wrath, which protects itself from its surroundings by taking refuge in inaction. It is similar to the rancorous revolt of Achilles. The Greek hero also sees his value system crumble, saying that war no longer has any meaning and that he'd rather die old and unknown.

When Llull, having attempted to transform the world with his philosophical system, feels disrespected and doomed to failure, he is overcome by a depressive ire that emerges from the highest feeling, from his passion for the eternal principles of the divine order. As such, this wrath has a very curious status for Llull: it forms part of his catalogue of deadly sins, but at the same time originates from a novel impulse and rebels against the degradation of human communities. In the poem *Lo desconhort* the character Ramon speaks. He obstinately clings to his painful ire, despite a hermit's attempts to console him. Finally, instead of calming down, he manages to awaken the ire of that seemingly smug hermit: it makes him acknowledge sinful earthly chaos and he is moved to act.

Wrath always points to the world's seams: those points where aspirations rub up against realities, truth and convention, social norms and innocence. Because of its ability to get to the bottom of things, it is logical that wrath presides over the spectacle of Judgment Day, when the seams of the world split and the difference between extermination and restoration is abolished.

V – BEFRIENDING WRATH

We are all too familiar with degraded forms of wrath. There is the constant bad mood of those angry with the world, who censure everything others do and take every reprimand as an unforgivable offence. There is the dark, self-destructive resentment that chains its victims to an unpleasant moment in their past and forces them to relive it over and over again. There is that tantrum that flares up before realising it's an over-reaction but that persists in order to avoid seeming unfounded and results in a directionless frenzy. In these forms, wrath has lost its exceptional impetuosity and retains only the sense of injury or has been reduced to an irritability that believes in nothing. It weighs on us, it eats us up inside, it embitters us and others, getting us stuck in unproductive obstinacy. These degraded variants are unable to find positive motivation or bang a fist on a desk, and perhaps that's what's wrong with them: they aren't wrathful enough.

Because wrath has an enormous force to it. It's been attributed to the most extraordinary epic heroes throughout history and even to the most powerful god of them all, because men have always perceived wrath as being more than human, even as a mark of supernatural powers. It makes reason revolt against chaos, justice rebel against evil, self-esteem protest against scorn and social norms protect themselves against innocence. And at the same time, it makes an unprecedented power grow within us with a determination that can surpass any other considerations. It is precisely wrath's intense radicalness that can be dangerous to our mental balance and others' physical integrity. Wrath is an innate and powerful gift, extraordinary and fearsome.

Seeing as it is inside of us, we'll never be entirely rid of it. What's more, it's probably foolish to want to destroy it, so it's best we befriend wrath. If we don't want it to degrade, and to degrade us, we must show wrath some respect.

That is what Aeschylus did in one of Greece's most disturbing tragedies, *The Eumenides*, the final play in the *Oresteia* trilogy. The play explains the end of a series of acts of revenge: King Agamemnon sacrificed his daughter Iphigenia to appease the gods; Clytemnestra murdered her husband Agamemnon to avenge her daughter; Orestes killed his mother Clytemnestra and her lover Aegisthus to avenge his father's death. In each case we find injustices that scrape harshly against the grain, the desire to punish them, and bloodshed within the family. We see slow and meditated wrath that overtakes the avengers and always ends with an outburst of violence and the proud display of the executed bodies. Once set in motion, the bloody wheel keeps on turning and that is why Orestes, despite acting on the orders of the god Apollo, cannot rest easy after his matricide. Thus begins *The Eumenides*: once Clytemnestra is dead, Orestes is followed by phantasmagorical women dressed in black with blood dripping from their eyes, likened to angry dogs, who drive him mad.

They are the Erinyes, divinities who avenge blood crimes whom the Romans – significantly – called the Furies. At the centre of this tragedy is a trial between gods and men that takes place in Athens. A jury from the democratic city must decide whether Orestes will be declared innocent or guilty. There is a hung jury, but the goddess Athena weighs in to absolve him: Orestes goes free. This political decision should have stopped the wheel of vengeance and bloodshed but when the Erinyes find out, they are even angrier; they declare they will unleash their wrath on the Athenian lands and poison them with crimes. Their vengeful fury threatens to destroy and divide the community before a strange and delicate solution is reached. The Erinyes are finally calmed by the goddess Athena presenting them with a place of honour in the city: a cave where they will be venerated. The Athenians offered their respects and, from then on, the Erinyes went by the name Eumenides (which means the 'benevolent ones') to win their favour. There, in the cave, sleeps good wrath, with its strength intact, not degraded; in the cave rest the truths too harsh to be exposed in the light of day.

This is the solution of the democratic city: accepting the supernatural power of wrath, honouring it with rituals and trusting that when it awakens (because it will awaken), it will come to protect us and not to destroy us.

This is the ancestral way of keeping close those things that are too intense and winning their favour: by making representations of them and transforming them into rituals. This is what has always been done in art, play and sporting competitions.

Wrath is the most disconcerting case because it is not easily controlled. When we make representations of it and ritualise it, we extend its duration, reflect on it and mould its unpredictable fury so we can take advantage of its strength without repressing it. In order to appropriate Medusa's destructive power, Perseus had to view her reflection in his polished shield. *The Iliad*'s representation of rage in speeches and battles is impressive in its precision and vehemence. Some of the most sublime moments in literature – just think of the first scene in *King Lear* – capture this passion.

Wrath's relationship with the art of movement is even more intimate. Since the dawn of time there have been dances of rivalry, stagings of warrior fury and wrath, gestures between representation and ritual. They glorify strength by stomping their feet, clapping their thighs with fearsome out-of-joint faces such as the Maori haka, now well-known thanks to the New Zealand national rugby team performing it before their matches.

Some urban dances also play with the cycle of challenge, offence, and outburst. Krumping, for example, which originated in South Central Los Angeles around the turn of the millennium. In 1992, after the police officers who had brutally beaten Rodney King were acquitted, there were major riots with looting, burned homes, dozens of deaths and thousands of injuries that didn't end until the army took to the streets. It was in that atmosphere of militarisation, discrimination and criminality that the future krump dancers grew up. Currently, this dance is usually presented as a discipline that offers an alternative to drugs, delinquency and rough streets. In other words, to real violence. It's the best alternative to shooting somebody, as one of the krump virtuosos, known as Miss Prissy, likes to say. All of the tension has passed into the muscles: one of the originators of the style, Thomas Johnson – alias Tommy the Clown – explained that krumping is: 'when you're dancing and your body is doing a lot of different moves.' 'It's really like you're fighting on the dance floor,' it's a kind of 'intensity.'

In the competitions, two opponents face off as if they were rival gang members. The first one advances and dances in fits and starts, defiantly provoking the other with gestures, perhaps knocking off a hat or pretending to push the opponent, humiliate them. But there's no need for them to touch each other: the convulsive motions are already a sophisticated way of attacking, spurred on by the circle of spectators. Every round is a crescendo. It begins gradually, then builds up faster, finally climaxing in a paroxysm of dazzlingly dexterous, seemingly spasmodic gestures. And when the dancer displays their most incredible skills, the audience leap up and start to dance with them in a furious burst of collective enthusiasm. Then the audience retreat and the other dancer's turn begins, continuing the battle. It looks as if they'll end up punching each other, but no: when the battle's over, the competitors hug and congratulate each other on their beautiful representations of wrath. The dancers often have painted faces and are both themselves and not themselves, commanding and freewheeling as they transform the everyday rage they carry within them. Emerging from a marginal environment with much violence, this art celebrates the strength of surviving amid danger, of taking the most dangerous human faculties and turning them into an empowering game and act of affirmation and sociability. The strength of the performance feeds on the power of wrath.

Representing a lack of control is already a way to tame it. The ritual accompanies the rage and leads its power in a different direction. It is like living with a majestic beast that could either kill you or serve you. No matter how hard you try to domesticate it, it will always be a wild animal, but if you treat it with sufficient respect it will be your protective spirit.

Beyond that vengeful itch, wrath can give you the strength to firmly say no to degrading commitments, to refuse to collaborate with mediocrity or evil. It can give you the power to change your point of view, to refuse the code of your surroundings and side with something worthwhile, to keep the violence at bay.

Wrath can disrupt us and strengthen us, it can free us from living a submissive life or from repeating a lesser version of others' lives. But the beast can never be completely tamed. It is always nearby, in the cave, half asleep. We have to visit often to pay our respects, and we must have faith.

ENVY

MARINA PORRAS

I – THE FURIES OF HELL

For a long time, my only relationship with the seven deadly sins was inside a theatre. When I was a little girl I loved to watch performances of *The Little Shepherds*, a traditional Catalan Christmas play. It must have been my great-grandmother who first took me to see it, and I found the whole show very strange and otherworldly. I would go each year to a community centre where they still performed the play, and it was like travelling back in time. The theatre was old and dark, the seats creaked and were uncomfortable and at the entrance to the stalls there was a mosaic of Saint George slaying the dragon that I found very unsettling. Since I didn't study anything about Catholicism until many years later, my idea of Christianity was formed by this play about some shepherds who defeated the devil. It sounds banal, but that play gave me my first idea of a universe where good and evil coexisted and battled. Every year I would insist on going back and it wasn't easy to find someone willing to sit through the three hours of amateur acting with me. I loved that the whole work was in verse, so much so that I bought the book by Josep Maria Folch i Torres and I still can recite some parts by heart.

One of my favourite scenes was when the furies emerge from Hell, the seven deadly sins represented by seven girls dressed in red tights, wearing a lot of makeup and headbands with devil horns. Satan wants to corrupt the soul of a little shepherd and he's enlisted the seven sins to help him, so that 'drop by drop the spirit of evil will filter into his heart and make him more evil than a viper.' The scene takes place in a forest and the devil can't see that the protective archangel Saint Michael is hiding behind the trees. Satan summons the furies and the seven girls appear onstage, surrounding the poor shepherds who are deathly afraid. Each girl explains which sin she represents and how she can tempt humans. I watched it all very intrigued because I had no idea what temptation meant. Over the years, I found those girls increasingly ridiculous, but also increasingly interesting, because I was beginning to understand what it meant to be tempted by evil. Of all the sins, I liked envy best because it seemed the most dangerous. The others were more obvious: lust compels you to possess; pride, to act superior; greed, to hoard money; sloth, to do nothing; wrath, to attack; gluttony, to eat. Envy compels you to desire without consummation. It is an empty, unending sin. It is also the most secret of the sins and, therefore, the most fearsome. There are hardly any outward signs that reveal when you've been tempted by envy.

Some years later I read a passage in an autobiographical text by Mercè Rodoreda that reminded me of that image of envy onstage, wearing devil horns. Rodoreda writes:

The evening when my parents went out for the first time to their drama lessons, which I hated, my mother got more dressed up than I'd ever seen her, and wore a new dress. I remember that, as she tied her sash in front of the large mirror in the entryway, I yanked the sash away in a rabid fit of jealousy and started kicking her ankles.

That burst of rage against her mother made me understand that envy is the most terrible sin because it always comes from a very profound feeling that's very difficult to explain to others but even harder to explain to yourself. It also helped me to understand why Rodoreda, with her cruel style filled with things that people do and feel but don't dare speak aloud, is one of the best writers to explain envy.

II – WHO IS THE FAIREST OF THEM ALL?

Rodoreda's memory of exploding with rage at her mother was surely the inspiration for a scene in her novel *Broken Mirror* between Sofia Valldaura and her mother, Teresa. Sofia is a girl who never loved her mother much:

When she saw wearing her embroidered shawls studded with rhinestones and her herringbone stockings, she wished she would leave and never come back. One day, when her mother scolded her and yanked her out of a flowerbed near the chestnut trees, she thought she should kill her.

Teresa Valldaura is an amazing, dazzling woman. Every man falls for her and she has an innocence and a kindness that make her not only more attractive but that also save her from certain fatalistic attitudes. Sofia has grown up in the shadow of this mother she can never surpass and who has never paid much attention to her. She wishes her mother had a stronger maternal instinct, that she would give her structure and make her feel wanted and loved. 'One night when her mother had come up to give her a goodnight kiss,' we read in *Broken Mirror*, 'Sofia ripped off her necklace and broke the clasp.'

That goodnight kiss is reminiscent of the scene that opens Marcel Proust's *In Search of Lost Time*, when the narrator explains how he suffers if his mother doesn't come to his bedroom to give him a kiss. Marcel has a very close relationship with his mother. She is his centre of gravity, his measure of all things. Marcel's mother, who is also pretty and seductive, always puts her son before any of her other concerns. Influenced and overwhelmed by that maternal kindness, all the women Marcel will love in his life will have to pass through the filter of comparison to the infinite, unconditional love his mother gave him. Marcel grew up as a child who was always treated with kid gloves, taken care of and spoiled by the women in his home. The bond of love he has with his mother will tint his life with the kindness and innocence he was surrounded by as a boy.

Rodoreda's female characters, and the author herself, do not have easy relationships with their mothers. Rodoreda explains that, when she was a girl, she wanted to be like her mother, 'liked and complimented by everyone.' Rodoreda spent her childhood in a villa in Sant Gervasi with a garden filled with plants and flowers. Her grandfather had a monument placed in the garden, topped with a bust of Jacint Verdaguer. It was made of stone and wood and was surrounded by plants, like some sort of rustic fairy grotto. The family took many photographs with the monument as a backdrop. There is one where Rodoreda's mother appears, very young, stretched out over the sculpture and dressed as a nymph. She is wearing a gauzy white dress, her black hair loose and flowing, and she has a chain of flowers around her waist and a bouquet of flowers at her chest. She is surrounded by laughing friends, also dressed as nymphs, but she has a very serious, brazen, provocative gaze. Mercè Rodoreda is in the photo, too. She must be about three years old and stands to one side of her mother, in a small white dress. You can't see her face because she must have moved and so was captured all blurry and insignificant in the photograph.

The Rodoreda family album is filled with portraits of her parents in costume and performing plays, adapting their home as if it were a stage. Rodoreda appears in all the photos with the big bright eyes of an innocent girl, except for in the image of her first communion. In that she wears an ugly, heavy dress and a necklace with a cross; she holds her hands together and looks upwards, as if praying. She explains that the day they went to the studio, the photographer told her mother that they couldn't use a black backdrop because that was for girls who had prettier features than her daughter.

Envy between mothers and daughters is an age-old story. We are all familiar with the flipped version: there are mothers who envy their daughters because they believe they've stolen their youth. They see in them the spectre of their beauty, the decline of their own body. Many fairy tales speak of this, and this is the source of the wicked stepmother, a mother who envies her daughter who is younger and more beautiful than she can ever be again. Snow White's wicked stepmother is actually a sad witch because there is another better than she. It is no coincidence that her revenge begins when she asks the mirror who's the fairest of them all and it answers not her but Snow White. The stepmother is displeased with the image the mirror reflects back. Rodoreda's literature is also filled with women who do everything they can to be liked and to like themselves. They are women who want to look into the mirror and be satisfied with their reflection. Envy is born when you look into the mirror and don't like what you see there. Everything about this sin begins with the eyes.

III – A DIRTY LOOK

Envy comes from the Latin word *invidia*, which is derived from the verb *invidere*, which means 'to look askance at.' Envy is a dirty look: a resentful look, filled with poison. The philosopher Francis Bacon calls it the evil eye, describing it as a poisoned eye that irradiates venom without realizing that the venom also falls on the one who spits it. It is not only that the envious don't see themselves in a good light; it is that they don't see clearly. 'And what are you looking at, with those little Japanese eyes?' one of the characters in *Broken Mirror* asks Sofia Valldaura, when she is still a child. Reticent and haughty, Sofia grows up hampered by a family atmosphere in which she never feels comfortable. She is a thin, nervous, uptight girl: despotic with the servants and reserved with her family. Everyone praises her elegance, but her eyes are most curious. They are half-closed, signalling that her gaze will always be oblique, askance, cutting: the gaze of envy.

Joseph de Maistre writes that there is no vice, no crime or chaotic passion that doesn't produce some sort of physical corollary. Sofia's eyes are the manifestation of the resentment she carries within her. Yet she considers them her defence because envy is her way of surviving. They demonstrate her uncomfortableness with the world, but she bears them with pride because they distinguish her from her family:

Not Japanese eyes. Strange eyes, thinks Sofia. A doctor had told her that with one little scalpel slice in each corner they'd be perfect, but she never wanted to go under the knife. 'She loved her eyes that she could never open fully, they were part of her charm. Would they gleam as much, if open? Would they be as unsettling for their unusualness as her raspy voice?'

The envious gaze is oblique; it is quick and devastating because the gazer seeks to conceal it. It is a gaze that can only be detected by another intelligent, experienced eye. Envy is a very instinctive and visceral sin, but it needs a somewhat sophisticated environment in which to act. During childhood, envy is a mostly material drive, which leads us to hate someone who has what we do not. Cruel and impulsive, it is also clean and clear. It is a sin that rapidly leads to fits of rage. Envy needs a slightly twisted mind, for example that of a teenager, to function in all its splendour. When we are growing up and constructing our personality in a weak and malleable environment, envy has a lot of latitude.

IV – AN ADOLESCENT VICE

As a little girl I would cling like a tick to any decently articulated fiction, and I would spend all afternoon watching truly awful American TV shows. Their plots were all based on cliched relationships at unbelievable secondary schools, and I formed a very American idea that adolescence was about fitting into a setting as a way to create a place for yourself in the world and, as such, learning to make others see you. In these shows, everything revolved around finding an image that you wanted to project to yourself and to others. The main preoccupation among my teenage friends was figuring out how others saw us. We wanted to know who was giving us 'dirty looks' and why, and how to react to that offence. Our answer to the question was very often that the reason anyone would look askance at us was envy, and we used that as a defence mechanism.

One of my girlfriends in that period was a petite brunette with the enormous black eyes of a snake charmer. We all had the half-baked bodies of fourteen-year-olds, but she seemed like a Greek statue, and had breasts that set all the hormones in the class aflutter. She was just as charming then as she is now, and she knew how to pull in any boy she wanted. She was the first to inaugurate the era of making out in public. I remember that it happened in school, after class. We decided that the make-out session would take place behind the peacock yard, which was called that because it had peacocks in it, strutting around and showing their tailfeathers in mating rituals – in a metaphor so obvious it was utterly ridiculous. The human couple in question went to the back of the yard to share absurd teenage kisses and we went along as friends to stand side by side to make a human wall. The idea was to conceal and protect them, but we clearly drew more attention to the spectacle. We called the line of shielding friends the 'wall of envy.'

Jane Austen's literature is filled with youthful envy. Emma, the eponymous protagonist, is the prettiest, cleverest, and most popular girl in her village. She tries to use the envy she provokes for her own benefit, looking to control those around her as if they were little figures in a diorama. Austen, a splendid moralist, teaches readers that this tactic doesn't get Emma anywhere, but she enjoys explaining how the girl has to figure that out for herself by tapping into her own goodness. Austen's literature is perfect for explaining the differences between good and evil, because virtue is always happily rewarded and vices, despite being minor and forgivable ones, are duly punished.

That is not the case with *Mad Men*, a morally ambiguous television show by Matthew Weiner that is a beautiful catalogue of the seven deadly sins. Betty Draper, the main character's marvellous wife, is so perfect she was born to be envied, and that is the source of her power. When she enters a room time seems to stop. Every eye turns to rest on her and that is what pushes her to continue surviving. Betty lives for the envy in others' eyes, but eventually she realizes that it is hollowing her out inside. She is only someone when other women compare themselves to her. Her drama begins when she sees that she is nothing to herself, when she discovers that she is no one if there are no eyes gazing upon her.

V – WHY HER?

Envy is relational and relative, it cannot exist without others. If we are sullied by envy, what we have and what we are is measured based on others' value, and the grass will always seem greener on the other side of the fence. Kant explains that envy is the resentment we feel when we see something of ours eclipsed or diminished by what others have. Envy's cry is often the question: 'Why her and not me?' It is a poisoned thought, because we can always find reasons to ask it of ourselves. Envy is also a question of distance: the closer we are to that which we envy, the stronger our drive to envy is. Therefore, our family, so close and so influential, is a place where envy can grow powerfully and cruelly.

Broken Mirror is the story of a house and the family that lives there. Rodoreda wants to explain the rise and fall of a clan as she explains the rise and fall of a city, a society, and a country. She brings together three generations of a family to explain them through comparison, envy's natural form. Rodoreda liked books about complicated family histories, like that of the Sartoris clan written by Faulkner, which tells of young men who grow up like wildflowers in the colonial mansions of the American South. Instead of an old plantation, Rodoreda chooses a villa in Sant Gervasi. However, her intention is the same as Faulkner's: to explain the fall of a family based on the place they live.

Every story of a fall from grace needs a hero. *Broken Mirror* has a heroine: Teresa Goday de Valldaura. Daughter of a fishmonger, Teresa's life changes one day when a rich man three times her age sees her walking past the opera house. He falls in love with her and they marry, and when he dies Teresa is now a part of high society. She is young enough to remarry and pretty enough to marry whomever she wishes. Salvador Valldaura takes a fancy to her despite his lingering trauma from a prior relationship, which is the first secret hidden in this novel. Valldaura had fallen in love with a gorgeous Viennese violinist who committed suicide shortly after they met. Resigned to live with the pain and remake his life, he marries Teresa and buys her a villa in Sant Gervasi. He knows that his wife, who was born to be a princess, will enjoy living in a fairy tale home. It is with the appearance of this house, the material stamp of a love that can never be spiritual, that the story of *Broken Mirror* truly begins.

Teresa spends her life in the pursuit of beautiful things and happiness based on the good things she finds within her grasp. Since she was not born rich, she's taken full advantage of everything luck has brought her, with a mix of intelligence and the spitefulness of a woman who is used to always getting her way. Teresa's life is filled with difficult, tragic events, but she pulls through because she never loses the innocence and goodness that is in her heart. Rodoreda knows how to imbue her main characters with a patina of humanity and greatness that makes them survive everything thrown at them, just as she did in her own life. Teresa is a good woman, but since the effort of remaining true to herself consumes all of her energy, when she has a daughter she cannot give unconditionally as mandated by the maternal instinct. When Teresa must choose between herself and anything else, she always chooses herself. So when she gives birth to Sofia, a child different from her in every aspect, she cannot find a way to bridge the gap. Sofia grows up lonely and marginalised by the splendour of a mother who shines too bright. All those years in the shadows she has plenty of time to ask herself, why her and not me?

The day Sofia meets Eladi, her future husband, he notices her mother before he notices her. Eladi Farriols is the grandson of textile industrialists and son of the owner of a haberdashery. He and his father work together at the shop. Teresa is one of their best customers and her visits are always a whirlwind of selecting and trying on things. Sofia, on the other hand, is uptight and demanding, taciturn. 'Sometimes a glittering mother gives birth to a washed-out daughter,' thinks Eladi the first time he sees her, 'but never trust still waters...' Ambitious and thinking of his own interests, Eladi is drawn to Sofia, despite her surliness, because he is able to project onto her a peaceful future, far from the slavish work at the shop.

He liked comely, cheerful, innocent girls with big black eyes. And Sofia's eyes were so small it looked as if she couldn't even open them fully; she parted her hair down the middle and pulled it back. He'd seen women with that same hairstyle in an illustrated edition of the novels of Balzac that his uncle treasured.

I couldn't say whether it was a coincidence or Rodoreda's infinite cruelty, but one of Balzac's most famous novels with a female protagonist is *A Woman of Thirty*. Balzac found 19th-century Paris the perfect breeding ground for describing envy, and in that novel he tells the story of a young woman trapped in an unhappy marriage, frustrated because her husband is unable to bring her to orgasm.

    Broken Mirror is a novel filled with sex, yet Sofia is one of the few characters we will never see in a satisfying sexual relationship. This is another of the reasons she envies her mother, who leads a life full of secret lovers who cause her suffering but also make her very happy.

'If only Sofia were more like her mother in certain aspects, even just a little!' Eladi rues. But Sofia was a secretive girl, with many admirable qualities that took a bit too long to discover.

Since Sofia has always felt threatened by everything, she's never felt safe anywhere. She can never go to bed with anyone because she never has enough confidence and trust to let her hair down. As a consequence of her self-repression, Sofia has become a cold, soulless young woman.

VI – A HARD HEART

Rodoreda admits she has a weakness for naïve characters who disarm and captivate her: 'Ingenuous literary characters arouse all of my tenderness, it makes me feel good to have them around, they are my best friends.' Ingenuousness is precisely what allowed Rodoreda to survive without becoming bitter and hardened. In the letters she wrote to Anna Murià from exile, we see a woman who is suffering but always finds some reason to love life. It's as if the author could live in her own world, and it was that capacity for imaginative isolation that saved her. That was why she enjoys creating women of angelical purity who walk without their feet touching the ground, who are both very close and very far from everything surrounding them. They can be calculating and have evil outbursts, but deep down they have an innocence that marks their actions, and that deep ingenuousness redeems them.

Teresa frivolously distracts herself with pretty clothes and shiny jewellery, but at every point she has something in her life that she loves in a serious, devoted way. Sofia is nothing like that. She is a new, unique character for Rodoreda, as she herself recognised: 'Sofia Valldaura allowed me to play with a hard heart, when I had only played with tender hearts before.' A hard heart is the heart of someone unable to love and, as such, someone much more capable of inflicting harm without emotional repercussions. Sofia could act with relentless cruelty because her heart had hardened over the years. Marked by her envy of her mother and by her inability to make the best of her situation, she became an ice princess.

When we have fits of envy, we always end up harming ourselves; it is a feeling that fuels self-defeat, self-sabotage. The envious are always on the defensive because they believe that everyone is conspiring against them. At one point when a boy approaches the house for a visit, young Sofia stops him at the door to the villa and says, 'My name is Sofia and I am the little girl in this house.' This statement sounds haughty because envy and pride are close neighbours: one is the flip side of the other. 'The common Way to do one's Business and rise in the World,' says La Rochefoucauld, 'is to use all possible Means of perswading [*sic*] People, that one's Business is done already.' Envy appears when power becomes impotence, when the feeling of superiority transforms into inferiority, when self-confidence turns into fear of failure. 'Those who are the most distrustful of themselves, are the most envious of others,' wrote William Hazlitt, 'as the most weak and cowardly are the most revengeful.' Envy is what we feel when someone interrupts our desire for expansion, our wish to stand out and assert ourselves.

The first time Sofia and Eladi touch they use the pretext of a green ring, a ring the colour of envy. It takes place at Eladi's store, a day when she and her mother go shopping together. While Teresa chooses crepe for her lingerie, Eladi notices Sofia's ring. She takes it off and shows it to him, and he furtively strokes her fingers. '"It's an emerald of very pure, dark green," says Sofia. He is silent for a moment and pointedly adds: "lovely".' The emerald is a gem of bright green colour, and Sofia's ring is set with a dark stone. Green has been the colour of envy and jealousy, probably since Shakespeare used it in *Othello*: 'O beware, my lord, of jealousy; It is the green-eyed monster which doth mock the meat it feeds on.' The colour green is also associated with bile, the liquid that corrodes the liver and can turn poisonous. Sofia and Eladi, from the moment their hands touch, are linked by that green-eyed monster, which will run through their relationship. Both resigned to it, they marry. He trusts that the marriage will bring him financial gain and she marries because her hard heart doesn't have the strength to put up any resistance.

On their wedding night, she forces Eladi to kiss her foot before touching her: 'That's it, little mister Eladi, like a good dog. And now, go wash up.' Sofia knows that her husband sleeps with as many women as he can, and she makes him pay for his promiscuity with her coldness. That same night Eladi confesses he has a daughter with a cabaret actress. When Sofia learns of his secret, she begins to build a wall separating her from her husband. It is an impassable wall that will never crack and that pushes her to be led by the darkest aspect of envy, the nihilistic impulse that cancels out life's optimism.

VII – THE GREEN-EYED MONSTER

While envy provokes an apathy that leads into the void, jealousy guides us into the most obsessive anxiety. Jealousy is the flip side of rage, just as envy is the flip side of pride. They both end up consuming you. It was a long time ago and now I laugh recalling it, but there was a time when I believed that love couldn't exist without the constant fear of losing everything. We fell in love fast because he was very powerful but very lost, which was a perfect combination for someone who wanted to save interesting men with gaping wounds. As we were completely different, we discovered in each other unknown universes and had a lot of fun together. I've never met anyone who filtered everything through sensuality and their body as he did, in such a physical way. One night, while he was driving very carefully along the twists and turns of Vallvidrera road, he put his hand between my legs and told me that, without even touching me, he could feel my magical emanation. He was crazy, but I loved it.

His entire life was devoted to seduction and he couldn't help but count all the women whose heads turned when he entered a restaurant. He used to tell me that he considered sexual relationships and sentimental relationships as two different worlds, and at the time I didn't believe him but now I do. He couldn't help proving that he could attract any girl he wanted to, and I couldn't stand the idea that there was room for something that wasn't me between him and the world. A friend told me that he'd said her blue eyes were lovely and I felt like I'd been stabbed. It hurt me so much that I began to try to control everything, and I started imagining twisted stories. The poor guy didn't even need to do anything because, as David Carabén sings, 'everyone knows that suspicion is the first form of faith that exists.' Since he loved me and didn't want me to suffer, he would restrain himself, and I felt like I was locking a lion in a cage at the zoo. It is one of the few times I've felt an impulse flooding all my attempts to control it and overwhelming me. Jealousy is a feeling that devours everything. We broke up when I realized that, if I continued along that path, I would end up loving anxiety instead of loving him. Luckily we can still laugh about it together, because at the time I thought the green-eyed monster's bile would corrode my brain.

The lascivious figure of Eladi is what brings jealousy into *Broken Mirror*. After he feels he's been treated with disdain by his wife and after the havoc caused by his confession, Eladi withdraws and seeks to bolster his self-confidence between the legs of the servants of the household, like 'Senyor Ramon' of the old song, who misleads the maids. That puts Sofia in the middle of romantic muddle that she hasn't the slightest interest in. Since she is more repulsed by than enamoured with her husband, she makes a game of making the maids suffer and be jealous of her. While envy is born of the desire to possess what we do not have, jealousy is born of the fear of losing what we do possess.

La Rochefoucauld says that jealousy is just and reasonable because it only tends to preserve a good that belongs, or that we believe belongs to us, while envy is the rage of someone who can't bear the happiness of others. This sentiment could have been spoken by Armanda, the cook at the villa in Sant Gervasi. Armanda is a clever, nimble girl, who is always attentive and concerned with being liked. She is an important character in the book because she represents the internal mechanism of the house and the family. She has been in love with Eladi since before he married. Sofia knows this and, when she leaves the house to go to her wedding, 'she only cares about Armanda seeing her, because she had sometimes caught her looking at Eladi with tear-flooded eyes.' Until he tires of her, as he eventually does of all the servant girls, Armanda is Eladi's first victim. Sofia, in turn, uses them as a weapon against her husband: she enjoys making him suffer over them.

She always chooses pretty ones, thought Armanda, she gets her fun where she can, by driving Senyor Eladi up the wall. If they're dumb, they fall into his arms; she likes that they have to be secretive and quick about it. If they're smart, they play hard to get, and then she finds the game priceless.

When Armanda and Eladi's relationship ends, Sofia makes her pay for the suffering she felt when it began. She had felt humiliated over what was happening right under her nose and she didn't fire Armanda because she was too proud, because that would be like confessing that she knew what was going on. Teresa, who is also aware of her son-in-law's affairs, knows that Armanda was truly in love with Eladi, a love that her daughter had never given him. In one chapter, Teresa tells the cook to eat cakes before bedtime so that the sweetness will bring her dreams of love. 'Don't ever let it die, Armanda, don't ever let it die.' Teresa takes the side of love even when it comes to her son-in-law's infidelities, even though that means going against her own daughter. That is the dichotomy that runs through the book: a heart of sugar versus a heart of ice.

VIII – A GAME OF MIRRORS

There is a poem by Gabriel Ferrater entitled 'The Mirrors' and it describes a woman strolling through a market, which is a metaphor for life. The woman doesn't go through the market explaining what she's chosen, like many other women do; she doesn't go about touching the fruit to see if it's ripe or asking if the eggs are fresh. She is 'loyal and mysterious. / She chose long ago, and has faith.' But sometimes the woman questions the wisdom of her silent choices. At those moments, the poet explains, men have the responsibility of being mirrors, of offering a reflective surface that gives her a clear, sure image of what she has chosen. The man's function is to understand what image the woman wants to see when she looks at him.

> Let her not be surrounded by murky shadows.
> Let us all be the mirrors where she looks
> when weighing the wisdom of her measure
> with which she chose hers forevermore,
> let her always find a crystal-clear image.
> Let's show her that we accept and understand
> her choice: great honour from those she's chosen.

This woman is asking to be shown the mask she's chosen to wear through the world. Envy works very well in societies that conceive of life as a theatre where everyone plays a role. In order to hide their imperfection and weakness, the envious, says La Rochefoucauld, relate to others through a mask they build, largely without wanting to. La Rochefoucauld, a 17th-century French aristocrat, is famous for his maxims, moralistic phrases that are as implacable as sword blows. These aphorisms were discussed in salons and wielded in conversations like a game, to the extent that Madame de Sablé said that writing maxims was like a sickness. These maxims are the perfect chronicle of what happens when a society transforms into a masquerade ball, in a theatre that is both where the farce is performed and what remains once the performance is over. What Ferrater's woman is searching for is to distance herself as much as possible from said farce. She seeks a refuge, a place where she can find 'great honour' from her chosen loved ones. She doesn't want to be forced to fake it, she doesn't want to have to go through the world carrying the burden of lies. She wants the mask she wears to be as close as possible to her truth.

The envious, on the other hand, are always surrounded by murky shadows, doubts, and suspicions. They are so used to camouflaging themselves in front of others that they end up wearing a disguise even for themselves. The envious have a very high opinion of themselves, and so are disappointed by the image the mirror reflects back at them. La Rochefoucauld says:

Self-Love is the *Love* of a man's own Self, and of every thing else, for his own Sake. It makes People *Idolaters* to themselves, and *Tyrants* to all the World besides. [...] It is an *Abyss*, too deep ever to be sounded, and too dark ever to be seen through; there it sits undiscovered, even from the nicest, and most penetrating *Eye*, and runs a thousand wild *Mazes* undiscerned: Nay, it is sometimes concealed from its own self, and conceives and cherishes, and brings up a World of *Inclinations* and *Affections*, without so much as being sensible when they are *born*, or how they are *bred*. And some of these

Conceptions are so monstrous, that when they come to the *Birth*, it either does not know them, or cannot be prevailed upon to own them. From this gross Darkness proceed all its extravagant and ridiculous Opinions of its self, all its Errors and Ignorances, and sottish Stupidities in its own Case.

The woman in the poem wants to remain distant from that darkness and she knows that a darkened image would distance her from herself and her choices. Envy is born of such a dark, secret part of ourselves that we dare not even look at it. Envy is born, to use another verse by Ferrater, 'of an instinct from long ago, simple, as is the blood of men and women.'

Broken Mirror begins with a quote from Laurence Sterne that says: 'I honour you, Eliza, for keeping secret some things.' This is a novel filled with secrets. The weightiest ones – such as her husband's illegitimate daughter – are borne by Sofia. She decides that the girl will live in her home and that they'll say she's the daughter of some family friends who died in an accident. Maria, Eladi's daughter with the music-hall singer, will be another antagonist for Sofia from birth. When the midwife sees her, she tells her mother: 'I've never seen a girl so keen to live, never seen a baby open such clear, pretty eyes at birth.' Maria's large, lively eyes will be competition for Sofia's Japanese gaze. This girl will be another mirror her stepmother won't want to look into, another unpleasant image for her self-love.

When Sofia looks for her reflection in her mirror, she finds the mirror broken. Unlike the woman in the poem, she has not chosen those who are 'hers forevermore.' Sofia, as Rodoreda says, 'defends herself by accepting, she makes acceptance her strong suit, and she turns the weapon of her acceptance against her enemies.' Maria, on the other hand, is a girl who's 'capable of everything and anything. Capable of obtaining and capable of renouncing.' The difference between the two is a question of strength. Sofia only knows how to accept; Maria also knows how to relinquish. And this is why one lives in resignation and the other commits suicide when she finds she cannot bear the reflection she sees in the mirror. The more we hide our passions, the harder it is to know ourselves and our own vices. It is in stifled, rotting societies like the one described by Rodoreda where envy can do real damage. In order to see our image clearly reflected back at us in a mirror, there has to be some light in the room. The day Sofia got engaged to Eladi, she carved his and her initials into a tree trunk with the tip of a knife. Years later, when she returns to search for the scar on the tree, she can't find it. Sofia, like the erased initials, is unable to find in her life any of the projected hopes she had before abandoning herself to resignation.

IX – THE CANKERWORM OF VIRTUES

Extreme climates are the perfect setting for wild characters. In Jefferson, a dusty desert town invented by William Faulkner, lives Eula Snopes. More than a character, Eula is an allegory, an almost mythological teenager. 'It was that there was just too much of what she was for any just one human female package to contain and hold: too much of white, too much of female, too much of maybe just glory, I dont know,' writes Faulkner. I've always imagined the Dionysian figure of Eula, both attractive and repulsive at the same time, as a living portrait of sin. Strutting shamelessly through her suffocating town, Eula awakens the sleeping envy in the heart of men.

In Jefferson, where 'blood's thick' and the earth is filled with rage, suspicions hide, silent and patient, behind the curtains of the homes. Eula has committed adultery with the town's mayor. Everyone knows it, but they keep it a secret so that when the scandal breaks it will do more damage. As one character says:

'Women are not interested in morals. They aren't even interested in un-morals. The ladies of Jefferson dont care what she does. What they will never forgive is the way she looks. No: the way the Jefferson gentlemen look at her.'

There are two types of sins: heated crimes of the heart and cold-blooded ones. Lust, wrath, and gluttony are corporeal sins, sins of action. They are physical passions, while greed, pride, sloth and envy come straight from the brain. And since they are calculated, they are crueller and warrant less forgiveness. The gentlemen of Jefferson spend their lives trying to make Eula pay for merely existing, preparing concealed revenge and spreading lies. They resemble the allegory of envy drawn by Cesare Ripa in his *Iconologia*. Ripa represents it as a pale, weak old lady, with a confused expression and rotted teeth. Instead of hair, she has venom-spitting snakes on her head and is dying in agony because she is eating her own heart.

Envy, according to artists, deserves an icy punishment in keeping with its cold nature. Amid the macabre brutality of the hellish penance in Dante's *The Divine Comedy*, the envious have their eyes sewn shut with iron wire, since they derived pleasure from seeing other people brought low. It is as harsh an image as that depicted in the Renaissance murals of the Last Judgment at the Cathedral of Albi, where the envious are left naked in the middle of a frozen lake, battered by a cold wind. Every representation teaches us that envy is a sin that hurts the sinner, like when Giotto painted envy as a man with a snake emerging from his mouth and eating out his eyes. Cervantes, in a metaphor that sums it up perfectly, calls envy the 'cankerworm of virtues' that devours the soul.

'Admiration is happy self-surrender,' writes Kierkegaard, 'envy is unhappy self-assertion.' Eladi is a character obsessed with the work of Marcel Proust. He reads him constantly, collects his essays and tries to translate him. At first it seems he idolises him, but his is not a happy admiration but a tormented vice. Eladi projects onto Proust all his failures and takes refuge in his pessimistic bookworm activity. Eladi is the epitome of Rodoreda's male characters. Many are helpless men, unable to take the reins of their lives, men who've given up before even trying. More than evil, they are just plain weak, and they make their wives hate them because they've left them out in the cold, having to fend for themselves, while their husbands search for all sorts of excuses.

'We want the author to give us answers,' writes Proust in his essay *On Reading*, 'but all he can do is give us desires.' It isn't strange that Eladi, surrendered to a life of unhappiness and boredom, becomes obsessed with the inconstancy in Proust's work. Over the years, he abandoned the vices that gave him joy in his youth and took refuge in reading the memories of *In Search of Lost Time*. It is a sort of apathetic nostalgia very typical of mediocre bourgeois men: when they believe they can no longer ardently defend anything, they close themselves up in their libraries to read. 'He kept the books on a small shelf, to the left of his bed, in arm's reach. He read them in fits and starts: never a whole volume from beginning to end.' His fondness for Proust makes his wife smile disdainfully. Perhaps Sofia is satisfied that her adulterous husband has to settle for the sighs of jealousy of the Proustian narrator instead of pursuing chambermaids.

She didn't like Proust in the slightest, because he had been ill in body and soul. For her, admiring the author, as well as the work, was essential.

Perhaps the truth was that she didn't like Proust because Eladi liked him.

Sofia can despise her husband when she sees him collecting books by his favourite French author because she knows that she married a small, effete man, a man who has been incapable of pleasing her. Their marital cohabitation is reminiscent of the fakeness and hypocrisy that Proust sees in the bourgeoisie of his time. Eladi is the very image of weakness, a portrait of the Catalan man that runs through all of Rodoreda's books. Cowardly and ineffectual, he is merely a passive spectator of everything that happens to him, so much so that he is not even able to truly comprehend his favourite author, who 'sometimes fascinated him and other times made him nod off.' When her husband dies, Sofia thinks that in Eladi's still gleaming black eyes there were the same lakes of melancholy as in the eyes of Proust. It is a mercilessly cruel epitaph: he can only truly resemble his admired genius hero in death.

XI – CAN'T SINK ANY LOWER

There are few characters as perfect to borrow for allegories as the bad guys in Disney films. One of the most famous is *Sleeping Beauty*, which had its premiere in 1959. The villain in this animated film, inspired by a story by Charles Perrault, is an evil fairy who casts a spell on a new-born princess that condemns her to sleep. Maleficent is thin and proud, her skin is greyish, and she wears a long black dress that trails behind her majestically. She has a long, narrow neck and speaks with a deep, foreboding voice. Two enormous black horns sit on her head and her companion is a crow. She carries a very long wand topped with an emerald-green glass ball that matches her eyes.

The story begins when, in the kingdom of Sleeping Beauty, the king and queen have had a baby girl. Like good Christians, they hold a big baptismal party and invite the entire kingdom, but Maleficent is excluded. Her star turn is appearing at the party to ask why she wasn't on the guest list. Once again we see the question: why them and not me? Maleficent takes her revenge by placing a fatal spell on the little princess, in turn becoming a spiteful witch who can't bear the sight of a pretty, happy child.

Envy turns ugliest when it is most pure, when someone's mere existence is too much for us. 'We saw him in a light that made him so happy and so beautiful,' writes Valéry, 'that it made us lose even our lust for life.' Maleficent, sensing that the princess may have a joyful life, condemns her even before that joy can be confirmed. If we take envy to its furthest extremes, we find ourselves with a purely destructive sin, nearing nihilism. Nietzsche speaks of the vortex of envy, because it leaves a void in its centre. When we don't get something we want, says Nietzsche, we'd rather the whole world crumble. Maleficent, condemned to rule over the world of darkness, wants to drag the entire universe down with her, to a place where everyone suffers the same fate.

Envy can also double down on its own twistedness, and from this springs *Schadenfreude*, a German term for the happiness at seeing others fail. Kierkegaard says that it is the ugly cousin of envy, because not only does it want what it doesn't have but it enjoys watching other people fall short. When Maleficent has finished casting her spell, she lets out an evil laugh and disappears into green smoke. She laughs at the parents who have just seen their baby daughter condemned to death, paying homage to the quote from Lord Byron that describes the envious as those who 'but breathe in others' pain.' For Nietzsche, happiness over the bad that happens to others comes from our existential unease with the world, because the pain of others makes them our equals, placating us. After all, Maleficent is merely a witch who feels hurt because she was left out.

Envy can spiral into the void and can twist, but it can also be long-lasting. Then it transforms into resentment, which is envy plus time plus powerlessness. Scheler says that it poisons your own soul, because when you become resentful you never recover from it. Envy can be cured, but resentment can only think from a place of unhappiness. Resentment makes violence grow inside of us, the poison pooling. Maleficent casts a spell that will last sixteen years, until the princess' birthday when she will prick her finger. The length of the curse is a reaction to its restrained violence: lengthening and postponing the agony is a way of seeing her pain compensated.

Yeats says that fairy tales are places of abandonment where souls can change from good to bad as quickly as a gust of wind. Maleficent wants to belong in the humans' kingdom, but since she cannot she turns against them. Resentment denies the value of what we want, like in the fable told by Aesop where there's a fox who wants to eat some grapes but can't reach them, and since he cannot have them, he says they must be sour. Resentment is the consolation of impotence, and this gesture is the origin of the Nietzschean slave morality: what we denigrate and hate is what we once loved and desired. Valéry wrote: 'If you look closely at scorn, you'll find a hint of envy. Our strongest hatred is for those we wish to resemble.'

XII – LIVING WITHOUT ENVY

My grandmother, who is not usually one for solemn declarations, says that she has always been happy because she's never envied anyone. One day she was telling me about a customer at her restaurant, where she was the cook and owner, who, to annoy her, said she thought that it was horrific to work such long hours. 'And I thought,' she told me, 'look, I've always worked hard, but because I wanted to, and precisely for that reason it never would've occurred to me to make a comment like that to somebody else.' I see a connection between my grandmother and Josep Pla because of their realistic, practical way of comprehending the world. In an interview, Pla once said that in order to be happy you have to not be envious:

I've never envied anyone, and if you were to give me a fortune right now I'd give it back to you, same thing with a Rolls Royce. Because I'd just drive it into this wall, or some tree. I mean, I'd be too distracted.

Envy, for Pla, is a distraction, and that's understandable, because envy distances us from the core of what we want to be. If we envy something, it's because we don't really know what we want. I would say that the antidote to envy is knowing what you want and being proactive about getting it. Pla wanted to write, and if they'd put something between him and writing it would have been an annoyance to him. Those who feel no envy are happy people with purpose, they know what they want and they are busy achieving it. La Rochefoucauld sums it up better: 'The surest sign of being born with great qualities is being born without envy.'

One of the aims of envy's poisonous darts is to knock the envied person off their path. 'I worry about writing about my childhood memories,' Rodoreda explains in a letter to her editor Joan Sales. 'What if they lead some envious wretch to start slandering me?' Rodoreda was probably putting on mysterious airs with that stance, because if she'd wanted to write about her childhood, she would have; but Sales, always astute and restrained, advises her:

Don't let fear of such contemptible people keep you from writing down those memories. I'll never spur you on to write when your reason for not wanting to is laziness, but I will when it's fear of the poisoned bite of the mediocre […]. They would only forgive you your talent if you weren't successful, and they would only forgive you your success if you weren't talented.

Envy is, clearly, a writer's sin, as writers are always quick to measure their success and talent against others'. Rodoreda wrote to her editor about reviews of her work, saying: 'I suppose he's part of a group who thinks this lady is too famous and we need to knock her down a peg. In other words, it's the same old story, when someone arouses such ponderous envy, they have to be called out.' Rodoreda, like Pla and my grandmother, also sees envy as an excuse for sloth:

What I find most strange is that he's irritated by someone like me, I keep to myself, I'm not a gossip, I just work and go about my business. Well, there's nothing to be done for it. I'm not acting out of vast disdain but rather because, deep down, people that are so burdened by envy arouse a certain amount of understanding and pity in me.

Rodoreda's strategy for avoiding viper tongues is isolating herself in her work, in Romanyà de la Selva, at a house where her only distraction is the garden. Sales tells her that she's doing the right thing, just as Víctor Català isolated herself in L'Escala, because if she had lived in Barcelona everyone would have got under her skin.

It's no coincidence that being famous in Catalonia is synonymous with having to distance yourself somewhat from the social stage. Envy is the sin that best describes our country and it is a central pillar of our society. Catalonia is a great factory for churning out bonsais, small people who are decorative and don't draw a lot of attention to themselves. Behind anyone who tries to stand out there is always an army of Catalans looking down on them and warning that so much attention will only cause problems. Pla writes:

In our country, anyone who does anything, who takes a step forward, who's in motion, who has an aspiration or two, is envied, hated, subjected to a relentless, horrible trial, either clandestine or public. […] Everywhere else, accepting one's authentic personal value, one's capacity for action, displaying some sort of powerful vitality, creates an aura of admiration. Here it's the opposite. Only mediocrity is socially plausible.

XIII – THE SLAVE MORALITY

This envy of anyone who stands out that Pla mentions, Kierkegaard calls lack of character. Nowhere have I seen this so clearly as on chat shows: spaces where people argue over small patches of power like petty landowners.

Some months back, on a radio chat show, the discussion grew heated as I tried to explain myself. I was speaking with a journalist who has much more experience and power than I do, a man with very small eyes who seems to have a chronic nervous condition. During the advert break, off the record and as we were taking off our headphones, he looked at me, appalled, and said: 'Your opinion is unworthy of a public media outlet.' I was so taken aback by his comment that, after I had regained my composure, I was tempted to attack him; but I saw that his despicable statement was the last recourse of a man who didn't know how to take someone disrupting his inner tranquillity. He couldn't tolerate someone shifting the horizon of his territorial expectations.

Looking for faults in others, explains Nietzsche, is a way to ameliorate a feeling of inferiority and powerlessness, as it is seen as a way to re-establish one's superior position. In Catalonia, mediocrity is rewarded by a defence of the discourse of equality. There is a desire to bring down anyone who stands out concealed within the demand that we think in a whisper to avoid offending anyone. When we mix envy with equality, the result is that we can disdain everything we want with the pretext that it will always hurt someone. Really, that is just a way to deny that some ideas, and some people, are better than others.

The powerful idea underlying our public discourse is that standing out too much will bring you harm. That it's better to move within the established limits and suck out all the good you can without taking any unnecessary risks. In Catalonia, all success is calculated and all praise is designed to domesticate. I've seen many intelligent journalists, politicians, writers and artists who, out of a fear of getting into problems, chose to give up before they got started.

When you don't have enough strength to defend a conviction, it's normal for you to try and get others not to either. If you have surrendered, everyone should follow your example. It is a form of envy that is intolerant of all difference, and willing to create strategies to place obstacles in the path of any attempts at distinction. No one is authorised to defend authenticity, or to try to do things in a different way. So moderation and nose to the grindstone have been the prevailing models: 'Moderation,' wrote La Rochefoucauld, 'is a fear of falling into that envy and contempt which those who grow giddy with their good fortune quite justly draw upon themselves.'

In Catalonia, envy is a great equalising monster. Since everyone needs a space where they can feel safe and approved by others, we end up behaving according to their expectations, even when that is prejudicial to us. Succeeding within these societal expectations, as opposed to reaching for the stars, means being complicit in maintaining a low level for everyone. The envious want to bring others down, but those who are envied also end up wanting to bring themselves down, even when that means giving up. As a consequence of normalising this, we renounce our own originality and difference. Not renouncing that would be too costly to allow us to live comfortably in society. It is an attitude of the Nietzschean slave who accepts losing before even starting to fight. That is why, over time, only those who have talent and intelligence, but also strength, are able to rise above through a trial by fire. Success is achieved only by those who know, as Scheler said of Goethe, that their rich and great existence is bound to make the poison flow. To put it in other words, with an aphorism that deserves to be better known: success is achieved only by those who believe that 'envy is better than pity.'

One of the strategies for transcending in this decadent environment that rewards mediocrity and punishes distinction is to pretend to be crazy to avoid having to be average. Rodoreda used to scare journalists with her histrionic, bold laugh. It was a provocative laugh, designed to create a wide rift between her and normality. 'What I remember best,' wrote Montserrat Roig after interviewing her, 'is the alchemy of her laugh and her strange gaze.' It was a hard gaze that imposed distance, that didn't want to fit in. 'I would say that in Mercè Rodoreda,' she wrote about herself, 'there is a blend of innocence and of bad faith or, to put it better, of seeing things clearly.' In a society that promotes dimming your light, the author preferred to be seen as a lunatic than to take part in that perverse game. Perhaps with that lucid gaze she had seen too many people broken by a mix of fear, vices and corruptions. 'I have the sensation, like every Catalan,' said Rodoreda, 'that for whatever reason I live a thwarted life, like mutilated, do you understand? And from that place comes the feeling that I haven't achieved what I would've liked to.'

XIV – A COUNTRY OF RATS

It's not something that's often mentioned, but the final chapter of *Broken Mirror* is told from the perspective of a rat. They are demolishing the house and the rodent runs through the garden looking for a safe place to sleep. It is right after the civil war and no one is left in the villa. Sofia fled to France and decided to stay. She married a Frenchman and changed her last name. Armanda, the cook, was taking care of the house during the war until she fell in love with one of the militiamen who came to expropriate it. The memories of the family who once lived in the villa have no place in post-war Barcelona. All that's left are the rats and, at the end of the chapter, even the rodent can't find a place to die in peace.

'When I came back for the first time, after the war, in 1948,' wrote Rodoreda, 'Barcelona looked sinister and depressing. People walked through the streets stunned and sad.' She still remembered how the city was in the 20s and 30s, when she used to read Dostoevsky and felt like a queen walking down the streets of Barcelona as it was beginning to shine. The violence of the contrast between before and after the disaster allows her to describe, from her exile, the decline of a city she no longer recognises as her own. The city Rodoreda writes about is not hers; it is a space written from the memory of what she has lost. It pains me to admit that *Broken Mirror*, one of the best novels about Barcelona, is the portrait of a city that does not exist.

The end of the novel is an allegory of this debacle. Towards the book's conclusion the symbolic images multiply, and the atmosphere becomes unreal. Catalan society appears in the metaphor of the villa with a splendid past that is now being demolished. The walls are crumbling. All the furnishings and objects of value are taken out into the garden and set on fire. The memory of that house burns in the flames of a bonfire that scares the rats. It is not incidental that Rodoreda ends with a portrait of her society, explaining that after the war the panorama was so devastatingly bleak that not even rodents could survive. The message can also be read the other way around, as the author's warning from beyond the grave: even if you're a rat, you won't survive.

XV – BROKEN MIRROR

In Latin, the verb *invidere* means 'to look askance' but it also means 'to look too closely.' When you lack distance from what you're looking at, you are more likely to look askance at it and therefore envy it. I found the distance I need in order to avoid envy in books, which serve as a filter between me and reality and give me space to imagine the distance between what is and what could be. I like to see the world as a stage, comparing what happens with what others have invented. Rodoreda, until the rug was pulled out from under her, said that she went through the world trying to put herself into complicated situations that made her feel like a character in a novel. She liked to see how the mechanisms of fiction played out in reality. It amused her to see which gears worked and which failed. This gesture, typical of people who partially live through books, is very effective for imposing distance and leaves a lot of space for relativising, but it makes you see the world as a match that has already been played.

Living in this way means constantly managing a game of

mirrors. You focus on the reality in fiction and fiction is reflected in reality. That works until you find yourself in moments where the game stalls, the calculations fail, the glass cracks and what you are left with is a broken mirror. It is only when you find yourself with shards in your hands, angular and sharp, that you understand why life is not an allegory explained by girls dressed as demons in a Christmas play. You also understand that there are realities that can only be explained by broken mirrors and that those are the most important ones because, as Leonard Cohen sang: 'there is a crack in everything, that's how the light gets in.'

When the distance between you and reality disappears, when your gaze is most vulnerable, you have to be able to look at yourself in the broken mirror and find a safe, clear image, like the woman in Ferrater's poem. 'There are magic mirrors,' wrote Rodoreda. 'Diabolical mirrors. Mirrors that deform. There are small mirrors for hunting skylarks. There is the everyday mirror that makes us strangers to ourselves.' Envy is surrendering to the mirror that makes us strange, and thus betraying ourselves; projected into infinity, it is a suicide. 'Love without desiring / All that you are not,' wrote Auden in one of his poems, and it is a very lovely verse against envious powerlessness. The best way to love without desiring all that you are not is to admire. In order to live with our mirrors, we must transform envy into admiration.

Admiration seeks to love the world with its virtues and its defects, but it needs room to elevate the gaze, to search out something beyond what's in front of our eyes. I've found this space in fiction, which is both escape and elevation, because it always reassures you that there is leeway. Envy, on the other hand, looks low and nearby because it is cowardly and afraid; it understands the world as a narrow, limited space, and it castrates the imagination. Envy's gaze is tempting, especially when you realise you are living in a degraded environment, but it pulls you down and traps you.

Yet seeing reality filtered through fiction reminds me that, despite the degradation in my surroundings, there is always another alternative. That is also why I prefer to admire rather than envy, and filling my cup with others' imagined universes has given me the space to do so. If you decide to elevate your gaze instead of lowering it, if you are constantly willing to be surprised and give yourself over to admiration, envy becomes a harmless temptation because you will never cease to find new mirrors through which to confront the world. That is why my worst envy, transformed into admiration, is for the talent of authors who know how to see and explain life through their broken mirrors.

GREED

ORIOL PONSATÍ-MURLÀ

I – INTRODUCTION

At one point in Ridley Scott's popular film *Hannibal* (sequel to *The Silence of the Lambs*), Dr Lecter (played by Anthony Hopkins) is giving a conference in Florence about the links between iconography and literature on the subjects of suicide and greed. Thomas Harris, author of the novel the film is based on, uses Canto XIII of the Inferno section of Dante's *The Divine Comedy* to justify making this connection. In that canto, Virgil and Dante enter a dark, sinister forest in the seventh circle of Hell. All the trees that grow there are the transfigured bodies of those who've committed suicide. Their punishment for having separated their bodies from their soul before their time had come naturally was being planted in Hell and imprisoned forever in these trees. The only birds that fly through the wood are the Harpies, who peck and hurt the tree trunks, causing them both pain and allowing that pain to pass to the outer world, since the condemned trees can only speak through the wounds inflicted by the sinister birds. The two poets stop in front of the tree-body of Pier Della Vigna, minister to Emperor Frederick II who, in 1248, lost the emperor's favour, was accused of treason, blinded and imprisoned. A few months later he killed himself in prison. As far as we know, the accusations against Pier Della Vigna were motivated more by envy of his diplomatic skill and the trust Frederick II had for him than for any actual treason and much less for anything having to do with greed. But for their purposes, Thomas Harris (and Ridley Scott) associate Pier Della Vigna's suicide with greed so that they can align it with the iconographical tradition that represents the avaricious traitor Judas hanging from a tree with his entrails out, often in the form of an unclean soul that the devil devours when it emerges. Actually, the cinematographic depiction departs significantly from the lesson Luke gives us in the

Acts of the Apostles (1:18), according to which 'with the payment he received from his wickedness, Judas bought a field; there he fell headlong, his body burst open and all his intestines spilled out.' It is not Luke but Matthew who describes Judas hanging from a tree: 'So Judas threw the silver into the temple and left. Then he went away and hanged himself' (Matthew 27:5). On the other hand, Matthew never mentions Judas' intestines spilling out. That's irrelevant. Art history is filled with cases where artists have departed substantially from the literal sacred text in their reliefs, engravings, reredos, miniatures, etc. And in this case, we find dozens of representations of Judas hanged and with his abdomen open (for example, in the anonymous wood carving from the late 16th century held at the Museu Nacional d'Art de Catalunya) and often, Judas opens his own belly with a knife as he hangs, despite how patently absurd that is. If iconographic tradition fuses two different passages from the gospel creating a new narrative with Judas hanged and disembowelled, Thomas Harris and Ridley Scott certainly have every right to turn Pier Della Vigna into a greedy man so covetous of others that, like Judas, he ends up hanging himself. That allows Harris and Scott to establish the thesis that Dr Hannibal Lecter (in a bizarre symbiosis of Josef Mengele and Harold Bloom) is defending: that greed carries within it the seed of self-destruction and that suicide is not only a consequence of avarice, but rather its corollary, the visible manifestation of a process of interior self-annihilation that begins the moment one starts to act greedily. 'Avarice, hanging, self-destruction, with avarice counting as self-destruction as much as hanging,' writes Harris. We must admit that, despite the textual and iconographic modifications, Dante himself seems to be confirming the thesis with the impressive verse that concludes Canto XIII: 'Io fei giubetto a me delle mie case' (translated by Longfellow as 'Of my own house I made myself a gibbet'). The suicides in *The Divine Comedy* can only ever recover their body in order to hang it once again from the tree that is their current body. The tree that became a gibbet is now their home; but what had been Pier Della Vigna's home (his body) simultaneously became a gibbet when he began to act (presumably) with greed. That said, there is an enormous amount of feelings condensed into just that one verse and we shouldn't get side-tracked as we wanted, rather, to begin this essay with a reference to that part of Scott's film for two relevant reasons.

Firstly because in just a few lines we were able to confirm what we all know but many of us have trouble admitting: that the transmission of elements that make up the nodes of a culture are articulated with at least the same amount of fantasy as of rigour. It is not only the psychopath Hannibal Lecter (in other words, Thomas Harris and Ridley Scott) who is allowed to distort and use at his convenience both the historical figure of Pier Della Vigna and Dante's verses. Long before him, dozens of artists over the centuries have used two perfectly incompatible passages from the gospel as if they were one and the same, giving rise to a third iconographic narrative in which Judas not only hangs from a tree with his entrails out, but also that those entrails become (out of hermeneutic requirements necessary to make comprehensible an incomprehensible image) his soul. In this case, Judas' soul emerges from his abdomen instead of his mouth, as was typical, possibly justified by his lips having kissed the Lord moments prior as an unclean, treacherous soul should not even brush the lips that had just kissed the Most High. The history of our culture is filled with incongruencies and inventions of this sort as, one presumes, is the history of Christian culture, seeing as for centuries it has been more explicitly our cultural history than any other. There are plenty of examples: Saul of Tarsus' fall from a horse doesn't exist anywhere in the Bible; Jesus' beloved disciple lying in an unrealistic position on his master's lap during the Last Supper (due to St Jerome misunderstanding the original Greek text); and the commonly accepted attribution of the phrase 'ora et labora' to *Benedicti Regula monachorum* by Benedict of Nursia (not only does it not appear a single time in the Benedictine monastic rules, but furthermore reflects a terrible summary of their contents), to cite just a few of the most glaring. A well-documented collection of these 'errors' of transmission can be found in the book by Valentí Fàbrega referenced in the bibliography.

Secondly, though, by referencing that part of *The Silence of the Lambs* I wanted to reject any negative evaluation of these defects inevitable to the cultural chain of transmission. Thanks to these sorts of errors, confusions, inventions and misunderstandings we have Caravaggio's *The Conversion on the Way to Damascus* at the Santa Maria del Popolo in Rome, which certainly wouldn't be what it is without the monumental horse atop the fragile, defenceless body of Saul/Paul stretched out on the ground; we have dozens of representations of the Last Supper – such as Giotto's Renaissance version at the Capella Scrovegni in Padua, the Romanesque version in La Seu d'Urgell (currently held at the Museu de Vic), and the Gothic version by Jaume Ferrer (at the Museu de Solsona) – that even a four-year-old can see don't work, but that doesn't keep them from being pillars of our iconographic tradition. And thanks to those same errors, confusions and misunderstandings, we have been able to test millions of students over decades, making them believe they knew something (and in Latin) about a monastic rule without having to oblige them (or their teachers, of course) to make the effort of opening up a rather eccentric 6th-century text. It might sound as if we are saying this sarcastically, but we aren't. We are convinced that simplifications, omissions, incongruencies and lies (in the extra-moral sense, of course) are a substantial and unalienable part of any given culture's secular transmission. They aren't marginal episodes or exceptions, but rather part of the natural means by which culture transmits from generation to generation the facts of the past (*facts* here is used in its widest possible sense: historical events, but also traditions, experiences, dogmas, concepts, etc). The recalcitrance with which every branch of the discipline of history – only since the 19th century, necessarily concurrent with of the arrival of the new faith in modernity, positivism – has tried to read the past as a coherent succession of events, ignoring (deliberately or not) all the incongruences therein, has ended up convincing us that the events of the past can be read like an open book, like a logical and ordered series of causes and effects.

Convincing us, in fact, that they are like a book we can write: still today, manuals *on* and histories *of* constitute fundamental instruments for the acquisition *of* knowledge, even (or above all) in higher education. But the errors of all sorts, the gaps, the many facts that remain inexplicable without extraordinary man-handling of the historiographic narrative, are too numerous to reduce to an anecdote. We may as well get used to the idea that it would not even be reasonable to think we could omit them. And that they often give rise to readings that are interesting, creative, and even amusing. Raising awareness of our basic fallibility at comprehending our cultural past and present is absolutely indispensable so as to avoid making dogmatic fools of ourselves and to stave off the temptation to defend as incontrovertible truth that which is nothing more than an attractive and suggestive interpretation that provides us with instruments with which we, in turn, can elaborate our own interpretations that are richer and more useful to our interests and needs. That is also true, it goes without saying, of greed.

Therefore, throughout the pages that follow, readers cannot

expect to find an *objective* look at the concept of greed, because greed is not something that can be analysed, neither synchronically nor diachronically, like an object in a laboratory. Readers cannot expect that, even when the writer of these lines is obliged to adopt forms of expression that could lead them to believe the contrary. Because statements like 'during the Middle Ages, the concept of greed...' or 'the ancients believed that greed...' are inevitable. But neither the Middle Ages nor the ancients are specific enough concepts to ever have more than a remotely approximate value to allow one to sketch a plausible trajectory for us to approach the notion from a suggestive, revealing perspective, allowing us to understand things, but never the thing itself. If the effort of sketching out that trajectory achieves those objectives, it will already undoubtedly have been worth it.

II – BETWEEN VICE AND VIRTUE

Though it may seem a slightly feeble methodology for approaching a subject, I've always found it useful to begin a deep dive into a concept with a simple definition from a common dictionary. Not to remain there or digress (although, sometimes, the simple dictionary definition can send you down some rabbit holes), but rather merely as a good starting point. Unlike specialised dictionaries, general use dictionaries usually give definitions that fit quite well with the meaning that we intuitively give to concepts in their everyday usage. While serviceable, they do conceal – as is to be expected – the buried problems and complexity that come to light when discussing them in more depth. It is also true that this act of transposing common sense into the form of a definition can be done in several very different ways, depending on who the writer is. And dictionaries are always written by someone, even if their authorship is generally invisible. In this sense, it is also usually productive to consult various dictionaries' entries of a single word. Since, unlike a table or a plant, no one has ever seen greed, it is unsurprising that different authors have different formulations of it – sometimes even contradictory or incompatible ones. So let us take a look at, for example, what the Catalan normative dictionary, published by the Institut d'Estudis Catalans, says:

> greed
> 1. Excessive and disordered desire to acquire riches to hoard them.
> 2. Excessive continence in spending.

The Spanish normative dictionary, published by the Real Academia Española, tells us:

> greed
> 1. Immoderate eagerness to possess and acquire riches in order to amass them.

In this case, the two dictionaries don't offer any relevant differences beyond the fact that the IEC has two definitions (*desire* and *continence*) for what the RAE condenses into one (*acquire* and *possess*). What is abundantly clear when comparing the two definitions is that both entail an explicitly negative connotation of the concept: *excessive, disordered, immoderate*. Obviously, that's why greed is a sin. So far, so good. The problem is that all of those adjectives presuppose a *relative* evaluation. In other words, nothing is excessive, disordered, or immoderate except in relation to a gradation that marks the point where excess begins: some order or some measure. Obviously, this is not exclusive to greed but is rather a common characteristic of many (though not all) moral attitudes that are traditionally considered negative. In the case of greed, however, this relativity is particularly accentuated. More, dare we say, than in the case of any of the other sins considered deadly. This highly relative nature has turned greed into a relative sin. Into a sin so relative, in fact, that throughout history it has even been able to make the transition quite smoothly to the terrain of virtue. So, it is a sin that fluctuates between vice and virtue. Which is an extremely strange way to be a sin.

Greed, a virtue? Readers may find that to be an exaggeration. Or, at best, as a characteristic of modern capitalism, but not any sort of constant that could be traced through the centuries. And it is undeniable that understanding the rise of capitalism would be difficult without the corresponding stimulation of a pecuniary eagerness that is often perfectly conversant with greed. The rawest expression of this association between greed and capitalism is surely found in the graduation speech delivered in May 1986 by Ivan Boesky at U.C. Berkeley's School of Business Administration: 'Greed is all right. I want you to know that. I think greed is healthy. You can be greedy and still feel good about yourself.' This phrase would have gone under the radar had it not shortly afterwards inspired part of the famous speech in front of a group of shareholders by the film character Gordon Gekko (played by Michael Douglas) in the 1987 Oliver Stone film *Wall Street*: 'Greed – for lack of a better word – is good. Greed is right. Greed works.' Thirty long years later, the course taken by financial capitalism and the growth of the purely speculative economy would make it even easier to situate greed at the very heart of the capitalist machinery, so that a Gordon Gekko of today would not show even his reluctance to use the word *greed*, 'for lack of a better word.'

This is not the right moment to dive into this question as it is one which requires profound and deliberate treatment. But nor should we completely ignore the discrepancy (at the very least, apparent discrepancy) between the supposed rationality needed to undertake economic decisions and the patent irrationality that motivates all forms of greed. We do not use the words *rationality* and *irrationality* here with any inflection, positive or negative. We are simply stating that modern economic theory, specifically from Adam Smith onwards, has tended to indicate only the aspects involved in economic previsions and decisions that can be calculated and quantified rationally in terms of maximising profit margins. Still today, contributions made by authors such as Daniel Kahneman and Amos Tversky, with their prospect theory, and the financial behaviourism of Richard Thaler do not exactly represent the prevailing way of understanding economic theory. On the other hand, it's obvious that however greed is understood and valued, it isn't possible to analyse it without taking into account the irrational mechanisms that set it off. As well as the glaring reality that these mechanisms are often contradictory, unpredictable and impossible to make universal. Risk, fear, need, victory, loss… these are concepts that make no sense outside of a framework of personal values and certain psychological traits. And even when framed around the same subject, they are volatile and inconsistent in nature. We are unwilling, for example, to make the same effort to earn a set quantity of money as to not lose that same amount. As such, we have to account for how we could possibly predict global economic behaviours when we are incapable of predicting individual economic behaviours. How can we consider greed, which is moved by irrational mechanisms, an engine of economic activity, which is considered rational? How can we embrace greed as an ally of capitalism when we don't even have a clear understanding of what relationship they should have? Perhaps more than two centuries of ignoring the irrational underpinnings of human economic behaviour has made us too naïve and we must now put this perspective front and centre in order to avoid the presumed rationality of capitalism leading us into a crisis that unmasks and unleashes all our worst irrationality.

Beyond the difficulties of considering greed as a true economic virtue, here we are only interested in demonstrating that this positive regard for greed is not anecdotal or rare, but can rather be traced throughout history to build a narrative of greed as a simulacrum of virtue in some cases, and as a virtue *tout court* in others. Setting aside the Wall Street sharks and travelling back to the early 18th century we find praise of greed as a motor of social change (economic, but also cultural, educational, etc.) no less brazen than that espoused by Oliver Stone's Gordon Gekko. In his famous *The Fable of the Bees* (1705), Bernard Mandeville strives to show to what extent a society moved purely by those attitudes traditionally considered virtuous would end up in a perfectly undesirable general stagnation. Acquiring personal profit – which necessarily involves setting into motion the mechanisms of greed – is an essential condition for any sort of social progress. Mandeville argues: 'Fraud, Luxury and Pride must live / while we the benefits receive.'

But let us travel even further back, because we can find this same idea three hundred years earlier, in the *Historia disceptativa de avaritia* (1429) by the Italian humanist Poggio Bracciolini. Employing the always ambiguous and suggestive dialogue form, Bracciolini has an interlocutor condemn greed as a vice while another exalts it as a virtue, remarking how 'strong, prudent, hard-working and wise' the greedy must be and the undeniable benefits their activity contributes to society.

We can even go back a further thousand years in this merely indicative retrospective, and find not exactly an elegy of greed as a virtue, but rather an acknowledgment of how blurry the lines between vice and virtue are in regard to greed. Prudentius, the poet and Christian apologist in Tarraco (Roman capital of Catalonia) who died in 405 CE, warns readers in his *Psychomachia* [*Battle of the Soul*] of the danger greed represents, precisely due to its facility for presenting itself under the guise of virtue. Prudentius goes so far as to describe it as a monster with two faces: 'Virtutum acies errore biformis portenti ignorans, quid amicum credat in illo quidve hostile notet' ('Wavering before the deception of this two-faced monster, the Virtues' line knows not whether to trust her as a friend or mark her as a foe,' in Louis B. Snider's translation).

In truth, Prudentius attributes an essentially deceptive character to greed. To a greater or lesser extent, falling into avarice always implies deceit. In Prudentius' symbolic imaginary, so finely depicted in one of the loveliest illustrated versions of the *Psychomachia*, the 10th-century *Manuscript 24199* held in the British Library, greed always holds out glittering trinkets that attract the unsuspecting and, at the same time, a concealed sword that will lead to the destruction of those tempted. Prudentius does not convert greed into virtue. He only warns of how easily it can pass itself off as something it is not. First by using material goods as bait that can trap the unwary and, when that doesn't work, greed knows how to appear – due to its two-faced nature – as virtue itself, justifying the accumulation of wealth not as an end unto itself but as a means to obtaining ulterior benefits that can be considered positively. Prudentius' warning does not provide us with tools for discerning when we are dealing with this two-faced monster, but rather merely affirms greed's slippery nature. In other words, the impossibility of even circumscribing greed in a definition that allows us to clearly determine whether it falls into the territory of fault, vice or sin, is a problem. As we've seen in these initial pages, it is a problem that is far from anecdotal or contained within a certain time period; rather it is structural and recurring.

III – EXCESS, DEFICIENCY, AND THE GOLDEN MEAN

Seeing that it's so difficult to define, that it can even sneak into the opposing camp and remain there concealed, how is it possible that greed made its way into the pantheon of deadly sins in such an apparently definitive way? In order to answer this we must first clarify, even if just very briefly, that the story of the consolidation both of the deadly sins and their antagonistic theological virtues is long, as is every process of dogmatic consolidation. To begin with, Christianity doesn't really ever invent anything but rather gathers and adapts ideas from classical tradition. This is, in broad terms, the explanation for the success of its doctrines alongside – of course – the inestimable help afforded by its official imposition throughout the Roman Empire since the late 4th century. The vast operation of translating – from Greek to Latin – and of conceptual transposing – adapting ancient philosophical notions to the Christian spiritual paradigm – that was entailed in moving Greek pagan wisdom to a religious imaginary (along, largely, the footbridge of neo-Platonism) still constitutes one of the most monumental and successful intellectual efforts ever carried out in the Western World. Without it, it is impossible to understand the course of the last two millennia of our civilisation.

Naturally, the deadly sins did not immediately appear in the Christian context, nor were they grouped as we now know them. They all have a Greek background and it was, in fact, a Greek Christian author, Evagrius Ponticus (4th century CE), who made the first attempt to establish a correlation between the cardinal vices and virtues. In his brief treatise addressed to those who want to embrace monastic life, titled *Praktikós* (or sometimes *Monachós*), he named eight, not seven. In fact, Evagrius didn't speak of sins but rather of bad thoughts (*logismoi*). In other words, thoughts that are not wise to have, instead of thoughts that are bad in and of themselves. The primary proponent of Evagrius' text was the monk John Cassian, who some years later translated the eight bad thoughts into Latin as gluttony, lust, greed, sadness, wrath, sloth, vainglory and pride. It would be two centuries before this list took on a slightly dogmatic aspect when, in the late 6th century, Pope Gregory the Great, in his commentaries on the Book of Job, recovered Cassian's translation of Evagrius' list. He, however, gave precedence to pride, converting it not only into the primordial sin, but almost the only one. Pope Gregory I maintained the list but removed pride and then renamed them as the seven sins of pride: 'Nam quia his septem superbiae vitiis...' [For these seven sins of pride...] It was not until the mid-13th century that Thomas Aquinas would take up the list again in his *Summa Theologica*, consolidating it as we know it today: pride; gluttony; lust; greed; sloth; envy; and wrath.

Yet neither Evagrius, nor Cassian, nor Gregory, nor Thomas, when writing about greed or any of the other six deadly sins, started from zero. St Thomas was the one who most explicitly stated his sources, which are primarily biblical and Aristotelian. Though Aristotle was an undeniable point of reference for St Thomas, the good Doctor Angelicus took what he needed from the Greek and left what he didn't. Earlier, we stated that the concept of greed was particularly difficult to define and showed how it was even able to slide easily into the realm of virtue. This difficulty is exacerbated by a binary perspective on greed, understood as the opposite of its corresponding cardinal virtue: generosity. Why? Well, because generosity is no less relative than greed is. When attempting to define generosity we also find ourselves devoid of any point of reference from which to determine whether an action is generous. There are no acknowledged generous actions that are not subject to a determined ranking in the giving arrangement. And now we'll complicate it even further with the giving and receiving arrangement. Because – as we see even in the definitions of the most basic general dictionaries – greed implies both acquiring (receiving) and not letting go of (not giving), just as generosity implies not acquiring (not receiving) and letting go of (giving), which forces anyone wanting to do a more than a superficial analysis of the matter to take into account the type of relationship (balanced or unbalanced) in the giving and receiving arrangements. Schematically, they imply a minimum of four possible double movements:

1) receive much and give much
2) receive much and give little
3) receive little and give much
4) receive little and give little

Very well, perhaps it isn't nearly as complicated as we were making it out to be: 1) and 3) correspond to the realm of generosity, while 2) and 4) belong to that of greed. Perhaps we could even muster the courage to organise the four typologies of action and conclude that 1) is less generous than 3) according to the sort of relationship between giving and receiving, while 2) is less greedy than 4) due to the same relationship. But, why don't we say it differently? Why don't we say that 1) is more greedy than 3) and that 4) is more generous than 2)? We could very well say it that way, but this simple possibility again forces us to face the problem of the *absolutely relative* nature of both greed and generosity. Their interdependence is so extreme that it's impossible to define one without invoking the other. What is greed? The opposite of generosity. And what's generosity? The opposite of greed. And we're back where we started, like the inexperienced ship's boy who asked the captain how he could tell the difference between portside and starboard, and received the sarcastic reply: 'Very simply; if you see seagulls on portside, starboard is the opposite one.' As you can see, the problem doesn't lie in the giving or the receiving, which are clean, transparent actions, but in the *much* and the *little*, which are vague and ambiguous adverbs.

Aristotle realised this as – it is sometimes tempting to think – he realised practically everything. The shame is that it seems pretty much no one paid him any mind. When writing about ethics, especially in chapters 1-3 of Book IV of *The Nicomachean Ethics*, Aristotle realised that he could not speak of greed and generosity (and, by extension, he could not speak of vices and virtues) in binary terms. So he introduced a third element that, while perhaps a seemingly small change, was actually a radical restructuring of the model based on antagonisms. To escape the closed circuit created by the reciprocally relative characters of both virtues and their opposing vices, Aristotle situated the negative and positive extremes of an action as far apart as possible. In the case of giving or receiving money, Aristotle conceived of a negative extreme he named *aneleutheria* (which we could translate as avarice) and, on the opposite extreme he placed *asopia* (prodigality). These two extremes allowed Aristotle to delimit the conceptual field into which he wanted to locate the virtue, not at either extreme but rather in the middle, in what he called the golden mean. Avarice and prodigality are two defective extremes, one as too much (excess) and the other as too little (deficiency). Using this model, it would be much easier to locate the virtue, which Aristotle called *eleutheriotés* (generosity), smack dab in the middle of those two extremes. Yet in morality there are no middle points the way there are in arithmetic and geometry.

This was probably one of the worst misunderstandings to arise around Aristotle's theory of virtue. The moral golden mean has nothing to do with a mathematical middle point. The golden mean between getting angry with everyone we meet and never getting cross with anyone is *not* getting angry at half of the people we meet. The golden mean between drinking an entire liquor cabinet and never tasting a sip is *not* drinking half of the bottles. In exactly the same way, what will allow us to avoid greediness is not donating fifty percent of our income, which would be the halfway point between giving everything and giving nothing. The appeal of Aristotle's tripartite approach is that the virtue is dynamic, meaning we are the ones who must determine it. In other words, it always occupies an indeterminate space between excess and deficiency, and that space is always situated closer to one or the other. If we take the case of bravery, this would be situated nearer to recklessness (excess) than to cowardice (deficiency). On the other hand, in the case of greed, it seems reasonable to think that someone who resides closer on the spectrum to avarice (deficiency) could be considered generous because we are not used to demanding, not even of those we consider most generous, that they give away more than a part of what they have in excess, beyond what they need to survive. And in general, most of us have more, at least a bit more, than what we need to live even a reasonable and modest life. So what is interesting about Aristotle's approach – and what he wanted to express with his concept of the golden mean – is that there is no liberality without an important dose of stinginess combined, at the same time, with a dose (in this case, smaller) of prodigality. Generous people are generous to the extent that they are both stingy and prodigal in proper measure. The change might seem small, but it is monumental. The tripartite model allows us to escape the presupposition that we can speak of vices and virtues in binary terms, as something static and identifiable. As such, it forces us to admit to the approximate nature of these notions and, to the extent that it's possible, establish them only after a process of reflection in the personal realm and of deliberation and consensus in the collective realm.

IV – FROM INDIVIDUAL VICE TO COLLECTIVE SIN

Let's set aside for a moment the difficulties inherent in greed's strictly conceptual framing and let's forget about the possibilities of reading greed in a positive light. We will now try to elucidate the glimpse we've got of why greed is judged negatively, not only in a Christian context, but also as part of the Classical tradition. Depending on your perspective, this may seem like a gratuitous question. Obviously greed is pernicious! But the question isn't entirely gratuitous, as whether greed is entirely pernicious or not remains to be seen. It isn't even clear who it harms. The greedy people themselves, or those who have to live with them? When putting forth these questions we are entering a realm that requires taking a close look at the reasons why each author discusses greed and in what terms. In order to obtain an overview, we'd have to individually analyse the most significant texts to have referenced greed throughout history and then this book's length would multiply by a factor of twenty, at the very least – something my editor would not find amusing in the slightest. Therefore, we will have to concern ourselves with a selection that, from our perspective, is both significant and enlightening. And since up to this point we've had an inverse structure, starting with the Wall Street sharks and walking backwards with brief stops in the 17th century (Mandeville), 15th century (Poggio Bracciolini), 13th century (Thomas Aquinas), 9th century (Gregory the Great), 6th century (John Cassian), 5th century (Evagrius Ponticus), 4th century (Prudentius), and 4th century

BCE (Artistotle), I assume you'll bear with me if we continue travelling back to the very beginning. And the very beginning, in this case, means the 7th-century BCE fable writer Aesop and the 5th century BCE Greek philosopher Democritus.

It is not merely our scratching the itch to complete this inverted itinerary that leads us to Aesop and Democritus. They are privileged with the prerogative given to all pioneers. And having some information about when and how a concept begins to circulate usually sheds light on its later iterations. What's more, in this case the association of a writer of fables and a philosopher (whose contributions about greed, it must be said, have received very little attention) allows us to approach the question from a perspective that combines logical and mythical discourse in a complementary way, taking refuge in an *idée-force* defended by the great contemporary anthropologist Lluís Duch. After all, it is not we who make the association between Aesop and Democritus but, as we will soon see, rather Democritus himself as one of his most relevant reflections on greed explicitly references Aesop's fable.

Sadly, of all the texts that Democritus wrote, we have access to only a fraction. Discussing him is made very challenging due to the fact that, on the one hand, only fragments of his work have survived and, on the other, the problems that arise from trying to situate a firmly materialist author in a fully Socratic and pre-Platonic context, something that has inexplicably led to his being relegated to the category of *presocratic*, despite lacking even the slightest chronological evidence to support such a characterisation. Democritus is the only presumably presocratic author who was born and died after Socrates, making this appellation quite a historiographic feat. Among the fragments we have from the work of this philosopher, there are half a dozen that reflect explicitly on economic gain and, among those, we find three (DK

68: B 219, B 224, and B 227) that are particularly interesting to us because they deal with the relationship between an eagerness for profit and the need to put limits on that eagerness, something that therefore allows the subject of greed to crop up. We can consider these the first philosophical texts that revolve around this question. Since they are brief, we will quickly look at them *in extenso*, in C.C.W. Taylor's translation.

> The desire for wealth, if not limited by satiety, is much harder to endure than the most extreme poverty; for greater desires cause greater lacks.

> The desire for more destroys what one has, as with the dog in Aesop's fable.

> The thrifty share the fate of the bee; they work as if they were going to live for ever.

First of all, we want to point out that greed still appears in Democritus as completely detached from the problem of generosity. In other words, we are dealing with three texts that put forth the accumulation of gains as not a problem of what we would now call distributive justice, or even as a social problem (the greedy who accumulate wealth at the expense of others), but rather as a strictly individual problem. For Democritus, greed is primarily a problem for the greedy themselves, because it forces them to adopt a way of life that tends to make satisfaction impossible and that, therefore, constitutes a conceptual absurdity: satisfaction (from the Latin *satis* meaning enough) has to tend, by its very nature, toward an achievable limit that allows one to say 'enough!' The greedy, as understood by Democritus, are insatiable, thus inevitably leading to dis*satis*faction. As a model of life, it doesn't seem particularly recommendable. As such, Democritus confronts us with the problem of spiralling greed: the desire to amass things (or money) places us in a perverse dynamic because if it is not focussed on concrete goals (amassing a specific amount or thing) or is an unlimited desire, it can paradoxically lead only to poverty. The relationship between greed and poverty is, in fact, the true axis around which Democritus' reflection revolves. And poverty as understood in at least two senses. In the first of the fragments quoted above, it is 'extreme poverty': a discrepancy between what one has and what one would like to have. We again find ourselves faced with a relational concept: whether one is more or less poor *in relation to*. If our desire to possess is greater, we will have an initial greater predisposition to feel poor because our very desire to possess already implies an awareness of not having what we consider we should. If, on the other hand, the desire to possess is slighter, it is easier to situate ourselves in the realm of satisfaction, of having enough. Therefore, with this reflection, Democritus is placing himself in alignment with the austerity of his contemporary Socrates (there's a delicious anecdote told by Diogenes Laërtius that describes the Athenian sage exclaiming at his city's market: 'Look at all these things I don't need!') and prefigures Diogenes of Sinope's total poverty as a form of philosophical life and the advice on the need to limit the scope of our desires in Epicure and, centuries later, the sermon of the Beatitudes in the gospel or the radical stripping of Francis of Assisi.

There is, however, a second notion of poverty related to the avarice that Democritus reveals in the next fragment: the greedy are more likely to end up impoverished than those who live with less concern for their material needs. But not in a relative or relational poverty, but abject, objective poverty. It is in this fragment that Aesop's fable appears as a justification of what is more of a sentence than an argument: 'The desire for more destroys what one has.' Let us revisit the brief fable to which Democritus makes reference. A dog has just stolen a chunk of meat and is crossing a river with the booty in his jaws. Seeing his own image reflected on the surface of the water, he thinks that his reflection is another dog with a bigger chunk of meat. He drops the piece he has and snaps at the water to grab the other dog's meat. As such, he ends up losing both the one he couldn't grab because it didn't exist, and the other that the river has already carried off.

The fable, number 133 in the index established by Ben Edwin Perry, appears in numerous variants over the course of the history of the reception and re-elaboration of the Aesopic corpus, but the moral is clear: he who is not content with what he has and covets what another possesses, ends up with nothing. Here Democritus signals a concept of poverty related to greed that is quite different from the one we found in the previous fragment. We could deem the first *reasonable*, in other words, one could reason – as we have tried to do – the sort of relationship established between need (or eagerness) and poverty based on a relational notion of poverty (the more I want, the further I am from having everything I want and the poorer I feel). In the second case, however, the reasoning comes up against obvious limitations. As a general rule, the desire for more doesn't end with what one has, as Democritus defends using Aesop's fable. The desire for more doesn't end with less, and much less with nothing, but rather with more, even when it isn't all the more that was initially desired. What happens to the dog is not only that he desires more, but that when he sees the reflection of what the 'other' dog has, he detects (erroneously) a chance to increase his own gains (in the fable it is fundamental that the dog thinks the piece of meat in the reflection seems bigger than the one he has) and this possibility veers him away from his initial plan. In other words, if the dog had stolen the chunk of meat and continued along his way, content with what he had instead of trying to grab a new chunk that seemed larger, he would not have lost the first piece. Here we are not faced with a fable from which we can extract a universal lesson. Perhaps it is true that, in some cases, coveting what others have (and that, even if equal to what we have, seems better for the simple fact that we are not the ones who have it) is not a good strategy for increasing our own assets. But in many other cases (we would even go so far as to say in the majority of cases), it is an excellent motivational carrot and even an engine of progress.

Clearly, the problem here is not how the dog attempts to acquire the chunk of meat, neither for Democritus nor for Aesop. In fact, the dog had already stolen his first (and only) chunk, and the fable doesn't moralise about not taking what belongs to others, but rather about the inconvenience of lusting after what we don't have in detriment to what we do have. In economic terms, this is a fairly conservative lesson. But most notable is that there is no display of logical argument, no reasoning that can be rebutted. Which is why Democritus, after announcing categorically that 'the desire for more destroys what one has,' instead of proceeding with an explanatory 'for…' that offers a motivation for the previous statement, he merely refers us to the fable of the dog which is obviously not, and does not pretend to be, a philosophical argument. Clearly, the sum of the statement and the reference to the fable can still offer us a pretext for reflection, possibly shifting how we see our relationship with material goods, or even affecting our behaviour out of fear of ending up like Aesop's dog, with nothing. This is what Duch terms an 'intuitive understanding of reality,' something valuable even though it is not articulated through strictly logical procedures. So, when reading the one fragment followed by the other, we find ourselves faced with myth and *logos* intertwined by the same author and around the same subject, which was a constant throughout much of the history of ancient thought.

The last fragment we've cited by Democritus ties in with the first because it again faces us with the question of the limits we must set in the acquiring of assets. His usage of the bee example allows him to highlight the ephemeral nature of life. Bees do not live longer than four or five weeks in their most active periods (the summer months). What's more, their longevity is inversely proportional to their activity: the less they work (in the autumn and winter months), the longer they live. Analogously, the same thing happens with the greedy: the more they rush about trying to obtain riches, the more they shorten their lives, not in the biological sense that happens with bees, obviously, but rather in the measure that their rushing about accumulating assets subtracts time for living their lives. Democritus' reflection presupposes, of course, that the time we devote to managing our chrematistic affairs is not time we spend living authentically or, to put it another way: there is an incompatible relationship between work and life. This may seem strange when seen through a modern lens (indeed, one would hope that is the case, given the number of hours we devote to work). But it was not strange in the least to a Greek person in the 5th century BCE, especially a Greek person like Democritus who, though living austerely, inherited a fortune from his father that allowed him to dedicate his entire life to nothing more than travelling, studying and writing. Life is incompatible with work because a life truly lived is a life entirely devoted to reflection, to knowledge, to reviewing life's guiding principles, to philosophical leisure (that which Aristotle would later call the *biós theoretikós*, the 'contemplative life'). It is highly significant that in a much later Latin context, the word leisure (*otium*) is the root while the word for business is created by adding a negating prefix to the first (*nec-otium*). This signals that the normal thing, the neutral and preferred option, is disposing of free time, time off from work, leisure time to live fully and devote oneself to philosophical and divine contemplation (the medieval *vacare deo*: dedicating one's time to God). The negation of this quality time, *nec-otium*, which survives in Catalan as *negoci* and in English as *negotiate*, distances us from full human life and brings us closer to an instinctive life devoid of meaning from a human perspective; an animal life that, like the bees, is spent toiling away with no awareness of the finite nature of existence.

As such, these first texts challenge us to consider an idea of avarice that is evaluated without taking into account its social implications. The greedy present no problem for others, but only for themselves. They are simply people who have made a mistake when establishing their priorities in life and allowed in an eagerness for wealth that can only lead to dissatisfaction instead of choosing a life governed by other motivations that make it truly valuable. This first way of understanding greed, as a pure personal accumulative zeal with no link to the consequences in the social order this zeal can cause (and, as such, no direct or indirect mention of the tension between greed and generosity, or the classic problem of usury), is merely the first chapter in the history of the concept. When – as we will soon see – the problem is put forth in social rather than personal terms, this first conception of it will be relegated to the back burner.

In broad strokes, we could say that greed does not begin to be considered a social problem until the 12th to 13th centuries, when urban centres began to consolidate. As we've seen, when some ancient Christian authors attempt to establish not only the list of the primary sins but also determine which one was the basis of all the others, pride and greed intermittently disputed for the top spot. The dispute almost always ends with pride as the winner, despite the fact that most medieval biblical commentators had plenty of quotes from the Good Book where greed comes out looking much worse than pride. From the categorical 'Nothing is more wicked than a greedy man' (Sir 10:8) from the Ecclesiastes, to 'Greed is the root of all evil' (Tim 6:10) in the Gospel. But naturally, it is not biblical authority that guides and forms the basis of a doctrine, but rather its ability to respond efficiently to the problems of its time. And amid the harsh economic stagnation of the still highly agrarian and autarkic Early Middle Ages, greed had little chance of beating out pride, the sin that could lead to challenging the immobile established order. Those chances improved, however, when the rigid feudal structure began to show cracks due to the economic momentum that began in the 11th century and that explains both the growth of cities and the development of a commercial activity whose impetus was only halted by the harsh crisis of the 14th century.

Yet the form of greed that begins to present a threat from that point on is no longer the *innocent* vice that corrupts one's personal life goals. The greed that starts to be fought in the 12th century is the greed that threatens to put pay to the *natural* roles that had been in place for centuries, the greed of subversion and destabilisation that opens the doors to social change: merchants with more economic power than minor nobility and the ecclesiastical class; usurers (Jews) who loan to merchants (Christians). A phenomenon like the one that led to a crisis of the Greek nobility at the end of the 6th century BCE and resulted in the Age of Pericles and the dawn of democracy. Similarly, this incipient destruction of the order that held medieval society together through a dense network of perfectly hierarchised loyalties and vassalages would gradually open the floodgates to modern society. The ferocity with which Cistercian monks and scholastic philosophers, along with Franciscan friars and Dominican orators, would attack greed (we might even say they were born to attack greed) only served to underline the central role of the greedy as, in this context, true social revolutionaries.

V – GREED AND PHILANTHROPY

Up until this point we have carefully limited ourselves to describing the presuppositions and perspectives surrounding greed's appearance at various moments of our history. We have resisted making any judgment – positive or negative – about greed as we strive to meet the challenge posed by Josep Pla when he declared that it is 'much more difficult to describe than to opine. Infinitely more difficult. Which is why everyone gives their opinion.' Because we strive to meet Pla's challenge and because the task of the philosopher (and, by extension, the task of all those who take up humanistic matters) seems to us not only much more pleasant but above all much more productive when one refrains from spreading their varyingly lucid opinions and instead offers an analysis of the language. In other words, when one begins by asking what a certain word actually means. Which equates to asking what X means when employing a certain word. Because that which is behind the word (in this case, greed) – if there is anything behind it – will tend to remain hidden while what we wanted to say when using the word *greed* is likely to be clarified.

Now, as we approach the end of this essay, we would like to set aside the historical perspective and focus on the here and now. What function does greed serve, or can serve, in our globalised, interconnected, liquid Western world? In order to respond to that question we will look at greed from the opposing perspective, in other words, from generosity. And we will explore what possibilities of synthesis or reconciliation we can find in this (presumed) opposition that will help us to answer what, in the end, we should do with greed. Here in Catalonia, the word most commonly associated with generosity is *solidaritat*, which could be translated as personal philanthropy. We began our look at greed with a dictionary definition and we will conclude with another. For *solidaritat*, the Catalan normative dictionary gives us:

1. Complete correspondence of interests and responsibilities.

While the Spanish Royal Academy's dictionary, under *solidaridad*, says:

1. Circumstantial adhesion to the cause or endeavour of others.

It would be hard to imagine two more antithetical definitions of the same concept. They not only reveal two variant notions of this desire to contribute to the welfare of others, but two fundamentally opposed mental universes, both from the perspective of human understanding (anthropological) and from the perspective of the relationship between the individual and society (political). Where the definition from the Spanish dictionary marks a distance from *others*, the Catalan dictionary speaks of correspondence, in other words, of *us*; the *circumstantial adhesion* becomes *complete* (so, structural, not circumstantial); the *interests and responsibilities*, which can only be one's own as opposed to others,' become the mechanism that activates and justifies the demand to be a community, while the *endeavour of others*, buffered by distancing, becomes in turn the explanation that the act of solidarity be necessarily ephemeral, circumstantial. Two definitions such as these perfectly delineate the suggested realm of solidarity and, therefore, also what is excluded from that realm. According to the Catalan definition, the feeling of correspondence is only activated when we are aware of sharing something with someone – and, as such, necessarily implies a certain proximity – is basic to the activation of the philanthropic act. In that sense, many of the gestures that we usually consider philanthropic, which are designed to benefit people who live in geographical, social, or economic realities very different from our own, would be excluded from the Catalan definition. While those same actions would fall under the Spanish dictionary definition and would be very similar to what we have traditionally understood as *charity*.

If we take into account the fact that the two definitions of the opposite of *greed* are opposites of each other, where exactly is *greed* at this point? Although we prefer not – as we've mentioned – to put the normative aspects of the discussion before the descriptive aspects, we cannot hide the fact that we feel much more sympathy toward the Catalan definition of philanthropic solidarity than the Spanish. And, in fact, that is because the Catalan definition seems to us to be much more efficient in that it makes no effort to hide what is impossible to hide: that there is no philanthropy without interest, which is tantamount to saying that there is no generosity without greed. In a conceptually transparent world, without the cloudiness that affects not only matter and sensory experience but also the swirled network of ideas, you are either greedy or generous. We construct definitions, exclusions and oppositions and we find our places within them because, frankly, we can live better there than in some tangle of hybrid, undefined territories, in the no man's land of scepticism where nothing is ever sure. But any tracing of the paths greed has travelled along – even one as schematic as ours – is sufficient to prove that if one tries hard enough greed can be turned into either the worst of sins or the most noble of revolutionary sentiments. Perseverance in our attempt to endow this concept with a well-defined outline that allows us to discern it from its also well-defined opposite does not appear to be a terribly worthwhile endeavour. In that case, why don't we try to bring the sin and the noble sentiment closer together? Why don't we have them sit down at the same table and have a discussion until they arrive at an understanding? If we were to do so and they did come to an agreement, it would be very similar to the philanthropic solidarity expressed in the definition in the Catalan dictionary, the moral sentiment that wants us to be generous because it knows we are greedy, that defines an 'us' because it knows we can only be responsible (in other words, fully respond) if we are capable of clearly delineating who we are, to whom we are indebted, with whom we are committed due to shared interests of whatever sort. This apparently paradoxical exercise of fusing egotistical and altruistic sentiments, of merging greed and philanthropic benevolence, situates us in an open field that lacks conceptual definition, which is not as comfortable a place to be as the well-marked terrain of closed notions. While not as comfortable, it is more realistic. It forces us to be the ones who combine the opposing extremes of this same semantic field in their (which is our) just measure, so that they cease to be extremes and become reasonable and feasible. But, of course, there's someone who already realised that – as, it's sometimes tempting to think, he realised practically everything – and that someone was Aristotle.

PRIDE

JORDI GRAUPERA

THE MORAL OF THE STORY

For what it's worth, in my experience your best virtue is your worst defect. This is the origin of tragedy, and why it is said that the road to Hell is paved with good intentions. That which saves you, condemns you. That which liberates you, enslaves you. Your strength is also your weakness.

I – THE WOMAN AT THE DELICATESSEN

I've never felt so defeated as I did the year I turned twenty-five. My father had died some months earlier and my mother a few years before him. I had a job I hated but that was too good to give up. I hadn't finished university and I smoked more marijuana than I'd like to admit. On the outside, I was holding up pretty well but, on the inside, it was just the opposite. Except on Friday evenings. When I left work, I would walk to a delicatessen two blocks away from my house. I entered that place like I'd just won the lottery and would buy up everything, as long as it was high in cholesterol. It was my moment of pure happiness.

The woman who worked there was about fifty years old and particularly slow; my manic energy threw her off. I would make a great effort to be jovial and kind, maintaining the tone I wanted to set for the rest of the night without appreciating that it was also Friday afternoon on the other side of the counter. Since I was spending much more than was sensible and very quickly, I figured she must be pleased. That was part of the pleasure I took in it: spending irresponsibly on cheeses, cured sausages and alcohol. I imagined my flat mates' excitement at the treasure I was bringing home, and felt euphoric.

One day when I was settling a bill even higher than usual,

the woman behind the counter said to me: 'You think pretty highly of yourself, don't you?' My whole world crumbled. I was about to tell her: 'Look, lady, I can see your flaws too. I can see you're not very clever, and you've obviously got less emotional intelligence than this potato salad, but I haven't said anything to you about it, have I? Haven't you noticed that nobody says those sorts of things, even though they're obvious?' But instead I just said: 'We're all trying our best.' I didn't go back to that shop again in the two years it took me to finish university, and after that I left the country.

For many years I've thought that the haughtiest aspect of my attitude was that response. If I'd confronted her, if I'd allowed myself to be consumed by rage and shouted at her, if I'd muttered something through my teeth – even an insult – I would have been treating her as an equal. But no. I decided it was more polite to not say anything, to restrain myself, to not engage in a dispute over the territory of the offence, which I thought wasn't really worth my time.

Since I have a tendency toward abstraction and mysticism, when someone disputes some mundane, dirty territory with me, I always concede immediately. I try to protect the higher ground, which is always inside my head. That usually infuriates my antagonists and for a long time I was puzzled by that, to the point that my most frequent defence mechanism isn't playing dumb like so many intelligent people I know, but playing the innocent. True humility consists of facing off in the territory chosen by your opponent, but I've never found the strength to feign aggression, and as a result I always end up sounding condescending.

There is a simpler way to explain the paragraph above, which is saying that I am arrogant precisely because I am only keen on debating subjects that interest me. Especially if I've mastered them and can be or seem superior to my interlocutors. It's irrelevant that I have a tendency toward mysticism and abstraction as I could just as easily say I lean toward football and film. The flip side of this accusation is to say that I have every right to some interests at the exclusion of others, and to debate only that which entertains or benefits me. And the flip side of the flip side is to say that this accusation I've made against myself is a *captatio benevolientae*, as is this entire first chapter: a way to make it seem as if I'm attacking myself in order to win readers' favour and be accepted even before I've really begun, so that my fear of writing a bad essay is balanced out by a love of my flaws.

The most bothersome symptom of pride, and the first one noticed by others, is not listening. It is a physical manifestation, an almost knee-jerk reaction or natural consequence, like gaining weight if you're a glutton. On the other hand, when there is an uncomfortable silence or when a subject you've some knowledge of is raised, you are embraced by a sensation that's the opposite of shame. This cold calm feeling that you're indispensable leads you to talk a blue streak. Because you are only interested in power. You are only interested in words that strengthen your mastery of yourself and others. Overcoming pride is essential to better living and a life with broader horizons. But it is often an exercise in hypocrisy: you listen in order not to appear arrogant. This effort is hard to conceal and eventually leads you to doubt all your criteria: you no longer know how to distinguish what is worthwhile from what is a mere spiritual exercise. Imprisoned by forced humility, you are consumed by doubt: what if you are just enabling people to tell you useless nonsense? I don't think it's a coincidence that I ended up writing a doctoral thesis against the idea of neutrality. As we can see, pride is not solved by a transformation of your personality, but rather by a fortification of your character. It is not cured in society by trying to adapt your gestures to moral expectations but rather in solitude, by attempting to create your criteria within the constraints of your self-knowledge.

Clearly, pride is a vice of perception and, as such, always has room for further reflection, leading to an infinite spiral. Perhaps that is why pride is often misunderstood, sometimes unintentionally and other times purposefully and malevolently. As such, this misunderstanding acts as a poison because social pressure against pride is also a way to destroy the finest angels in our natures and the few original thoughts that emerge throughout our lives. The antidote to pride is not merely humility; it is also a social space where a genuine interest in different, better things is seen as a win-win. It makes life richer and more open.

Beyond my purported tendency toward abstraction, there is also a specific question that interests me, and that is why that woman at the delicatessen couldn't just let me enjoy my shopping. I will now try to answer it.

II –THE TIGHTROPE WALKER

The more fragile a community is, the more we have to censure its strongest figures.

For centuries we have cultivated the idea that of all the defects of strong characters, the most dangerous is pride. The prideful man is the father of tragedy because his excessive attitude incites violence. He is irresponsible and must be kept at bay.

And keeping him at bay is everyone's job. The streets of this side of the Mediterranean are filled with citizens committed to their civic duty of letting you know when you get too big for your britches. At any moment, anybody walking by feels free to give you their opinion. I don't know where the custom of laying into the timid comes from, but I suppose it could be that no one wants to miss out on an opportunity to wallow in the weaknesses of others, especially when they are innocent. Everyone knows that the timid are afraid to put themselves out there because they are pessimistic about what others think of them. What I'm saying is that, when given the opportunity, everyone commits the sin of pride.

In any case, neither the timid nor the proud can use ignorance as an excuse. We are never surprised when someone calls us arrogant or shy. These are traits children are scolded for from a very early age and, as a result, the first time it's mentioned buries itself in our childhood oblivion.

The fact that I come off as arrogant to people is so internalised that the only humility I know is work. It has taken much effort for me to reach this state of inner peace, and yet sometimes I still spiral into guilt because I can't stand my shows of affection being interpreted as disdain. Obviously, the opposite would be worse: my disdain being taken for affection. To have been humbled to the extent that I only knew how to send signals of submission. But that only happens to the fake humble.

Like all vices, coming to terms with pride requires a significant amount of accumulated experience, sometimes even an entire life. Working on it is inevitable because it follows you like a shadow: the more enlightened you believe yourself to be, the more it shows. Those convicted of pride work on their vice in front of an audience, as reckless as a circus tightrope walker. The audience wants them to fall because everyone prefers to witness an exception rather than a circus routine, and because death puts everybody in the same boat, even more so in the case of a reckless person's death. But tightrope walkers feed off that death wish; they can sense it clearly in the massive silence and it is the force that keeps them upright. Upon reaching the end of the tightrope, they are aware of having travelled the infinite trajectory that separates commiseration from true self-knowledge. And then they no longer need the applause; they are free.

III – PRIDE AND VANITY

In the beginning, there were eight deadly sins. In the 6th century, Pope Gregory I (the Great) reduced them to seven – the number of completeness in the Bible. He (rightly so, in my view) merged sadness with sloth, vainglory with pride and added envy. Perhaps because he was a very practical man – a genius of bureaucracy and administration – he didn't realise that the costs of merging vainglory and pride were much higher than simply bundling together two for one.

Psychoanalysts maintain that there are two kinds of sane person – in other words, two types of neurotics: the hysterics and the obsessives. The hysterics depend on others' opinions and the obsessives have plenty with their own. It is the same distinction that separates vainglory from pride. A hysteric who trips and falls ridiculously in front of a group of strangers will first check to see if anyone witnessed the fall before checking for injuries. An obsessive will first assess any physical damage and then look for any spectators.

Vanity arises from an inner insecurity, but with it comes a talent for reading others. Pride, on the other hand, is what's left to loners who've lost their sensitivity. The vain believe they know how to see through the eyes of others; the proud barely glance at you. They are opposing survival strategies. The vain, if they know their trade, are those who come over to ask you for a favour only for you to end up thanking them when all is said and done. The only scenario the proud could imagine is that you are the one asking them for a favour.

Behind all their comedy and desire to seduce, the vain are essentially sceptics. They're never sure that the world exists and, once they've more or less convinced themselves that it does, they then begin to question their own existence. That's why they seek out applause. They need constant reassurance that the world is responding to their presence. There are actually two extreme ways to prove that others exist: a cry of pain or applause. If you are unable to perceive the pain of others, then you opt for cruelty. You generate pain in order to get a response. Taken to its final conclusion, you would become a sadist, cruelly interfering in the lives of others until you'd completely destroyed them. The definitive evidence to confirm the world's existence and your place in it would be your best friend's head on pike, raised as a trophy.

The vainglorious, however, are empathetic. They have a great talent for reading the emotions of others (or at least they're convinced they do, which is enough for them). When they receive love, they recover their faith, yet it doesn't last long because they experience love only through the visible manifestations of affection which give them pleasure. And pleasure is a chemical discharge that retreats like the tide when its stimulus disappears, leaving an anxious void. Even their memories of it fade quickly and they grow distrustful. The repetition of that injection of endorphins eventually leads to the object of pleasure losing all meaning, and what they are left with is their need to satisfy that chemical urge. The vainglorious evoke the same compassion and repulsion as a body wracked by abstinence syndrome.

The vainglorious are easy to dominate – you need only flatter them and let them speak, and they'll do the rest – but they are very hard to emancipate because they can only get past their intrinsic insecurity by reconciling themselves with the world's uncertainty. They must accept that they are alone. And they don't know how to be alone. Attempting to raise their self-esteem so they don't need external approval only feeds their addiction. It's like trying to quit cigarettes by smoking heroin: you are more likely to end up addicted to something worse.

The vainglorious are useful when put to the service of a higher cause. When they decide to create, they are able to swap their scepticism for an act of faith, before setting aside their constant flighty searching for absolute certainty in others' affection. Then, the ultimate truth is their creation. If they can introduce some of the vitality they miss in the outer world into it, then their weakness for trying to glean the effects of their presence in others can turn into a code of conduct. If they continue to try to make everyone like all they do, they will build up a tolerance for accepting the unacceptable.

Yet everything has its limits. Sooner or later, life forces you to choose between your own or others' criteria regarding something truly important. If the vain don't know how to impose themselves, they end up being doormats, the good people who everyone takes advantage of. And there is no creative work or talent that can remedy that.

That explains why vanity without a counterweight leads to naïve art. The strength artists derive from creation, which is something that rescues them from vanity, makes them lose their edge. Unable to offend, they become blunt, flat and dull. And they evoke the same pity as those who engage in online social media with a lot of vanity and little pride: their need for 'likes' is so strong that they warp themselves to get them. Their statements come from pride, not vanity.

I submit for the reader's consideration that this is seen in humanity's most universal creation: children. In the beginning, your children murder your ego because they weaken you physically – I'm sure you can recall the classic torture of being awoken every few hours throughout the night – and because they unleash your imagination to the extent that you can visualise every potential danger that could possibly harm them. Any trifle that affects your children takes precedence over even the privacy of your thoughts: there is no space to say you'll deal with it tomorrow, or five minutes or ten seconds later. It has to be now. Your survival instinct loses its number one position in the ranking. In that simultaneously fuzzy and highly alert state, it is common to find the old seduction tricks pointless and to feel awkward at carrying them out. The same thing happens with an artistic work when the author takes it seriously: the superficial aspect of vanity loses interest. All very well and good, but how many of us parents have seen our vanity transferred onto our children? Parents who shamelessly show off their little masterpieces to the world. The children become a social black hole sucking up the light of others' tender gazes. They are enslaved by the vanity of their parents, who end up dependent on the approval of their children. The temptation to live through the affections of your descendants, to see your efforts validated by their love, is very significant and the leading cause of spoilt children.

Everyone knows that for some, the love and freedom in parenthood only come to light when they are able to say 'no' and then the children will inherit this same love and freedom. The strength that parents need to defend their boundaries is not emotional but rather moral. In this battle, the ego is wounded and, with it, vanity.

There must be something in you that stands up for itself; a bit of pride. This is the most surprising part of Gregory the Great's decision to merge the two vices: pride is an antidote to vanity. If vanity is redeemed by listening to others, then pride is redeemed by the morality of standing strong. Otherwise, vanity sinks into dependence, and pride into misanthropy.

Since the proud are as impermeable to praise and criticism as they are inaccessible through words, they are much more complicated to dominate than the vain. The proud live as if they need nothing. Notwithstanding, pride is much easier to cure. In fact, there's no need to do anything. Sooner or later, life will bring them down a few pegs. And then, if they are weak, they'll become lazy because all effort is worthless and no amount of encouragement can pull them free from their sloth. If they are strong, they will become wrathful because all imperfection reminds them of their own. Solitude eats away at sensitivity so it doesn't lead to compassion but rather a deaf uneasiness and, like the sound of a stove's hood fan, which is a relief to everyone when it's turned off even though a few seconds before no one was aware of it at all, the proud suck all hope out of the room and no one can relax until they're gone.

The proud and the vain would do well to speak to each other with the sort of sincerity they are lacking. Their shortcomings are complementary: the proud could teach the vain that the world, despite its indifference to their manoeuvring, exists, while the vain could refute that by saying that solitude for solitude's sake is nothing more than a prison. In *El criterio*, published in English as *The Art of Thinking Well*, Jaume Balmes says that pride is more malicious and suggests great crimes, while vanity is weaker and rather suggests ridiculous miseries. It is hard to imagine how such antagonistic defects could be merged, as Gregory the Great envisioned, into one vice. Balmes somewhat resolves the contradiction by saying that the conceited have moments of both vanity and pride. It is true that we are led by different impulses at different times, but it is also true that we are never so susceptible to becoming one thing or another depending on which way the wind blows. We have a core that is the basis of our character, and this character has aspects that compensate for our excesses. Those aspects are usually the same but they are never what ultimately defines us, in a way similar to how ascending signs introduce elements into our horoscopes but don't define them. Therefore, it isn't enough to say that we waver between pride and vanity depending on the moment.

When we say that someone is arrogant, we say something different to when we say that someone is vain or proud. You can have a lot of vanity and a lot of pride at the same time: it is the inaccessible spherical being. When you try to prick that person's haughtiness to get them to trip up, their vanity shows up with the full force of its seductiveness and ends up winning you over without breaking a sweat. When you try to soften them up with flattery, they refuse to budge and savour their victory without ever lowering their chin.

The combination of vanity and pride makes the arrogant person a public danger because they believe they will always find a way out. And because of their vanity, this way out never surrenders. At key moments, they have a hero complex: they want to challenge the gods. They don't hide and are very ambitious. They don't care what others say because they're convinced that everything will work out in the end and that just thinking that will make it so. As such, they often end up devoured by their ambition. I think that was what Gabriel Ferrater meant in his poem 'Literature' when he says the writer was 'devoured: the ineffable tempted him.' That temptation is a sign of pride. The proud cannot resist dominating the most sacred – the ineffable – in a duel to the death. Yet when Ferrater says that the writer was devoured, he is concealing the chaos unleashed by that temptation. This danger is what must be killed before it destroys the world.

IV – THE DOG-MAN

The book *Leviathan* by Thomas Hobbes is named after a monster found in the biblical Book of Job. Hobbes references it because God defines Leviathan as the king of all the sons of pride. Pride is the utmost political sin because it is the enemy of public order, forcing the sovereign even further towards pride. It is unsurprising that *superbia*, the Latin word for pride, shares a common root with the word 'sovereign,' but the key to Leviathan is the difference between them. A sovereign rules above others while a proud man believes himself to be above others. Tranquillity on the streets, stability and a healthy economy are only possible if the sovereign subdues the arrogant.

The task that Hobbes took up was to transfer his century's scientific spirit – Newton's physics and Descartes' geometry – to the political realm and this is why he is considered the father of the modern state. He is also known as the father of conservative liberalism due to his view of mankind and its place in the world. Hobbes was a liberal because he believed that each person's inner freedom could not possibly be controlled by the government, and he was conservative because he had a pessimistic view of mankind.

That pessimism is reflected in one of the most famous quotes in the history of secondary education: 'man is a wolf to man.' Isolated from its context, the quote seems to say that violence is natural in the sense of instinct. Hobbes wanted you to think like an animal. Stripped of civilisation, we are wild beasts that kill each other for no other reason than the fact that we have no morality. But the wolf is not just any animal. Aside from the fear its howling causes in all cultures, there is fascination of its life in its strictly hierarchical pack. The wolf is a political animal and, as such, susceptible to being domesticated, like us. Wolves that wanted to be dogs signed into a social contract with humans: they would stop stealing their hens in exchange for food and mutual protection. Humans made the same pact with them. We are the dog that forgot its origins.

Hobbes said that in our natural state, we are entitled to everything. And that we cede that right to a sovereign to spare us the poverty and brutality that goes along with perpetual war, of 'all against all.' He can be called a conservative because he is more interested in conserving that provisional, fragile peace than in risking it in the name of utopias. His passion for science also protected him against important ideas such as justice and its universal pretensions, and words inflated with hubris.

If that were as far as he went, Hobbes wouldn't be modern. He would be just another vile despot and the monster Leviathan would be indistinguishable from any feudal lord, obsessed with creating docile breeds of human dogs (like Socrates in Plato's *Republic*). But I've already said that Hobbes was a liberal, not just a conservative, because he believed that inner freedom remains uncontrollable by the government in office. This is one of the great inventions of modernity: the conscience.

Now that we've been modern for many generations, we're very used to thinking of the state as a vertical order. Think about the courts: there are local courts and above them, the *supreme* court (again sharing an etymology with *superbia*) the European and international tribunals and beyond that the United Nations. Not everything can everything be tried in every court, as they do not all have the same legislative capacity, and in some, shall we say, horizontal vestiges remain such as in questions of extradition or international custody battles. But these are exceptions; the basic form is pyramid-shaped, like the issues at stake: an unfair traffic fine does not fall within the jurisdiction of the Court of Human Rights, but if the procedure for issuing it and the trial involves a human rights violation or is an example of ethnic persecution ending in genocide, the highest-ranking officer in the city might well end up committing suicide with a thimbleful of cyanide in The Hague.

Modernity is the process that led to that simplification which, despite what the propagandists for absolutism say, is not a merely administrative matter. There were once many forums for disputing injustices. A violation could be resolved and judged simultaneously at the bishopric, the count's home, in royal audience, the assembly of commons, at the parish or even within the family. Each forum had an explicit power and freedom for the judge to punish, as well as a different perspective on justice and peace. Modernity reduced all of that to two authorities: the state and our own consciences. The state extended its reach to the limits imposed by the soul, not for lack of desire to take it further, as today's propaganda wars reveal, but because the soul possesses a freedom that is hard to tame. Or at least that's what we believe, and that is enough to make our consciences the state's most feared enemy.

Hobbes saw this danger more clearly than any of his contemporaries. In the contract the wolf-man signs to submit to a sovereign and become a dog-man, there is a clause preserving the right of conscience, even if it is exercised in the most private way possible – Hobbes was not a democrat.

Hobbes' finding is important because the most violent political problem of the 16th to 17th centuries was the religious wars that arose from the schism within the Catholic Church. The relevance of separating state and soul is greater than that of separating Church and state (in fact, one is a consequence of the other). It is a distinction that reaches all the way to conscientious objection today and, in our still post-war cultural imaginary, finds its climax in the argument that Eichmann used at his trial in Israel, and which the Americans had already dismantled at Nuremberg: that of due obedience.

The conflict boils down to this: do you obey the law and the hierarchy even when they go against your principles? Much of American cinema deals with this subject of taking the law into your own hands and this is the moral dilemma moviegoers are most interested in: whether we can continue to use Clint Eastwood as a model now that the anarchy of the Far West – where only the morality of the gunman counts – has been tamed.

The conflict as Hobbes saw it was clearer. A sovereign has the power to punish you for the sake of peace and progress. OK, understood. Now: the sovereign can put you in jail for life, torture you with the most sophisticated devices and even kill you and your family, but none of that can ever match the threat of Hell. There is no temporary pain that can outweigh eternal damnation.

It's a problem, especially when the sovereign is Catholic and you're Protestant, or vice versa. If the sovereign orders you to do things that go against your religion, or you believe that mere obedience to a heretical king condemns you to eternal hellfire, what incentive do you have for obeying him?

The solution is revealed in the third part of Hobbes' book. The first – and most brilliant – part is a psychological treatise in scientific vocabulary; the second – and most influential – deals directly with politics; the third is a reinterpretation of the Christian scripture that has always been read as a pathetic justification against the – still prevalent – suspicion that *Leviathan* is an atheist book. But that is not true: it is the first great attempt to solve the problem of freedom of conscience.

In it, Hobbes says that obedience to the sovereign is a religious command, even if the king is a heretic or sinner. If the king commands you to commit a sin, it is he who sins, not you by obeying. On the contrary: if you disobey him, even if in keeping with your religious or moral conscience, you are committing a deadly sin because you imperil social peace, have no possible salvation and so off you go to Hell. If the king condemns you, it is God who condemns you. With one stroke of his quill, Hobbes gives the king the power of Hell. To give it a nice, mysterious spin, I call this the secularisation of Hell, and I believe it to be the seed that bore its ripest fruit in Auschwitz.

The sovereign needs to curve the verticality of the arrogant and, to do so, he must become the most supremely proud: both the devil and the angel who believes he is wiser than God. The sovereign must first prevail over the wolf-man, who trusts in his strength and cleverness to dominate others and profits from a chaotic, violent world of constant war. When blood runs in the streets, he buys property. He is dangerous and must be tamed or killed. If you tame him, he becomes a soldier; if not, he becomes a bandit.

He is arrogant because he hasn't understood that he is not as strong or as clever as he thinks he is. A person can be better than someone else in some aspects, but the distance between the best and the worst is never so vast that a well-organised group can't subjugate and kill you. It is this fundamental, empirical equality that turns the war of every man for himself into a never-ending anarchy: no one can ever fully prevail.

When someone does prevail it is because they are leading a strong, well-armed and a very violent group, who – if they are smart enough – end up creating what is known as a monarchy. Since the struggle against this primitive form of arrogance depends on equality, the state needs to homogenise everyone to avoid the temptation to revolt. For this reason, Leviathan, the king of all the sons of pride, is a monster that subdues and makes all things uniform. Any distinction is dangerous, and any superiority a social menace. The sovereign is the only human who, like an untamed wolf, retains a natural state with the right to everything.

In the end, once the state is in place and things are level, the proud one is no longer the wolf-man but he who has a conscience, the last vestige of difference and distinction. His sin is to think that he knows God's will (or morality, or justice, or freedom) better than the sovereign and act accordingly. He walks on two feet because he has left the dog behind, and has no need to revert back to a wolf. Against him, the sovereign can only leave behind the wolf-man that he is and transmute himself into a God-man: taking all the liberties of the universe until he masters the forces of Hell, to which he ends up enslaved. Against the man who has a conscience (in other words, the man who imposes limits on himself and is free because he knows how to choose), the state can only respond with a total lack of boundaries with the force of a worldwide flood or an extermination camp. Anti-semitism has this exact moral origin: the Jew has a conscience, does not respond to the values of the state, and is too proud to even revolt against it. Leviathan can only annihilate him.

The verse from the Book of Job which inspired *Leviathan* has a hidden ambiguity that attests to this tension between the proud man-wolf and the proud free human being. The Hebrew scripture literally says that Leviathan: 'looks on everything that is high' (in the sense that he 'looks down on it haughtily') and 'it is king over all the sons of pride.' But the Hebrew dictionaries explain that 'sons of pride' is a way of referring to the imposing animals of prey, such as lions.

The Catalan translation follows the Christian Standard Bible with both saying that Leviathan is 'king over all the proud beasts.' In contrast, the King James Version, which was what Hobbes used, and the Latin Vulgata both opt for a more literal translation and as such speak of the children of pride and *superbiae*, respectively.

The gap between the meaning of the original Hebrew phrasing, which points to the wild animals in the ancient – literally wild – world and the later translations, in an eminently social world, that omit the metaphor to go straight to the moral value – pride – signals the shift in Hobbes' *Leviathan* from the original enemy of the early humans – physical violence – and the enemy of the state, which is the freedom of conscience. It is the hierarchy of our fears: first, we fear the physical pain inflicted on others and finally, we fear only the harm that our own freedom exacts on us. If you've understood this distinction and its political power, you understand what religion means when it uses the word *sin*.

From this distinction, it is easier to see something that our secular culture has forgotten: that the original Christian sin is pride. Adam and Eve are expelled from paradise for having disobeyed God or, in other words, for believing themselves better than divine law. From that expulsion comes the awareness of being free to do evil and the experience of pain, shame and mortality. Christians celebrate the *povera* birth of Jesus and the vulgar crucifixion of a political criminal as proof of humanity's redemption through humility: God impoverished and defeated man. You don't have to be a Christian to realise the power of this way of understanding life, and you don't have to be an atheist to see the problems that arise from it.

V – FALSE CONSCIOUSNESS

My childhood ended the day we were sitting around the table at my grandfather's house, a man we all addressed with the utmost respect. My sister said some silly thing and I burst out laughing, roaring loudly and unguarded, my head tilting back.

My grandfather, who was a man of few words, looked up from his lentils and said, curtly: 'You laugh like a simpleton.' And he continued eating. Almost immediately my face turned hot and my eyes brimmed with tears. I resisted crying, repressed it, held it in and finished my meal. I don't want to exaggerate, but I don't think I've ever laughed again the way I did that day when I was ten years old. Of all the ways of laughing, the most important is the one that comes from a feeling of safety. Unguarded roars of laughter resonate with the cultural values of their surroundings and are social in their entirety. You could stop them if you wanted, but there's no need: unguarded roars of laughter indicate that you know your place in the world, even if it's just in the small world of your family. That comment my grandfather made probably meant nothing to him, it perhaps being more a symptom of his mood than of mine, and he might well have forgotten all about it immediately. But for me, like all children in the face of a beloved authority figure, it meant the appearance of a moral and social standard, and taught me to contain my emotions in keeping with the atmosphere around me. I date the appearance of my self-awareness to that day.

The dictionary of the Institut d'Estudis Catalans makes a useful distinction between the first and second entries for *pride*. The first: 'Excessive estimation of one's self, one's own merits, that makes one feel superior to others.' The second: 'Legitimate feeling of one's own dignity or one's own work.' In this difference lies the primary reason for wanting to overcome the vice of pride. The distance between loving yourself excessively or legitimately could start with an error of perception – a poor assessment of your merits – that ends up translating into a moral flaw. A life that tends to over-estimate itself is a lie. Instinctively, everyone likes to think that what they consider to be their place in the world is synonymous with what it actually is. Knowing your place on the trophic chain is a survival tool.

That is why the codification of pride as a sin is an effective instrument of social control. After all, each and every one of us has, at one point or another, made the mistake of being overly fond of ourselves, and not realising it until it was too late.

This exact mechanism spurs the Marxists' idea of false consciousness. The notion of false consciousness serves to point to those who have a class identity that is incoherent with their pockets, those who don't identify with the working class out of ignorance and alienation: a proletariat with bourgeois values or a right-wing salaryman. Their brains are so fried that they don't realise they should be Marxists. Messianism feeds on a real fact – we often defend positions contrary to our interests by thinking that we are protecting them – and exploits that insecurity to erode confidence in our beliefs.

Given that, by definition, you don't see your false consciousness until it is pointed out to you, illegitimate pride is a mirror of social standards. It is your environment that tells you whether who you are and what you do is worthy of esteem. Among the forbidden sorts of pride there is that which attempts to repress social groups. Each cultural group has a series of repressions that are the memory of some danger whose origin has been half-forgotten and, for this reason, those who live outside these repressions seem to underestimate danger out of their own overconfidence.

I'll give an example: my paternal grandmother lived in the 'Gaixample' – a gay neighbourhood in Barcelona's Eixample – and would often grumble about the public displays of affection seen out on the street. One day, when I was about twelve years old, I accused her of being intolerant of gays. She looked at me in astonishment and replied: 'I don't care if it's two men or two women; Grandpa and I never kissed in the street.' Their offence was having freed themselves from a repression that she had imposed on herself and internalised as moral. The fact that the loudest vindication of the LGTBI world is now called *pride* seems to me to be more than poetic irony. In the face of repression enforced in the name of modesty, the only possible response is ostentation. The dictionary is again useful to us when it describes *pride* as first 'excessive estimation of one's self' – in other words, illegitimate pride – before adding: 'that manifests as ostentation of one's own superiority, and contempt for others.'

The relationship between ostentation and contempt as encapsulated in pride is the essence of the perverse uses of false consciousness because the feeling of superiority can be as illegitimate as the feeling of being the object of contempt. The centuries have already shown us that every truth spoken for the first time is ostentatious and contemptuous of prevailing common sense, just like any extravagance. Extravagance could be taken as a danger if you believe that everything hangs by a thread, as happens in periods of scarcity, as has always happened. But extravagance and truth spoken for the first time look too much alike at the outset: outside of the limits and with no clear direction within a given context. They have the same structure as a simpleton's laughter, the riotous guffaw of someone who has failed to pick up on the social tone.

The reaction against an incoherent presence – truth, extravagance or laughter – is identical: the instigators are persuaded to repress themselves and made aware that they are out of sync. Instead of resistance to all temptation, humility is turned into submission to any social pressure.

There is a false consciousness that manifests itself when we feel looked down on by what appears to us as a display of pride. It is the shock of seeing yourself faced with a new truth when you still live within old, obsolete metaphors. Then we convince ourselves that the new truth is mere extravagance, something that allows us to repress it like the laughter of a simpleton. The false consciousness of the proud and of those who feel scorned function as mirrors of each other and this explains why everyone understands the idea that pride was invented by the envious, while at the same time knowing it is not the whole truth. At the depths of our cultural preoccupations beats the difficulty of distinguishing the education of character from cruel repression. But this very contemporary preoccupation hides the fact that pride is a cultural tool that serves to triumph over cruel repression. Ostentation has always been available to the brave.

VI – SELF-LOVE

One of the first human needs has always been to transcend mere survival. Anyone who has ever forgotten it was lunch time when spellbound by something beautiful or caught up in a fantasy knows that. And this is why sybarites gain weight and lovers lose it. The former never escape the need, while the latter seem immune to it. Sybarites are usually sarcastic people who can't make any firm statement without feeling ridiculous or grotesque; they end up loving the cage that we've all agreed to call – out of mere pity – *hedonism*. Lovers, on the other hand, live inside a freedom that is made entirely of submission and madly chase the sensation of eternity that is produced by the combination of pleasure and duty: the strident pleasure of climax and the mute duty that is imposed by the biological imperative to perpetuate the species. This binomial is so powerful that it affects every sexual identity. And by that, I mean that this chapter is written with metaphysical, not sociological, pretensions.

Self-love allows you to avoid humiliation, especially the

most intimate, inevitable ones, born of necessity. Stripped of all self-esteem, you wake up in the morning to go to work compelled by the need to earn money. But earning money is also a way of showing yourself love, and not only because self-love is hard to improve from inside a coffin, but because money turns into dignity as long as you use judgment when spending it. On the other hand, a lack of money rapidly leads to undignified situations that are hard to manage. No one has ever needed to end up destitute to know that an economic downfall has many a perverse moment hidden within its layers. Moments that place you at a crossroads where none of the paths seem to lead to a place where trusting yourself or valuing your own virtues is easy. In a most basic way, getting out of bed to make some money is a form of self-esteem.

Despite that, getting out of bed just to make money is a small, daily humiliation. All our needs, all the things we do out of necessity, have a common base of pride and love. But living only through necessity ends up demeaning and impoverishing life. Leading an entirely practical life is as efficient as it is unsatisfying. Sometimes there is no other choice, but if pragmatism is an option, it is most effective at begetting psychopaths without imagination. And without imagination there is no morality or love, if you forgive the redundancy. When the briefest moment meets the most persistent atavism, as in the case of lovers who spend it reaching ecstasy, it becomes impossible to imagine life as a chain of basic needs. It not only becomes impossible, but it even allows us to consider Homo sapiens as being at the centre of the story or the protagonists of the universe. Putting humanity at the centre of creation via this divine gaze is what allows self-love.

Pure hedonists, on the other hand, hate themselves because they have the impression of being totally eccentric, even in regards to themselves. They believe that true eternity is the moment and live in the hope that the moment can last forever if their senses are sufficiently inundated. Within the apparent flippancy of their gestures is the whole weight of isolation. Theirs is a moral confusion about love: they trust no one, especially not themselves. Like a shipwrecked survivor who knows that drinking sea water is fatal and yet decides to die by sating his parched throat, they only know how to escape their thirst by running towards another, deeper, sadder thirst.

The gods and the creatures of Hell wage war in the gap that separates one archetype from the other. The lovers who awaken in the pure pleasure of the early months of love are too exhausted to look further into the distance. They are trapped in a labyrinth that quickly reveals its only exit: the door through which they entered, the return to solitude. Like Odysseus on Calypso's island, they can only flee or live the fiction of an unchanging life. At the same time, the hedonist who succeeds in falling in love may find a greater sensory inundation in the mysticism of the encounter with the other. If he overflows with the temptation to redeem himself through the other and does not fall into the addiction of looking only at the long term - or of focusing only on the drive for eternity - he can for a moment embody a fragile balance. Flesh and spirit seemingly beating to the same rhythm: each seeing the other in themselves. Since that is a paradox, experiencing it requires a considerable dose of humour: the correct dose, impossible to predict *a priori*, will save them the headaches of its innate moral relativism.

Very difficult to see from the outside, the limits are all marked by the needs of each moment. Awakening with purpose, with hope, is the way to manage the humiliation that your basic needs measure by the balance in your bank account. Self-love overcomes need without denying it and spares you humiliation and loneliness. That is, it allows you to get closer to others.

The fact that self-love is generous and its opposite is stingy can be seen in the universal truth that elegant people are hospitable and the haughty are suspicious. The elegant put their sensibilities to the service of lifting others up, making strangers feel safe with a combination of qualities and attitudes. It shows without telling: 'Being powerful is like being a lady: if you have to tell people you are, you aren't.' Elegance illustrates the fact that all human actions are deliberate choices and that every choice excludes other available options. There tend to be few available options, and the epitome of freedom is simply limiting those options even further until they are narrowed down to just one. The elegant delicately point to the place where sensibilities overlap and they do not show contempt for any convention, especially when they want to transgress it or find fault with it.

The haughty are cruel both to themselves and to others, and fight fiercely because of the insecurity that is eating them up inside. They try to distance themselves from the absurdity of the world to avoid paying the price for their choices. They need to satisfy an anxious desire for superiority by which they compensate for the vulgarity of life's necessities, especially the biological ones. They are obsessed with publicly camouflaging their deep conviction that they are frauds. They want to enslave others through their eyes and force them to have contempt for themselves. The elegant give us hope because they have self-love; the haughty do not.

VII – THE GOLDEN MEAN

Since your virtue is your defect, and what saves you condemns you, the virtue of self-love can also be a vice. But the vice of self-love is not a problem of excess, as is often said. It is not a question of intensity, rather the price to pay for each thing: loving yourself means understanding yourself. Self-love becomes pride when you displace the object of your love: you love what you are not and hate what you are.

There is no golden mean between the elegant and the haughty, just as there is none between the lover and the sybarite or the person with hope and the mere survivor. The idea of the golden mean is as pernicious as it is illogical, because it is designed to discourage imagination and substitute creativity in favour of calculation. The idea comes to us from Aristotle as he gathered the tacit understanding of traditional Greek culture to educate the sons of the elite of his time, which was the expansion of imperial Hellenism at the orders of Alexander the Great. In other words, and just as Catholics did centuries later, Aristotle needed to contain the pirates inside the hearts of the sons of good families.

The vice that Aristotle was attempting to contain is pride's predecessor, hubris. It is excessive self-confidence according to the idea that the golden mean is the midpoint between two vices: one a vice of excess and the other of deficiency. Just as bravery would be a virtue because it occupies the midpoint between cowardice and recklessness, hubris makes people believe they are like gods and that excessiveness leads them to failure, like a condemnation from the gods themselves to re-establish the world's balance and teach humans a lesson. But outrage, the origin of hubris, sheds even more light on the problem. It is a vice of war: finishing off a defeated enemy, raping the conquered women, or dismembering a body that is already a corpse.

I suppose there is a way to construct the vice of outrage as excess, but it is not entirely clear what an extreme version of it would be. After all, there is also rational calculation behind outrage as breaking a people's biological continuity is the quickest way never to have another problem with them, the right to conquest is a warning for sailors and a way to release pressure in the life of the soldier. Booty and cruelty are rewards for victory and investments in future peace. Kant was of the opposite opinion: in war he believed that you should never do anything that would stand in the way of a future peace treaty. Doing the unforgivable is feeding a future war. The difference between Kant and the young Greek nobles Aristotle was trying to educate is that Kant was already Aristotelian, and the Greeks weren't. The problem of outrage is that it always comes back to haunt you because the peace in the cemetery is paid for with the mental health of the executioners who then return home and have to be sensitive to the setbacks of civilian life.

The most powerful scene in *Schindler's List* shows a Nazi commandant on his balcony shooting a concentration camp prisoner exhausted by forced labour. He has the habit of picking one off every once in a while, like a fickle god whose mission is to show mortals that there is no other law than arbitrariness amid tragedy. It could be said that the commandant suffered from hubris, almost in the original Greek usage. While in the extermination of the Jews there was an indisputable rational calculation based strictly on logic – since logic functions in absolutes – the commandant's random killing has a touch of jovial irrationality, the seriousness of child's play, a crack revealing that, as humans, we are inherently flawed.

In the conversations Schindler has with the commandant, he tries to make him understand that power is something else. He appeals to the Nazi's pride with a tailor-made argument: everyone knows he can kill whomever he wants, yet true power lies in not doing it, in abstaining. What seduces the commandant is not that he tells him that killing like that is barbarously excessive, but the moment when he shows him a superior form of power: becoming implacable. He doesn't tell him to restrain himself, he tells him to surpass himself. Obviously, this tactic fails: the commandant's humanity is pure vice and can only be expressed as rage.

Aristotle needs a solution for the flaws inherent to humankind. And he finds it in calculation. The golden mean between two extremes: if you are starting out slow, accelerate; if you've hit the brakes too hard, retreat. But everyone knows that calculation in and of itself is not worth much. Plato, Aristotle's teacher, knew that: when he tried to imagine a country governed by reason he came up with such a totalitarian fantasy that we're left wondering whether it wasn't all just a joke. The message of this irony is that the main enemy of justice is desire, and that reason can only govern by imposing itself through totalitarianism.

Rage is not an excess that can be addressed by calculation. Aristotle knew that, which is why he suggests we also employ habit. Virtue is the child of habit because just deciding to be better, or calculating it well, is enough. Will and reason on their own are not enough. It takes habit, repetition, discipline. But seriously defending this position is like saying that moral excellence comes out of a fanaticism emptied of humanity.

In his essay 'How Tracy Austin Broke My Heart,' David Foster Wallace explains that elite athletes have to be unsophisticated, a bit dim-witted, and obsessively repetitive in order to be truly great. It is essential that they are not too self-aware, that they cannot see themselves from a distance, that they always live only in the moment, and that nothing exists for them outside of the game. In order for Tracy Austin to reach the ball in a match, she has to do the impossible. The impossible always lies a millimetre beyond our reasonable expectations. Reaching it requires a superhuman effort to empty your mind of all thoughts: you can't think that you'll reach it, you have just reach it. And you will only reach it if you've been trained to not think about reaching it. Athletes who are too intelligent will not reach it because in a fraction of a second they will see themselves from the outside, and that fraction will be the delay that makes them not reach the decisive return.

Habit is the creation of an instinct through repetition, an automatism. It strengthens discipline until becoming unconscious. It is thoroughly excessive. Sometimes it is a necessary excess and can give us a bit of domestic freedom that allows us to take care of other things, but it is always slightly sad, because it's tedious and reveals our limitations. Even when we are happy in our routines – in other words, grown-ups – we can only maintain a bit of hope and some creativity if we remember that all our habits are defeats.

When I was a little boy, my parents gave me an illustrated book that promised, on the cover, to contain the one hundred best jokes in history. They were so awful that I only remember one of them, and only because it made me sad for weeks. I still think about it quite often. It showed a boy my age, about seven and wearing pyjamas, sitting on the edge of his bed with his legs dangling off the side. In one corner was his mother's silhouette. 'Why are you crying?' she was asking him. And the disconsolate boy replied: 'Because I'm thinking that I'll have to dress and undress myself every day for my entire life.' I still can't understand how someone could put something so cruel into a book for children.

The problem with the joke is not that it's bad, but that it's evil. It points to the suffocating, meaningless part of life: it forces you to think about the countless petty trivial aspects of life like getting dressed in the morning, and it lines them all up together in an unbearable row. A child or adult who tries to count all the times they've have to button up their pyjamas will, of course, end up losing their mind, trapped in a rational prison that's indistinguishable from delirium. Aristotle's habits are the exact same thing, that mix of fanaticism and calculation.

At this point in history, it is not terribly polemic to say that logic is a superstition. Don't misunderstand me: it's my superstition. Like all superstitions, it is a very effective tool for transmitting information. Yet logic – especially Aristotelian, which was hegemonic until the late 19th century – is a closed system like a board or video game. It has rules and within these rules things function without exception. Logic never goes beyond the limits of its own set of rules. You can only fit authentic pieces of life into the logic if you trim off all the bits that stick out. It works well for scientific experimentation, vital for understanding the world and mastering it and dying of old age. However, in its most basic form, logic is not very different to animal instinct. Within their system, animals function very well, as long as they are not removed from those established norms or their trophic context.

This is the case with the golden mean, and so while I began this chapter by saying that it is illogical, what I meant that it is deficient because it is logical. Aristotle is smart enough to apply the golden mean more to character than to specific actions. If the golden mean were a behavioural rule and not a way of educating one's character, the absurdity would be even more palpable. If, for example, you were given the incorrect change at the supermarket checkout, then your two extreme options would be either doing nothing or decapitating the cashier with an axe. The golden mean between the two might perhaps be giving the cashier a loud smack to the face. Alternately, the two extreme options could be thanking them for reminding you that life is full of imprecisions, or doing nothing. The golden mean would perhaps be smiling at the cashier so good-naturedly that they felt slightly ill at ease. I believe that, if we could find a person able to imagine the two extremes as real options – the axe or the effusive thank you – that would be a way of obtaining a minimally reasonable golden mean since they would obviously be no role model and deserving of all our compassion.

Nevertheless, most people contemplate much more moderate extremes, and the contrast between one and the other is not substantial. This is why the golden mean has been popular for centuries. It helps modulate character and offers a certain feeling that one is able to control oneself. That, however, is fiction. In order to rein in the extremes, the opinions of the people in the queue, the supermarket security guard, the police, or a judge would all have more weight. The regulation offered by Aristotelian prudence is just a way to get used to those limits. As such, saying that the golden mean between pride and cowardliness is a sincere blend of self-love and modesty means nothing unless we are thinking about the Greek conquerors and their hubris. Moderation for its own sake means nothing without having the trophic context in mind: without knowing the pecking order of who is weak and who's in charge, who makes the laws, and who obeys them.

VIII – 'QUE LA SOMIO COMPLETA'*

'In private life, as in public life, one's own position is very difficult to grasp; man is made up of thousands of illusions which lead him to err about the scope of his forces and his opportunities to deploy them.'

This quote from Balmes doesn't say much of anything and yet at the same time captures a truth as easily recognisable as common sense: measure your strength well. It is perfectly suited to our country and has remained alive and well as an ideal

* A line from the poem 'Corrandes d'exili,' by Pere Quart.

in our public sphere in the last one hundred and seventy-five years since it was published. We have, in fact, been discussing this correlation of forces and how they are generated for centuries. Calculating well may save you from being reckless but it is very quickly put at the service of reducing creativity to aesthetic gestures designed to be evasive. It extends even to me dealing with the woman who works at the delicatessen near my house. It begins by taming the arrogance of political adventurers and ends by placing so many conditions on self-love that only the most basic skeleton remains: the survival instinct.

The woman at the delicatessen couldn't just let me shop happily for the same reason that during the ten years I lived on the East Coast of the United States no one ever told me I had a problem of thinking too highly of myself. Social customs are always an expression of the violence buried in the memory of generations. Americans are afraid of the violence of diversity that emerges from having different human groups who, simply by living one way and not another, compete to impose a hierarchy of values and priorities. Their predilection for private medicine and the freedom to bear arms comes from this same fear: If I pay for your health care and trust the police entirely, then we might end up killing each other.

Catalans' fear of provoking the state is expressed in specific terms through our aversion to people who can find independent formulas. This extreme individualism is accepted as reasonable only when they act in a crazy way. Most indulged in male artists, they are also required to pay the price for being explicit madmen, be it in the naïve version such as the Galàctics and Albert Pla, the misanthropic Josep Pla and Miquel Bauçà version, or the hyperbolic version of Salvador Dalí and Albert Serra. Gaudí doesn't fit into this, which is perhaps why we want to make him a saint.

Jaume Balmes was a priest from Vic in northern Catalonia

who wanted to save Spain from French influenced liberalism and rancid traditionalism. He came up with a modern Spanish Catholic nationalism that would influence the whole south of Europe, including Rome. As always happens with reformist notions, Balmes' ideas were more popular in Catalonia than in Spain. The quote opening this chapter comes from *The Criteria*, a manual for the nouveau-riche. It is a book designed as a behavioural guide for the bourgeoisie newly created by the first industrial revolution and the state bureaucrats, allowing them to continue to be Catholics. This manual continued to serve the interests of industrious people until the later Francoist period, but later lost all its prestige. My uncle told me that my grandfather would have him and his siblings take turns reading sections aloud at bedtime every night. That said, I only learned about it in passing, despite my studying philosophy at a department located on Carrer Balmes, the Barcelona street named after him. It is a religious manual of good manners that teaches you to navigate the contradictions of modernity and mollifies the metaphysical complications of the rise of materialism. It educates you in moderation and the repression of excesses. Read dispassionately, it summarises what many Catalans call *seny*: good sense and judgment and considered an essential aspect of the national character.

The criteria it endorses is that of repressing yourself both moderately, and to prosper, if that makes any sense; avoiding moral missteps and seeking the precise balance between energetic productivity and personal discretion.

Now that it is possible to read and write with relative freedom and without the Marxist professors in Barcelona's abuse of power, the debate over when the political movement for Catalan autonomy emerged keeps pushing the date further and further back. I see its origins in the conspiracies around the Compromise of Caspe and think that the emergence of Catalan regionalism in the 19th century is actually a decadent phase marked by a mentality that Balmes' Catholicism was the first to make explicit. Catalan regionalism is where those who feel the need to rid people of the idea of independence, which is an idea common in stateless countries, meet up with those who are convinced that what's most urgent is preparing for the long term. Some are cynics while the others, from all their preparation, often end up becoming overly staunch. It has always been said, and I think with some justification, that the 19th century didn't leave intelligence many alternatives. Nor was it easy to foresee the resulting cynicism and civil puritanism. Today, on the other hand, the only intelligent alternative is to run away from it all as quickly as possible, which isn't always fast enough.

Balmes published *The Criteria* in 1845. Spain was a violent country, unable to leave behind intermittent civil war, with a per capita income similar to Somalia and Afghanistan at the start of our century and a level of illiteracy similar to the poorest country in the world today. The army served as arbitrator and the federalist revolts in Barcelona ended with its leaders executed. In 1837 there'd been an uprising in Barcelona whose members identified with the postulates of 'La Bandera' [The Flag], a pamphlet that demanded a. murdering the politicians and b. Catalan independence. It was quelled by Baron de Meer, famous for his cruel repression of Catalonia in the 1820s. In 1841 and 1843 the army bombed Barcelona. The revolt of the Barcelonian progressives and Republicans of 1841 was described by Van Halen, the Captain General of Catalonia, in his *Reasoned Diary*: full-blown urban guerrilla warfare forced the army to retreat to Montjuïc. 'This combat with the army,' writes Van Halen, 'was to the battle cry of death to the Castilians!' It was, however, the Catalans who did most of the dying.

The context demanded that the Catalans be given a good reason not to be revolutionaries. A good reason means a reason that can define one's character. It has to be a reason that can hide the fear or at least make it bearable; if not, it is more worthwhile to burn it all down. *The Criteria* tries to define and promote this character as the character of a good, high-quality Spaniard. The implicit political assumption that Balmes is putting forth and taking for granted in his book is that the Spanish imagination has enough tools to create a modern Catholic nationalism, a prosperous and anti-capitalist conservatism and a European scientific line of thinking. Remarkably, Balmes manages all of that in *The Criteria* without talking about politics.

Since *The Criteria* is a manual for learning how to think, there are many disquisitions on perception, sensibility and reasoning, which form a not terribly original – but very well put together – compendium of St Thomas Aquinas passed through the cheesecloth of the Enlightenment. There are many examples, and all of them were aimed at the kind of man who reads the newspaper every day. Something that, in that period, defined a social class that at the least aspired to the bourgeoisie. Significant philosophical problems of modernity such as the difficulty of knowing the relationship between a cause and its effect, are posed but the response is a defence of common sense. The peasant, the rustic and the new uneducated bourgeois are placed above the analytical, the eloquent, or the 'man of talent.' The practical man gets it right more often than the visionary, whose words and writings 'drag others along with growing fascination.'

The Criteria's keystone is the idea that errors in judgment stem from a moral error that is summed up by the sin of pride. The proud do not realise that the victims of their character are 'their most dear interests, the same glory they so anxiously pursue.' The pages that Balmes devotes to pride, vanity and haughtiness are powerful because they are laden with the entire Catholic tradition and have the eloquence of a priest who is well travelled and rhetorically gifted. But his whole arsenal is put at the service of a warning against 'men who set out for adventure.'

One thing we have learned in the 175 years since the publication of *The Criteria* is that the quickest and most effective way to control an arrogant leader is democracy. The system that forces leaders to persuade the electorate that they embody deeply ingrained, instinctual values and have a vision for the future also forces them to work more with the tools of the vain than with those of the proud. In Machiavelli's dilemma over whether a ruler should be loved or hated, democracy responds that the best, safest way to take the sovereign down a notch is to force them to be loved in order to rule. What governs in a democracy is the queen's magic mirror in the story of Snow White; the queen is utterly dependent on its verdicts and the vain are always listening to it. Yet, too much dependence on vanity leads to increasing mediocrity. Politicians end up flattering the people to win their support, and they all become trapped in a vicious circle, smug and soothing, that leads to decadence. That is why, for greater prosperity, countries elect leaders who combine this vanity with pride. They must be arrogant enough to contradict the people, especially on those things that only a person of action can imagine. It is a precarious balance that calls for harnessing the virtues of the visionary without being a slave to the tendency to unleash chaos for its own sake. The morality we have constructed in this occupied Mediterranean territory makes this kind of leader impossible.

The counterexample is the 1213 defeat at the Battle of Muret where King Peter the Catholic died leaving Occitania to the French and veering the history of the Principality of Catalonia toward the south and the Mediterranean, where it was led by his son, James I. It was said that Peter II's pride made him lose to the pious Simon de Montfort. Though it was a religious war waged against heresy, or perhaps because of that, the excessive and sinful ways of the Catalan king led him to an excessive estimation of himself and in the epic battle (the setting where spiritual questions are disputed so the Lord can watch and make a ruling), God condemned him. Since our weakness is also our strength, King Peter's hubris had made him a hero the previous summer, in the Battle of Las Navas de Tolosa. The battle, which marked the slow decline of the Almohad world on the Iberian Peninsula, was won against all prognostics because, according to the propaganda, the passion of the allied Christian kings inspired their soldiers.

This counterexample shows that the codification of the sin of pride has always been an efficient instrument of political control. Pride is the political sin *par excellence* and has always struggled to distinguish brave leadership from vice. In this context, the worst that can be said of Balmes is that he shared a century with Friedrich Nietzsche, and that it was the Prussian and not the Catalan who saw that the Archimedean point from which Christianity emerges is the revolution of the weak against the strong that became – in its most banal 19th century version – all strength is excessive and all superiority is haughtiness.

The origin of the monarchy is the moment when the biggest, best trained and best armed thieves staked claim over the lives of the productive stratum of society, exchanging material goods for protection, just as the mafia has always done. And the control mechanism for their cruelty and crazy ventures was a religious education about the character flaws of hubris and pride. Nietzsche attributes the beginning of European spiritual decline to these ethics that transform the humble into role models and stupidity into currency. Democracy is the *coup de grace*: it directs the self-control demanded of the monarch toward the elector, the new sovereign. *The Criteria* is practically a caricature of the ideology of moderation that Nietzsche saw as proof that humanity, in Europe, was dead inside.

After two world wars and a domestic one waged against Catalonia, the only mentality that remained in the country was a post-war one. James I responded to his father King Peter the Catholic's profligate pride by earning the title of 'Conqueror.' When the best sons of every house were either killed or sent into exile, Catalonia responded by expanding the scope of what we consider haughtiness over the last three quarters of a century. The massification of cruelty that Europeans saw in the 20th century wars led the survivors to perceive danger as an implacable chain of people who think too highly of themselves, to the point that it was considered perfectly reasonable for intellectuals to question – out loud – whether one could write poetry after Auschwitz, which is ridiculous. In Catalonia, this spiritual impoverishment extended into every refuge of hope and the question became whether one could have a backbone after the lessons of Francoism.

The democratic space that we've allowed in afterwards is still being disputed by the cynics and the staunch purists of the 19th century, but in such a hopeful context that all that remains of those dangers is a common lack of self-love. All told it makes us perfect prey for exploitation in the name of each and every prevailing propaganda.

While people always talk about the violence of the past, we shouldn't conclude that the only way out of danger is the negation of character. No American has never reproached me for thinking too highly of myself for the same reason that their civil war, filled with heroes and hubris, taught them a practical lesson that is the polar opposite of ours. American pragmatism is anti-Balmesian because it defends the idea that judging character as a means to halt fanaticism leads awfully quickly to dictatorship, which is what they fought for independence from. It's better to focus on the consequences of who we are and what we do, and not so much on the myths that explain our origin and original sin. The truth is that winning wars helps to forge this perspective, but the main difference I've found between the American and Catalan political cultures is that the former have concluded that it's better to have a country full of arrogant people if that allows for the emergence of good ideas or genius. We Catalans, on the other hand, have concluded that it's better to keep our good ideas in a drawer and our geniuses repressed and isolated if that avoids having some arrogant person getting us mixed up in a conflict. Better to just settle for a tie, right out of the gate.

IX – THE USEFULNESS OF PRIDE

The woman at the delicatessen is the oracle of a people offering a very specific transaction: some delicious food in exchange for a long, ancient silence. She couldn't just let me shop happily because it was too dangerous to allow me to be purely happy in such a desperate, frivolous and arrogant way, even for a moment. Arrogance leads to wars. And don't you forget it.

Barcelona has become the capital of the inquisition against pride. It is a cheap honour that subjugates a vast territory within the borders of three European states. Beneath a layer of moral and political repression lies an indulgence in traditional customs – how Mediterraneans have tolerated low points throughout history – and some claim to universalism, both of which attempt to compensate for the feeling that we're living in a powder keg. But no one is fooled for very long.

If what I've explained in this essay is true, or at least approximately true, then we live in a geographical and historical atmosphere where tightrope walkers are not allowed up on the tightrope – who do they think they are, being so reckless – and where the vain are accepted only if they are completely dependent on others' opinions. As for the proud, they can expect only a radical marginalisation which never produces anything, ever. The man-dog is our paradigm and we aren't allowed to have any self-regard outside of the privacy of our own homes. The only self-love that's permitted is related to survival: if you adapt to the dominant power and build some slight happiness within the occupation, it is understood that you have a healthy self-esteem. Moderation is legal tender, but it too must be moderated to ensure it doesn't become an ostentation. It has to seem natural, just a shrewd bit of common sense, or some entirely rootless conservatism.

In conclusion, I maintain that the proud are useful to dominated societies. Their nose for power makes them impervious to subjugating propaganda and the indignities of the slave dependent on pleasing his master. While their vain side knows how to rescue the hope hiding in repression, their superior side is good at drawing lines in the sand. But the only way the proud will not become sterile aesthetes or incendiary and reckless is if they are allowed to work out their vice in public. If they can transform their zeal for superiority into a vehicle that allows the collective to overcome. They function as a buttress that permits others more space to grow and to dare. That is the humility they can aspire to.

At this point in time in Catalonia, however, pride defines even the most ridiculous transactions at a delicatessen and threatens to damage another generation's ability to summon the courage and frivolity necessary to get through their anxious yearning for truth and freedom. Since it is only human to believe that what has worked for you will also work for others, my prescription includes worrying less about the pyrotechnics of personalities and more about the gunpowder strength of character. In other words: put your vices at the service of something greater than yourself. Be proud, even if others say you're arrogant.

BIBLIOGRAPHY

Aristotle, *The Nicomachean Ethics*, translated by David Ross, Oxford University Press, Oxford, 2009

Baudelaire, Charles, *Les fleurs du mal*, translated by Richard Howard, David R. Godine, Boston, 1982 (1857)

Berger, John, *Ways of Seeing*, Penguin Books, London, 1972

Berman, Marshall, *All That Is Solid Melts into Air*, Penguin Books, New York, 1982

Bloomfield, Morton W., «*The origin of the concept of the seven cardinal sins*», The Harvard Theological Review, vol. 34, no. 2, p. 121-128, 1941

Bourdieu, Pierre, *La distinction. Critique sociale du jugement*, Minuit, Paris, 1979

Brontë, Charlotte, *Jane Eyre*, Penguin Classics, London, 2006

Bukowski, Charles, *Notes of a Dirty Old Man*, City Lights, San Francisco, 1969

Camus, Albert, *The Myth of Sisyphus*, translated by Justin O'Brien, London, Penguin, 2013 (1942)

Cervantes, Miguel de, *Don Quijote de la Mancha*, Instituto Cervantes / Real Academia Española, Madrid, 2015 (1605, 1615)

Claret, Antoni Maria, *Camí dret i segur per arribar al Cel*, Llibreria Religiosa, Barcelona, 1888 (1843)

Cleland, John, *Fanny Hill*, Wordsworth Classics, London, 2012

Cohen, Joel / Ethan Cohen, *The Big Lebowski*, Working Title Films, United States of America, 1998

Dante Alighieri, *The Divine Comedy*, translated by Henry Wadsworth Longfellow, George Routledge & Co., New York, 1902

De Voragine, Jacobus, *The Golden Legend: Readings on the Saints*, translated by William Granger Ryan, Princeton University Press, Princeton, 1993

Delgado, Manuel, *Las palabras de otro hombre*, El Aleph, Barcelona, 1998

Díaz-Plaja, Fernando, *Shakespeare y los siete pecados capitales*, Alianza, Madrid, 2001

Douglas, Mary & Isherwood, Baron, *The World of Goods: Towards an Anthropology of Consumption*, Penguin Books, New York, 1979

Duch, Lluís, *De la religió a la religió popular*, Publicacions de l'Abadia de Montserrat, Barcelona, 1980

–, *Mite i cultura. Aproximació a la logomítica I*, Publicacions de l'Abadia de Montserrat, Barcelona, 1995

Eliade, Mircea, *Histoire des croyances et des idees religieuses. De Gautama Bouddha au triomphe du christianisme*, Payot, Paris, 1978

Esteban, M. Luz, «*Promoción social y exhibición del cuerpo*», in María Teresa del Valle, (ed.), *Perspectivas feministas desde la antropología social*, Ariel, Barcelona, 2000, p. 205-242

Fàbrega Escatllar, Valentí, *La dona de sant Pere i altres oblits de l'Església*, Fragmenta, Barcelona, 2017

Graeber, David, *Bullshit Jobs: A Theory*, Simon & Schuster, New York, 2018

Gregory the Great, *Sancti Gregorii Magni Moralium libri sive expositio in librum beati Job*. Pars ii, XXXI, 87, MPL076, 1849

Han, Byung-Chul, *The Burnout Society*, translated by Erik Butler, Stanford University Press, Stanford, 2015 (2010)

– , *Good Entertainment: A Deconstruction of the Western Passion Narrative*, translated by Adrian Nathan West, MIT Press, Cambridge and London, 2019 (2017)

Harris, Thomas, *Hannibal*, Delacorte Press, New York, 1999

Hénaff, Marcel, *Sade: The Invention of the Libertine Body*, translated by Xavier Callahan, University of Minnesota Press, Minneapolis, MN, 1980

Hinojosa, Sergio, *Santa anorexia. La noche oscura del cuerpo*, Maia, Madrid, 2009

Horace, *Satires and Epistles*, translated by John Davie, Oxford World's Classics, Oxford, 2011

Huxley, Aldous, *Brave New World*, Vintage Classics, New York, 2007 (1932)

Ignatius of Loyola, *Spiritual Exercises and Selected Works*, Paulist Press, New York, 1991 (1548)

Kahneman, Daniel / Amos Tversky, «*Prospect theory: an analysis of decision under risk*», Econometrica, núm. 47(2) (1979), p. 263-291

Le Goff, Jacques / Nicolas Truong: *Une histoire du corps au Moyen Âge*, Liana Levi, Paris (2003)

Lévi-Strauss, Claude: *Mythologiques. Le cru et le cuit, vol. 1*, Pion, Paris (1964)

Llull, Ramon (1901-1903): *Libre de la primera e segona intencio*, edited by Jerónimo Rosselló, prologue and glossary by Mateu Obrador i Bennassar, Hijas de Colomar, Palma (1905)

Luria, S.Y., *Democritus*, translated by C.C.W. Taylor, Nauka Publishers, Leningrad, 1970

Maffesoli, Michel, *La part du diable*, Flammarion, Paris, 2002

Meeuws, M. D., «*Ora et labora: devise bénédictine?*», in Collectanea Cisterciensia, vol. 54 (1992), p. 193-214

Miller, Henry, *Tropic of Cancer*, Grove Press, New York, 1994 (1934)

Montaigne, Michel de, *Essais*, Gallimard, Paris, 2009

Nietzsche, Friedrich, *On the Genealogy of Morals: A Polemic*, translated by Douglas Smith, Oxford Classics, London, 1996 (1887)

Ortega y Gasset, José, *Estudios sobre el amor, in Obras completas, vol. V*, Revista de Occidente, Madrid, 1961

Orwell, George, *1984*, Penguin Modern Classics, London, 2004 (1949)

– , *Coming up for Air*, Penguin Modern Classics, London, 2001 (1939)

Pascal, Blaise, *Pensées*, translated by A. Krailsheimer, Penguin Classics, London, 1995 (1699)

Perry, Ben Edwin, *Æsopica: Greek and Latin Texts*, University of Illinois Press, Urbana, 1952 (2007)

Pico Della Mirandola, Giovanni, *Oration on the Dignity of Man*, Regnery Publishing, Washington D.C., 1996 (c. 1486)

Pigem, Jordi, *Àngels i robots. La interioritat humana en la societat hipertecnològica*, Viena, Barcelona, 2017

Pla, Josep, *The Gray Notebook*, translated by Peter Bush, New York Review of Books Classics, New York, 2014 (1966)

Plato, *The Republic*, translated by Desmond Lee, Penguin Classics, London, 2007.

–, *Gorgias*, translated by Robin Waterfield, Oxford World's Classics, Oxford, 2008

Poliâne, Lionel, et al., *Supplique au Pape pour enlever la gourmandise de la liste des péchés capitaux*, Anne Carrière, Paris, 2004

Prose, Francine, *Gluttony*, Oxford University Press, Oxford, 2003

Pujol, Adrià, *La carpeta és blava*, LaBreu, Barcelona, 2017

Rabelais, François, *Les cinq livres des faits et dits de Gargantua et Pantagruel*, Gallimard, Paris, 2017

Rebull, Nolasc, *Llegenda àuria de Jaume de Voràgine segons un manuscrit de Vic*, Aubert, Olot, 1975

Rigotti, Francesca, *Gola. La passione dell'ingordigia*, Società Editrice il Mulino, Bologna, 2008

Rivera, María Milagros, *Textos y espacios de mujeres (Europa siglos iv -xv)*, Icària, Barcelona, 1990

Rodoreda, Mercè, *Aloma*, Edicions 62, Barcelona, 2006

–, «Rom Negrita», in *Els set pecats capitals vistos per 21 contistes en homenatge a Víctor Català*, Selecta, Barcelona, 1960

Roth, Philip, *Portnoy's Complaint*, Vintage, London, 1995

Rougemont, Denis de, *Love in the Western World*, translated by Montgomery Belgion, Princeton University Press, Princeton, NJ, 1983

Savater, Fernando, *Los siete pecados capitales*, Random House Mondadori, Barcelona, 2013

Segarra, Marta, *Escriure el desig. De la Celestina a Maria-Mercè Marçal*, Afers, Barcelona, 2013

Shakespeare, William, *Hamlet*, Wordsworth Editions, London, 1992 (1603)

Smith, Adam, *The Wealth of Nations*, Bantam Classics, New York, 2003 (1776)

Snider, Louis B., "*The Psychomachia of Prudentius*" (1938). *Master's Theses*. 372. https://ecommons.luc.edu/luc_theses/372

Soldevila, Carles, *Fanny*, labutxaca, Barcelona, 2008

Stendhal, *On Love*, translated by Sophie Lewis, Hesperus Press, London, 2009

Swift, Jonathan, *Gulliver's Travels*, Penguin, London, 1994 (1726)

Thaler, Richard, *Quasi rational economics*, Russell Sage Foundation, New York, 1994

Theros, Xavier, *Burla, escarnio y otras diversiones. Historia del humor en la Edad Media*, La Tempestad, Barcelona, 2004

Toole, John Kennedy, *A Confederacy of Dunces*, Grove Weidenfeld, New York, 1987

Trías, Eugenio, *Tratado de la pasión, in Creaciones filosóficas, vol. I*, Galaxia Gutenberg, Barcelona, 2009

Vigarello, Georges, *Les metamorphoses du gras. Histoire de l'obésité*, Seuil, Paris, 2010

Wallace, David Foster, *The Broom of the System*, Penguin Classics, New York, 2016 (1987)

Weber, Max, *The Protestant Ethic and the "Spirit" of Capitalism and Other Writings*, translated by Peter Baehr and Gordon C. Wells, Penguin Classics, New York, 2002 (1905)

Winterson, Jeanette, *The Passion*, Vintage, London, 2014

Zamyatin, Yevgeny, *We*, translated by Gregory Zilboorg, E. P. Dutton, New York, 1954 (1924)

Zweig, Stefan, *Letter from an Unknown Woman and Other Stories*, translated by Anthea Bell, Pushkin Press, London, 2013